Rx for Life

By God's Grace Alone,

TULSA

ISBN: 978-1-954095-99-1
RX for Life

Yorkshire Publishing
1425 E 41st Pl
Tulsa, OK 74105
www.YorkshirePublishing.com
918.394.2665

Published in the USA

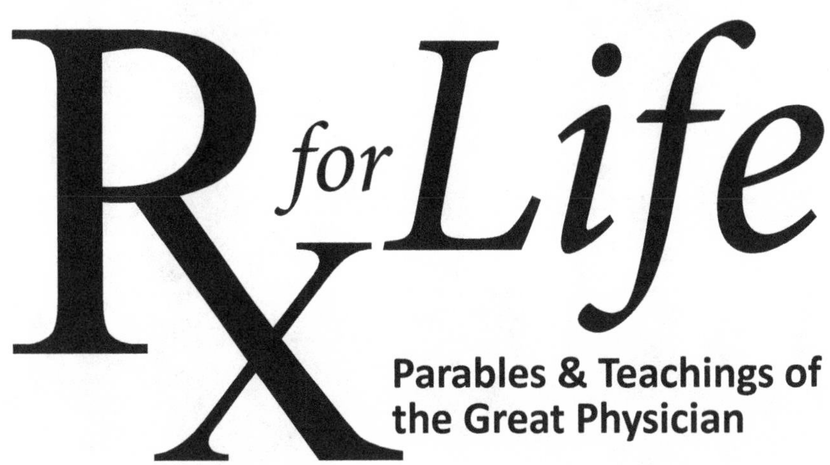

By

Daniel A. Tomlinson, M.D.

Endorsements:

Words matter… and Dr. Dan Tomlinson understands that! "Rx for Life" is a prescription for living that is uniquely clear and unlike most written prescriptions, can actually be read and understood clearly and powerfully. Dan has found the antidote for life that all of mankind needs – It is Jesus – nothing more, nothing less and nothing else.

Jim Wright
Pastor: Mountain Church, Medford, Oregon
Author: Shipwrecks & Storm Clouds

Dr. Dan Tomlinson has provided us with an in-depth study of virtually everything Jesus taught us during his earthly ministry. It is both profoundly theological and practical, explaining not only why, but how we follow the Lord. I plan to use this book as a resource in my college Bible classes. It has a place next to everything I read in seminary. Reading it has led me into a more loving walk with Jesus.

Charles B. Lutz
Bible College Faculty, Flagstaff, Arizona
Teaching Pastor, Big Arm Church, Big Arm, Montana
Author: The God Anonymous, Eyes to the Sky, A Bible Creed, Amazing Golf Stories

Truth & Love. In Rx for Life, Dr. Dan Tomlinson unfolds the message of the gospel in the best way possible. He shares his heart for you & me from a lifetime of learning and being loved by his Father in Heaven. You will be blessed as Dr. Dan invites you to sit at his table and study with him the teachings of Jesus.

Bruce Smith
Pastor: Fresh Life Church, Great Falls, Montana

All know what the Hippocratic Oath is and why it has been considered important in the realm of medical ethics. As a doctor himself, Dr. Daniel Tomlinson has applied his own, self-imposed oath to his writings about the Holy Scriptures, to remain true to the real meaning of each of the passages he illuminates in "Rx for Life". Enjoy reading this with the confidence of truthful insights.

John Creamer
Bible Teacher: Campus Crusade for Christ (CRU)

Contents

Introduction

Jesus of Nazareth, born in Bethlehem, the son of David, the son of Abraham, the son of Mary, the son of Adam, the Son of God, is undoubtedly the most influential and famous person who has ever lived. It is unlikely that anyone alive today, past the age of awareness, has not heard His name. This cannot be said of anyone else.

There are two reasons that this is true. First, over one-third of the people on this planet believe He is the only person who has risen from the dead to never die again. Second, after His ascension back to Heaven, Jesus sent the Holy Spirit to His followers, keeping the memory, purpose, and plan of His life front and center in the world's narrative.

His significance is felt in all aspects of our lives. He is present in our art, music, conversation, schools, government, health care, relief organizations, and ethics. The way women are viewed, the way we look at marriage, family, and social issues, e.g., slavery, the sanctity of life, and care for the poor and less fortunate have all been focused in our world by the life He lived and the legacy He left.

But His significance reaches infinitely farther than just His effect on our culture and worldview. That is because, as the Son of God, He revealed the very nature of God to mankind.

You see, all men intuitively understand that there is more to our experience than what we can see, hear, taste, smell, and touch. In the amplified words of Solomon, He has set eternity in our hearts (Ecclesiastes 3:11). We perceive something greater than ourselves at work in the universe, as design screams at us from all directions saying there is a God. But God is outside of our five senses, so without His help we cannot experience Him, we can only speculate about Him as has been done throughout the ages. Men have always been very adept in making God after the image of beasts and birds and after the image of men and women. But, in the fullness of time, Jesus arrived and made known to us the true nature of God. As He told His disciple Phillip, and by extension us, "he that hath seen me hath seen the Father" (John 14:8).

Along with revealing the nature of God, Jesus showed us the heart, plan, and will of God. The Bible's most famous verse states this clearly:

> For God so loved the world (*heart*) that He gave His only begotten Son (*plan*), that whosoever believeth in Him should not perish, but have everlasting life (*will*).
> John 3:16 (italics added)

But in this, the critical thinker sees a problem. That is, God is holy and we are not! The Bible states, "for all have sinned, and come short of the glory of God" (Romans 3:23). It goes on to state that the wages of sin, the result of sin, is death (Romans 6:23). Thus, God had to give His Son as ransom for the bad choices we make on a day-to-day and hour-to-hour basis. He had to do the second part of the famous verse because of the first part. That is, because of His great love for us.

Jesus Christ came to die! He did not come to make sick men better or bad men good; He came to make dead men alive!

Businesses and organizations often have a mission statement. It's not a bad idea for people, too. I have one as a physician. It has three bullet points: Love God and my neighbor wholeheartedly, become more like Christ, and help people medically and spiritually.

Jesus has a mission statement too. It is found in Matthew's gospel.

> For the Son of man is come to save that which was lost.
> Matthew 18:11

He came to seek and save the lost! If He did nothing else for us, that would be enough. For we were dead, headed for death and destruction, and He reached down and rescued us. We were the unfaithful and runaway bride that He just couldn't live without! He gave it all, went to Hell in our place, to bring us back to Him. For this, I am truly grateful!

But along with this great salvation comes one very important stipulation. We must receive that redemption, we must choose it. He does not force it upon any person. The Bible clearly teaches that an individual's salvation is a choice that each must make, that each must act upon.

> That if thou shalt confess with thy mouth the Lord Jesus, and shalt believe in thine heart that God hath raised Him from the dead, thou shalt be saved.
> Romans 10:9

It is a door that all who would must open.

> Behold, I stand at the door, and knock; if any man hear my voice, and open the door, I will come in to him, and will sup with him, and he with me.
> Revelation 3:20

In this, we come to the second reason for His visit to us. That is, He came to live beautifully! He came to reveal our need for a Savior. The people on the *Titanic* were not scrambling for the life-boats until they realized the ship was going down! So it is with us; we don't see our need for a Deliverer until we see how far short we are from His beauty and holiness. As the Great Physician, He came to heal us, He came to teach us, He came to show us the way.

Indeed, Jesus is the greatest of all teachers, philosophers, gurus, and religious leaders. That's because, unlike all others, His words have life! John, in opening His gospel calls Jesus the Word, the Logos; that is, the essence of God.

> In the beginning was the Word, and the Word was with God, and the Word was God.
> John 1:1

Jesus and God's Word, unlike any other writings, are insepa-rable. God's Word, the Logos, is alive. I know this is a difficult con-cept but the Bible nonetheless teaches it, so I choose to believe it. Later on, in Revelation, we again see Jesus with His title of the Word of God. (Revelation 19:13)

So, when we have words from Jesus, we need to grasp that we have something eternal, dynamic, and other-worldly. Something that we should pay attention to!

Unfortunately, sometimes when I read the Bible, I miss the tone of Jesus' message. Maybe you do, too. Sort of like reading a text message from someone. Are they being funny, sarcastic, playful, or harsh? Without the body language, that twinkle of the eye, or the tilt of the head, their message can be blurred and misinterpreted. Often this has happened with Jesus' words.

Take, for instance, the many times Jesus has what may seem as severe interactions with the religious leaders of His day, the Pharisees. We know that Jesus acts in love, as God is love (1 John 4:8), so how do these uncomfortable interactions jell with our Lord's character and personality? Think of it this way, filling in the tone: He is love so, if His words seem unkind, they are still given in love. In the Pharisees' case, the Teacher's arguments to them were like a three-year intervention! They had destructive attitudes and beliefs they were not even aware of that needed to be shaken up.

Filling in the tone needs to be done and I will endeavor to do so whenever we consider words from Jesus. We need to understand His personality. We need to stop reading the gospels like a text message.

Generally, when people are asked about the personality of the greatest One who has ever lived, they will speak of His wonderful compassion, love, and humility. But how often do people appreciate His other great personality traits that are ever-present in the gospel narratives? His characteristics of wit, playfulness, steely resolve, scandalous freedom, disruptive honesty, passion, and beauty, among others. This is what we must seek out. We need to stop thinking of Jesus as a two-dimensional historical figure but as the three-dimensional life force that He is!

Lastly, a point needs to be made concerning our Lord's most famous teaching method, that of teaching with parables. Jesus is known for His many wonderful and timeless parables that paint a picture in a way that mere lessons could never do. Earthly stories with heavenly meanings.

But parables can also be hard to understand. Why would Jesus use a teaching method that often can fly over our puny little brains, leaving us none the richer?

Jesus quoted the prophet Isaiah's words as being fulfilled in His preaching in parables. Let me show you.

> Therefore, I speak to them in parables; because they seeing, see not; and hearing, they hear not, neither do they understand. And in them is fulfilled the prophecy of Isaiah...
> Matthew 13:13-14

> And He (*God*) said, Go, and tell this people, hear ye indeed, but understand not; and see ye indeed, but perceive not.
> Isaiah 6:9 (italics added)

You see, Jesus being the Logos could blow away every human with the power and persuasiveness of His words. But that is not what God wants in His children. He desires us to love Him and not be "forced," so to speak, to choose him. He does not want us to be obligated to believe the truth without loving him. Love requires a choice, thus He will not manipulate people into loving and following Him. There is a tension present, a fine balance that God maintains between keeping His presence evident, yet subtly masked, so that people who want to believe have the ability to do so while people who do not want to follow Him will also be free to make that poor choice. What it comes down to really is: Who is on the throne of my heart? Is it me, or He? When I am on the seat of power, death is the result, but when He is allowed to reign, life and peace are the end.

So, let's study and examine the parables and teachings of the Great Physician. Lessons for life, prescriptions for life! Let's look at His words, unmasking them, so to speak, letting them move us with the power and potency of the Logos.

Repentance

I've taken a couple of ocean liner cruises with my family over the years. Early in the adventure, everyone is required to partake in a muster drill. You know what that is? All on board need to learn what to do should the ship encounter trouble and begin to sink. We needed to know how to put on our lifejackets and where the lifeboats would be in the case of an evacuation.

Boring!

You can imagine why I call it boring. That's because we don't really think the ship is going down. Same with the pre-flight airline briefing. We just don't see the need to give our attention to these informative sessions. But what if we knew ahead of time that the ship was going to sink or that the plane was going to run out of gas in mid-flight. Certainly, we would then pay much more attention. We would desire to know ahead of time what we could do to keep ourselves safe, what to do to be saved!

So it is for life in general. Souls move about on our little planet, for the most part, with little attention and incentive to live with God's standards and precepts in mind. Much like the muster drill, we don't see the need to make any changes to the way we live. Unfortunately for us, this is where the analogy breaks down. That's because, in the case of the ship or the plane, they are not likely to sink or crash, but in the world's case and for the souls of this orb, we are all going down, we all are in the process of dying. We are all going to meet our Maker.

Thus, secondary to our dire predicament, repentance was our Lord's first message. Before He taught about the Kingdom of Heaven, before we could learn from Him how to be born again, about forgiveness, hypocrisy, Heaven, Hell, money, and faith we had to understand about repentance. We needed to learn that we are not really all that good, we're not that all together. In fact, for a person to perceive that he needs a Savior, he must comprehend that he is a sinner, that he frequently, if not continually, misses the mark. Hence, we learn from Paul that the Law, i.e., the Old Testament, is our schoolmaster to bring us to Christ (Galatians 3:24), to show us our need for Christ and His saving sacrifice.

Thus, our Lord's initial message after His baptism in the Jordan River and the forty days spent in the wilderness preparing for His ministry was to speak of repentance.

> From that time Jesus began to preach, and to say, Repent; for the kingdom of heaven is at hand.
> Matthew 4:17

Interestingly, this was also His last message. His final instructions to His disciples before ascending to Heaven sounded this way:

> Thus, it is written, and thus it behooved Christ to suffer, and to rise from the dead the third day: And that repentance and remission of sins should be preached in His name among all nations, beginning at Jerusalem. And you are witnesses of these things.
> Luke 24:46-48

Not coincidentally, this was John the Baptist's entire message in preparing the way for the Messiah. "Repent and be baptized, for the Lamb of God is among us!"

In our day, the word repentance is somewhat misunderstood by most. The common perception of repentance is to be apologetic, to have sorrow or remorse for a bad attitude or action that one may do. But, while having godly remorse over sins committed is good, this is not the Bible's primary definition of repentance. This is not what Jesus and John were teaching when they both came on the scene preaching repentance for the Kingdom of Heaven, the Kingdom of God was at hand. No, the primary meaning of repentance is to do an about-face, to change directions, to go from thinking one way about something to thinking the polar opposite. The secondary, more commonly held but less important, definition of repentance is to have remorse over sinful acts and to confess them.

In light of the gospel message, in light of the "good news," to repent means changing the way I think about salvation. To change from a works-based theology of salvation to a sacrifice-based one. Specifically, to go from believing that I can save myself by having more good works than bad verses realizing that I am hopelessly doomed and need the blood of the Lamb of God to secure my salvation.

Despite the Jews having a sacrificial system in place for covering their sins, two parables of Jesus found in Luke's gospel display where their hearts were. What follows illustrates that many pseudo-righteous people were being tricked by Satan, the culture, and their flesh into thinking they were pretty good and not in danger of losing their salvation based on their lifestyle. As you may consider, this worldview is still very prevalent in our day. Let's visit a couple of Jesus' timeless responses to this type of thinking.

> And He spoke this parable unto certain which trusted in themselves that they were righteous, and despised others: (*Self-righteousness always leads to a legalistic critical spirit!).* Two men went up to the temple to pray; the one a Pharisee, and the other a publican. The Pharisee stood and prayed thus with himself, God, I thank thee, that I am not as other men are, extortioners, unjust, adulterers, or even as this publican. I fast twice a week, I give tithes of all that I possess. And the publican, standing afar off, would not lift up so much as his eyes unto heaven, but smote upon his breast, saying, God be merciful to me a sinner. I tell you, this man went down to his house justified rather than the other: For every one that exalts himself shall be abased; and he that humbles himself shall be exalted.
> Luke 18:9-14 (italics added)

The Pharisee was a "good" person. Not being an extortioner or an adulterer is moral. Fasting and tithing are virtuous. But unfortunately for him, though, he missed the point of life. This works-based worldview cannot save, works are the response to God's grace, not the end in themselves. Contrastingly, the publican realized he had been missing the mark and begged for God's mercy. You see, a prayer of repentance is always about mercy and not about merit! Really, when I confess my sin, I don't even want to promise that I won't do the same thing again. This confidence in my flesh will only lead to embarrassment later when I inevitably fail!

In addition, when discussing God's mercy toward us, many of us who follow Christ realize we are forgiven but forget that others are. We lack mercy toward other sinners and can be harsh toward them, forgetting that both we and they have been granted grace from our Lord. Since we have been given grace, we want to pass it forward. As Jesus taught, mercy should triumph over judgment. When I am judging over living graciously, I need to have a "love" check because often the problem is a legalistic, loveless rut that I have fallen into!

Continuing, in Luke 7, Simon the Pharisee invited Jesus and His disciples over for dinner. Given the Teacher's notoriety, many others, some invited and others not, attended. One such party-crasher was a woman of ill repute.

> And one of the Pharisees desired that He would eat with him. And He went into the Pharisee's house, and sat down to meat. And, behold, a woman in the city brought an alabaster box of ointment, and stood at His feet behind Him weeping, and began to kiss His feet, wash His feet with tears, and did wipe them with the hairs of her head, and kissed His feet, and anointed them with ointment. Now when the Pharisee which had bidden Him saw it, he spake within himself, saying, this man, if He were a prophet, He would have known who and what manner of woman this is that touches him; for she is a sinner. And Jesus answering (*demonstrating that He was indeed a prophet, as He read his mind!*) said unto him, Simon, I have somewhat to say unto thee. And he saith, Master, say on. There was a certain

> creditor which had two debtors; the one owed five hundred pence, and the other fifty. And when they had nothing to pay, he frankly forgave them both. Tell me therefore, which of them will love him the most? Simon answered and said, I suppose that he, to whom he forgave most. And He said to him, thou have rightly judged. And He turned to the woman, and said unto Simon, see thou this woman? I entered into thine house, thou gave me no water for my feet, but she has washed my feet with her tears, and wiped them with the hairs of her head. Thou gave me no kiss, but this woman since the time I came in has not ceased to kiss my feet. My head with oil thou did not anoint, but this woman has anointed my feet with ointment. Wherefore I say to thee, her sins, which are many, are forgiven, for she loved much. But to whom little is forgiven, the same loves little.
> Luke 7:36-47 (italics added)

This parable teaches that sin is a debt we owe to God. Differing amounts clearly, but unpayable by all. Again, Jesus is using a parable to show the pseudo-righteous person the fallacy of thinking they can make the payment.

This brings me to the second great benefit of true repentance (the first being losing the self-righteous critical spirit), which is that the forgiven one loves much. When we see that an about-face is needed, not just a little clean-up, we love much and start to live beautifully, basking in the light of God's forgiveness, like the women in this parable. That is what I want; you, too, I suspect. Remember, repentance leads to reconciliation. And oh, how good that feels!

A third benefit to repentance is that it leads to revival. Revival for individuals, revival in congregations, and even revival of nations. The great Welsh revival of 1904 was centered upon four points starting with national repentance. Evangelist Evan Roberts said that the keys were confession of sin and restitution, the forsaking of sin, responding to the spirit promptly, and professing Jesus publicly.

A beautiful picture of repentance being followed by revival is seen in the names of the gates of Jerusalem. Specifically, the Dung Gate, which was used to take out the city's refuse, preceded the next gate, called the Fountain Gate. So, track with me here. That Dung Gate pictures repentance, taking out the trash of our lives. Next, the Fountain Gate pictures the filling of the Holy Spirit, the spirit-filled walk! The order is most relevant and important. Spirit-filled living always follows confession of sins, not the other way around.

> If we confess our sins, He is faithful and just to forgive us our sins, and to cleanse us from all unrighteousness.
> 1 John 1:9

Truly, it is like taking a bath to repent, to confess, to agree with our Maker.

The fear of the Lord is also very much an important ingredient both to repentance and revival. The Bible teaches that the fear of the Lord is the beginning of wisdom (Proverbs 9:10). It proclaims that our God is a consuming fire (Hebrews 12:29), that He is a warrior. It is important to always remember who we are dealing with when we come to the God of the Universe. He is not some impotent, out-of-touch deity, no, He is the Author of Life, He is a Man of War! (Exodus 15:3)

The balance of this healthy fear is our Lord's great love, grace, and mercy toward us. Because of this, we understand that the proper fear of the Lord is not being afraid of Him per se, but because He is so awesome, it is to be terrified at the thought of being away from him.

The Proverbs teach that the fear of the Lord, that is, the reverence of him, leads to repentance.

> By mercy and truth iniquity is purged; and by
> the fear of the Lord men depart evil.
> Proverbs 16:6

Truly, when I fear the Lord, I don't want to disappoint Him by sinning.

Revival is also spoken of in the wisdom of the Psalms.

> O fear the Lord, ye His saints; for there is no
> want to them that fear Him.
> Psalms 34:9

> The secret of the Lord is with those who fear
> Him; and He will show them His covenant.
> Psalm 25:14

How cool is this? God will give revelation to the soul who fears Him!

Lastly, I want to show you that God reveals Himself in His glory to those who venerate him. In other words, His palpable presence is perceived when He is reverenced.

> God is greatly to be feared in the assembly of the saints, and to be had in reverence of all them that are about Him.
> Psalm 89:7

A better rendering of the latter part of this verse is that God will be present with those who draw near to Him, to those who are around Him, to those followers who reverence Him.

So, repentance is a major doctrine of the Bible. It is not necessary because God demands it, but God demands it because it is necessary! It is primarily the confession of our Savior from sin and then, secondarily, the confession of our specific sins. Confession of the Savior leads to our salvation, losing the legalistic critical spirit, and having much love. Confession of our sins leads to revival and reconciliation on all levels...individual, corporate, and national.

Lastly, in closing this discussion of repentance, a good Bible picture I have in my mind concerning our confession of the Savior, not self, from sin is seen in the yearly Passover sacrifice in which the Jews partook. Every year, the sinner and his family would come to Jerusalem with a lamb to sacrifice for their sins. Before the sacrifice was made, the priest would inspect the lamb, not the sinner. Likewise, our Lamb was inspected and found spotless. That is why my sins, which are many, are not seen by the Father. They are covered by the Son. He was inspected, not me!

Summary:

1. The road to salvation begins with repentance.
2. The primary definition of repentance is to change one's thinking concerning salvation. Realizing works won't save, only His sacrifice.

3. The secondary meaning of repentance is to remorsefully agree with God concerning specific sins in my life.
4. Benefits of repentance: Develop mercy over judgment. Love much. Revival.

For Further Study:

1. What is the purpose of the Law?
2. How does sorrow over sin sometimes not equate with true repentance?
3. What are some of the benefits of having the fear of the Lord? Of not ever wanting to be apart from Him?

The Kingdom of Heaven: Its Bill of Rights

"Repent: For the kingdom of heaven is at hand" (Matthew 3:1 and 4:17) were the first public calls from both John and Jesus. The King from Heaven had invaded the planet that belonged to our Adversary, Satan, and was beginning His campaign to take it back. The need for this invasion occurred after Adam transferred the authority given him by sinning.

Under Satan's leadership, our world is indeed a sick place. Evil is pervasive. Pride, greed, and pleasure-seeking are the default settings of His subjects. The world's system is invited into people's homes and hearts daily via the internet and television networks. Truly, we humans are living in a "matrix" of evil that we are, for the most part, not even aware of as being abnormal and desperately wrong. It is this upside-down world's system that King Jesus entered to begin setting up His Kingdom. It is a system that briefly did, and in the future will, turn the world back to right-side-up.

To learn what His kingdom looks like, we need go no farther than Matthew's gospel and to Jesus' very famous, and equally misunderstood, Sermon on the Mount. Specifically, the Constitution of the Kingdom of Heaven (also called the Kingdom of God) is described in detail in the sermon. We will see that Jesus' words of this constitution, for the most part, directly oppose the conventional wisdom of our present world. But, as we would expect from God, whenever man actually puts in use principles from the sermon, life actually works! The misunderstood portion of the sermon is that followers of God over the centuries have believed they could follow the teachings put forth despite our fallen, sinful nature. While the precepts are meant to be lived out as He taught, Jesus' primary intent was for us was to realize that we cannot even come close to this goal. The sermon's primary insight is to drive us to the important realization that we need a Savior!

To that end, the key verse, which unlocks the rest of the teaching, is found in Matthew 5:20: "For I say to you, that except your righteousness shall exceed the righteousness of the scribes and Pharisees, ye shall in no case enter into the kingdom of heaven." This would have challenged the listeners greatly because the scribes and Pharisees were the ones the people believed were most likely to populate a future heaven. Jesus T-bones this thinking, saying that God is looking for perfection! That people must be one hundred percent holy, complete, mature. Yes, we must be perfect. The conclusion He is looking for is that we obviously can't live this way completely, showing our need for a Savior. He was confirming our need for the many Old Testament types picturing this reality, e.g., the Kinsman Redeemer of Ruth, the Brazen Serpent of Numbers, the Daysman of Job, and Queen Esther from the book of the same, among many others. In seeing our need, this drives us to Christ, which then drives us in Christ as we live the Kingdom mentality, ever trusting in Him for guidance and confessing to Him when we invariably falter.

So, let's examine the Kingdom's Constitution, the Sermon on the Mount, starting with its famous Bill of Rights. Nine awesome statements that directly come against the world's wisdom yet nonetheless promise happiness to the kingdom saint who practices them.

The Beatitudes

> Blessed are the poor in spirit; for theirs is the kingdom of heaven.
> Matthew 5:3

Wow! Happy ("blessed" in King James English means "happy") are those who realize they do not have it all together, who understand that we can't make it on our own. Happy am I when I grasp how great God is compared to me, when I make Him my God and not myself! This flies in the face of the common worldview that happiness comes to those who make it! To the winner, to the man or woman with the most money, the best job, and/or the most accolades.

Its dependency upon God versus the pervasive competitive spirit that says, "If it's to be, it's up to me." It's the Tree of Life versus the Tree of the Knowledge of Good and Evil. It's walking by the spirit versus walking in the flesh. It is God has been so good to me versus I'm a self-made man.

Think with me here. Who in the above four examples are the happy ones? Why, it is those walking hand-in-hand with God, not those going it alone. Even for the few who do make it by the world's standards, the World Series champ, the billionaire, or the mega-movie star, when you look at their lives, often they're a mess. Many of these "champions" will say, when they finally reached the pinnacle of fame and success, that it was hollow, not being the pot of gold at the end of the rainbow that they thought it would be.

No, Jesus is right in starting the articles of His government with the need to realize that childlike dependency is better than adult-like independence. To the poor in spirit, theirs is the kingdom of heaven, for, indeed, they're going to feel right at home!

> Blessed are they that mourn; for they shall be comforted.
> Matthew 5:4

The Bible has many statements that seem to be paradoxical, yet are oh so true. The first shall be last; It is better to give than receive; If you die, then you will live, etc. This is another one of those great declarations: Mourners will be comforted.

This idea of sorrow to joy is peppered throughout the Word of God. Hannah cried unto the Lord at Shiloh to remember her barren state. God answered her prayer and her mourning turned to joy with the birth of Samuel. King Darius fasted and mourned all night after he was tricked into sending Daniel to the lion's den. How happy he was the next morning when the Angel of the Lord protected his prime minister from the predators. Of course, Jesus illustrated this principle in a way that warms my heart in describing the sorrow His disciples would experience upon His departure, followed by the joy they would feel upon seeing Him again, as He used a woman and a child for His promise.

> Now Jesus knew that they were desirous to ask him, and He said unto them, do you enquire among yourselves of that I said, a little while, and ye shall not see me; and again, a little while, and ye shall see me? Truly, truly, I say unto you, that ye shall weep and lament, but

> the world shall rejoice; and you shall be sorrowful, but your sorrow shall be turned to joy. A woman when she is in travail hath sorrow, because her hour is come; but as soon as she is delivered of the child, she remembers no more the anguish, for the joy that a man is born into the world. And you now therefore have sorrow; but I will see you again, and your heart shall rejoice, and your joy no man takes from you.
> John 16:19-22

A prophecy of Jesus' ministry compassing both His first and second advent speaks to His ability to provide comfort to the mourners.

> The Spirit of the Lord God is upon me; because the Lord has anointed me to preach good tidings to the meek; He hath sent me to bind up the broken-hearted, to proclaim liberty to the captives, and the opening of the prison to them that are bound: To proclaim the acceptable year of the Lord, and the day of vengeance of our God: To comfort all that mourn...to give them beauty for ashes, the oil of joy for mourning, the garment of praise for the spirit of heaviness.
> Isaiah 61:1-3

Indeed, Jesus is ultimately the reason, that in His Kingdom, those who mourn will be comforted.

Lastly, in considering Matthew 5:4, I recall Jesus' promise to send the Comforter shortly after His return to Heaven.

> If you love me, keep my commandments. And I will pray the Father, and He shall give you another Comforter, that He may abide with you forever. Even the Spirit of truth, whom the world cannot receive, because it sees Him not, neither knows Him: But you know Him, for He dwells with you, and shall be in you. I will not leave you comfortless: I will come to you. Yet a little while, and the world sees me no more, but you see me: Because I live, you shall live also.
> John 14:15-19

As an application to this Kingdom of truth, never judge the rest of your life by the present season you are in. There will come hard times in all of our lives. We live in a fallen world presently. But sorrow will turn to joy, beauty will come from ashes. Often, we are tempted by our flesh and the dark spiritual powers of this world to want to give up during a season of mourning. Some will even be challenged with suicidal thoughts and intentions. This spirit of heaviness is exactly what the Devil wants for us all. How very important it is to remember this second precept of the Kingdom: Blessed are they that mourn, for they shall be comforted.

> -----
>
> Blessed are the meek: For they shall inherit the earth.
> Matthew 5:5

In Jesus' only autobiographical statement, He said He was meek (Matthew 11:29). Moses, in penning the Torah, commented upon his meekness (Numbers 12:3). Indeed, meekness is a personality trait that God's Word seems to shine much positive light upon. Biblical meekness can be defined as strength under control, like a powerful stallion that is ready for battle yet attentive to his master. Solomon paints meekness with these potent words:

> He that is slow to anger is better than the mighty; and he that rules his spirit than he that takes a city.
> Proverbs 16:32

In the Kingdom mentality, the meek shall inherit the earth. But this is not how many alive today see it. Those who would inherit the earth think they must seize it! They need to grab for all they can get. It's "Out of my way, I'm going to get mine!" We're in a competition and, to inherit my little piece of the earth, I must put my best foot forward, I must promote myself, I must press forward even if others are injured along the way.

Obviously, this is not the way of our Lord. He taught that the one who seeks to save his life will lose it and the one who loses his life will save it (Luke 17:33). Of course, Jesus modeled this concept to the infinite degree when He took the sins of the world, the sins of all of us, the sins of you and me, and went to the Cross, dying to pay our unpayable debt.

Meekness contrasts with pride in that the former is others-oriented while the latter is always self-positioned. Outward signs of a meek person include his love for others, her awareness of the presence of God in her life, and his trust in God over self. One of the reasons meekness is so valued by our Maker is because it is a human personality trait that enables a soul to see his or her need for the Savior. A meek person can much more easily receive the "good news" of salvation over a prideful individual. Meekness opens the door to the Father by way of the Son and energized by the Spirit so that we have the victory that overcomes the world. Let me show you:

> Whosoever believes that Jesus is the Christ is born of God...For whatsoever is born of God overcomes the world: And this is the victory that overcomes the world, even our faith. Who is he that overcomes the world, but he that believes that Jesus is the Son of God.
> I John 5:1, 4-5

Faith in Jesus as the Christ, as the Anointed One of God, is the victory that overcomes the world. Or in Jesus' words, faith is the victory that "inherits the earth," which often is energized by meekness.

Lastly, the world says faith is a fantasy. God says faith is what makes me victorious. Jesus said that we are blessed because we have not seen Him, yet believe (John 20:29). You see, belief in God is rational, based upon so much evidence from His past dealings with us. Faith just extends the belief that He will do what He says He will do in the future, i.e., save us, take us to Heaven, etc.

> -----
>
> Blessed are they that do hunger and thirst after righteousness: For they shall be filled.
> Matthew 5:6

The soul who longs for "right living" shall be filled. In looking around our world, it seems this is not the case. Evil is rampant in our lives. The internet, news media, entertainment centers, and even the educational system feed the follower of Christ a steady diet of falsehood, deception, and evil. We long for the righteousness our Lord promised when He made this statement.

C.S. Lewis famously has written about the God-shaped hole with which we were all born. It has been said that people have a need to fill this space but, without God, all attempts fall short. Pleasure, prestige, adventure, drugs, and alcohol, etc., are all used in this effort. Every good novel or movie repeats the same story we all love to dream of: That of tension and near disaster followed by the rescue of the main character by a superhero. It's the gospel story told over and over again without giving credit or mention to the true superhero the story always reflects.

But the soul who calls Jesus Lord does have access to this filling presently.

> For the Kingdom of God is not meat and drink;
> but righteousness, and peace, and joy in the
> Holy Ghost.
> Romans 14:17

We can be filled with His righteousness internally, despite the world we live in not sharing in that. As the Word declares, we are in the world but not of the world (John 17:16).

In contrast, when the Lord returns visibly to our planet and sets up His external reign, then righteousness will be available to all. The Bible tells us in that day that the earth shall be full of the knowledge of the Lord as the waters cover the sea (Isaiah 11:9).

One of the many names for God is Jehovah-Tsidkinu, meaning "the Lord our Righteousness." Truly, the Godhead is the Alpha and the Omega, the source of all life and the goal for all life. Jesus, as the revealed image of the Father, is what we are all hungering and thirsting after. And He is available to all.

> Behold, I stand at the door, and knock: If any man hear my voice, and open the door, I will come in to him, and will sup with him, and he with me. To him that overcomes will I grant to sit with me in my throne, even as I overcame, and am set down with my Father in His throne.
> Revelation 3:20-21

> Blessed are the merciful: For they shall obtain mercy.
> Matthew 5:7

It would seem that the world's system prefers judgment over mercy. Rules and regulations are the staple of our lives in this fallen state. They provide security and boundaries to our uncertain world.

Not so with our Lord. He favors relationships over policies and procedures. And He deals with us in a circle of fellowship, where He is at the center, not a hierarchy of laws with Him at the top of the pyramid.

The definition of mercy is withholding of merited judgment. It is similar, yet different, than grace, with is to bestow unmerited favor. Both of these attributes we see in full display in God's dealings with us. In fact, when Moses asked God His name, this is what he heard:

> And the Lord descended in the cloud, and stood with him there, and proclaimed the

> name of the Lord. And the Lord passed by before him, and proclaimed, The Lord, The Lord God, merciful and gracious, longsuffering, and abundant in goodness and truth.
> Exodus 34:5-6

The many names of God in the Bible always tell of His nature. This first attribute, this first virtue which we learn characterizes our God, is mercy! He is a God of mercy. Thus, as we extend mercy to others, we become imitators of God. How cool is that? Of course, the merciful are promised to receive mercy as Jesus confirmed as part of the Kingdom charter. This energizes the words of Paul concerning reaping and sowing:

> Be not deceived; God is not mocked: For whatsoever a man sows, that shall he also reap.
> Galatians 6:7

This principle of sowing and reaping applies to many categories of life, including the giving of time and money as well as that of bestowing mercy toward others. The opposite of this principle, of course, is embedded in these promises. He who is stingy with his time, money, and mercy will receive a stingy portion of these blessings back to him in the future when he needs them most.

We learn of the importance of mercy from an encounter that Jesus had with the Pharisees.

> And it came to pass, as Jesus sat at meat in the house, behold, many publicans and sinners came and sat down with Him and His disciples. And when the Pharisees saw it, they said to His disciples, why eateth your Master with publi-

> cans and sinners? But when Jesus heard that, He said to them, they that be whole need not a physician, but they that are sick. But go ye and learn what that means, I will have mercy, and not sacrifice: For I am not come to call the righteous, but sinners to repentance.
> Matthew 9:10-13

In dealing with the four people groups which will populate the Kingdom of Heaven, that of Pharisees, publicans, sinners, and disciples, Jesus emphasized mercy over judgment. How we live is more important than what we give. He told the Pharisees, those learned men who studied God's Word, that they still had studying to do. He was pointing out that mercy is the highway to salvation and healing. When publicans and sinners realize God's great mercy as extended by our Lord, they readily receive the call to repentance. In contrast, when pharisaical believers extend judgment, no desire for change will ever be seen in those same publicans and sinners who are far from him.

Tragically, we see from an Old Testament picture of how death is the result of removing mercy to get at the Law. In 1 Samuel 5 and 6, the children of Israel were under a time of bondage by their enemy, the Philistines. They had lost the Ark of the Covenant a year prior in an ill-advised attempt to obtain victory over their perpetual enemy by bringing the ark into the battle. Their hearts were not right and God allowed the ark to be captured. Subsequently, the ark proved too hot to handle for the Philistines. Their god, Dagon, was decapitated when the ark was placed near it in that false god's temple and the people of the land were comically plagued with hemorrhoids! They correctly realized that the God of the Israelites was too potent to keep in their land, so they sent the ark back to Israel. They put the ark on an ox cart and sent it down the road to the nearest Israeli town of Bethshemesh. The men of Bethshemesh were working in the fields when the ark came ambling home. They were overjoyed to receive back the most revered icon of their faith. But what happened next is the lesson for all time which is pictured. The Ark of the Covenant contained the two tablets of the Ten Commandments as well as a pot of manna and Aaron's rod, which budded. Over the ark was the mercy seat where God had said He would meet His people. So, when the ark returned, the men of the city could not be faulted for wanting to know if the other icons of their faith were still in the ark or if the Philistines had plundered them. The result of this needing to know involved removing the mercy seat to get at the law. When they did this, the Bible tells us that a plague was released in the area of Bethshemesh and thousands died. As sad as this story is, it portrays for all time the importance of mercy over judgment.

Of course, the world's system does not accept this truth. Fact-finding and finger-pointing are the way of life for the masses. But, for those of us desiring to live in the Kingdom mentality, let us choose mercy over judgment, life over death.

In closing this discussion of mercy, let me show you a proverb demonstrating how beautiful and glorious it is to live a life filled with mercy toward others.

> The discretion of a man defers his anger: And it is his glory to pass over a transgression.
> Proverbs 19:11

> Blessed are the pure in heart: For they shall see God.
> Matthew 5:8

No man has seen God at any time (John 1:18). But this declaration is speaking of the Father before the revelation of the Son was given to men. The man or woman, the boy or girl who call Jesus Lord, realizing that He indeed is the Son of God, that He is part of the mysterious Godhead, they will see God as they gaze upon Jesus. Let me show you:

> God, who at sundry times and diverse manners spoke in times past unto the fathers by the prophets, hath in these last days spoken to us by His Son, whom He hath appointed heir of all things, by whom He made the worlds: Who being the brightness of His glory, and the express image of His person, and upholding all things by the word of His power, when He had by himself purged our sins, sat down on the right hand of majesty on high.
> Hebrews 1:1-3

You see, Jesus is the express image of God. He is the One we see when we see God.

Now, the confession of the Savior and the forsaking of sin give a person a pure heart. David, whom the Bible calls a man after God's own heart (1 Samuel 13:14) had many flaws, many sins. But he knew God as his Savior and forsook his sin (see Psalm 51). And he knew he would see God. "As for me, I will behold thy face in righteousness" (Psalm 17:15).

Isaiah saw the second person of the Godhead high and lifted up, as noted in Chapter 6 of his prophecy. John tells us in his inspired gospel that it was indeed Jesus whom Isaiah saw (John 12:37-41). This is called a Christophany, which is an appearance of Jesus in the Old Testament before He came as the babe of

Bethlehem. So, as Isaiah saw the Lord, he realized how undone he was, being a man of unclean lips among a people of unclean lips. One of the angels that appeared with the Lord took a coal from the altar (representing our Lord's sacrifice for our sins) and touched his lips saying "Lo, this has touched your lips; and thine iniquity is taken away, and thy sin purged" (Isaiah 6:7). Isaiah's heart was purified, seeing God, as his sin was forgiven and forgotten.

Looking forward to the redemption of our bodies being forever with the Lord also gives one a pure heart, enabling him to see God in this life:

> Beloved, now are we the sons of God, and it doth not yet appear what we shall be: But we know that, when He shall appear (*either at our death or His return*), we shall be like Him; for we shall see Him as He is. And every man that hath this hope in Him purifies himself, even as He is pure.
> 1 John 3:2-3 (italics added)

We know that Jesus is pure, thus, looking forward to being with Him puts one in the same category as the Lord. How awesome is that?

In contrast, if one does not want to see God, then don't have a pure heart. Keep sinning, keep living for your flesh, counting on self and denying the Lord, and indeed, that one will not see God. Jeremiah told Israel that if they would seek the Lord, they would find Him if they sought Him with all their hearts (Jeremiah 29:13). King Asa was told that if the people of Judah and Benjamin pursued the Lord, He would be found but if they forsook Him, He would forsake them (2 Chronicles 15:2).

Isaiah explained this relationship of an impure heart and the inability to see God with these words:

> Behold, the Lord's hand is not shortened, that He cannot save; neither His ear heavy, that it cannot hear: But your iniquities have separated between you and your God, and your sins have hid His face from you, that He will not hear.
> Isaiah 59:1-2

Sin indeed blocks my view of God. He is all around, but I don't see Him. I miss Him in a sunrise or sunset, I don't see Him in the mountain vista or the soaring eagle. When I hear a beautiful song, I don't connect the dots to His gifts or, when the love of a man and a woman is blessed by Him, sin will cause it to fall far short of what He intended it to be. Indeed, sin stinks! To get the odor off, I want to confess Jesus as my Savior and forsake my sin. That purifies my heart (along with looking to His return) and, as Jesus promised, I will see Him.

> -----
> Blessed are the peacemakers: For they shall be called the children of God.
> Matthew 5:9

The Almighty is the God of Peace. Therefore, it goes to reason that His sons and daughters will resemble Him. Peacemakers are doing what comes naturally because they look like their Father. Brothers and sisters also often look alike. Jesus, as our brother, is called the Prince of Peace (Isaiah 9:6). In this instance, peacemakers again take on the appearance of their brother!

Children of God spread peace wherever they go as they operate in the power of the Holy Spirit.

> Now the God of hope fill you with all joy and peace in believing, that you may abound in hope through the power of the Holy Spirit.
> Romans 15:13

Hopeful believing brings joy and peace! Of course, one of the fruitful manifestations of the spirit-filled life is peace (Galatians 5:22-23), along with love, joy, patience, gentleness, goodness, faith, meekness, and self-control.

Peaceful words and advice are also associated with godly wisdom. Let me show you:

> But the wisdom that is from above is first pure, then peaceable, gentle, and easy to be entreated, full of mercy and good fruits, without partiality, and without hypocrisy. And the fruit of righteousness is sown in peace of them that make peace.
> James 3:17-18

These verses are so loaded! Godly wisdom is peaceful and gentle, it is easy, it shows mercy, and does not show favorites or self-glorification. This *is* the barometer by which all wisdom is to be judged. If it brings strife, anger, envy, favoritism, and pride, these words of wisdom and advice are not of the Lord but of the Evil One. God's words always are associated with a combination of the eight characteristics noted above. The Adversary's words and the world's advice often are not.

These verses also are the benchmark for reading God's Word and understanding His tone. When I read the Word, if strife and anxiety are released, then I absolutely have the tone incorrect in my mind. I am not really understanding what He is saying. The Author is not the God of conflict and discord but the God of Peace. Brothers and sisters, always use these words concerning wisdom in rightly dividing the word of truth (2 Timothy 2:15).

A peacemaker understands that an important key to life is to put Jesus on center stage. When I do that, then the differences we have with each other fade away. Also, with the Lord at the center, I no longer need to demand my privileges and rights but will concentrate on my responsibility. I'm able to die to myself and my little kingdom as I elevate my Lord. This is extremely important for those among us who are married. If I am sowing peace over demanding my rights, things will go well. Often, men feel that, as the "head of the home," they can and should rule. This, of course is not promoting peace, and is not what the Lord is saying when He put the man over the woman. It's about authority, not importance or equality. Same as the Father and the Son. They are equal in importance and equality but in authority the Father is over the Son. This authority the man has over the woman is not the ticket to rule but actually is the charge to lead. Every good leader knows that he must go into the battle first if the followers are to be inspired for the fight.

So, dear believer, with God's help strive for a life of peace. Spread peace wherever you go. Use peace and peacemaking as your gauge for evaluating wisdom and God's words. And, along with that, have peace in all of your marital life. Things will go well when you do! As has been said: "No God, no peace; know God, know peace."

> Therefore, being justified by faith, we have peace with God through our Lord Jesus Christ.
> Romans 5:1

> Blessed are they which are persecuted for righteousness' sake:
> For theirs is the kingdom of heaven.
> Matthew 5:10

What is your life's metaphor? Is life like a party? A merry-go-round? Sometimes I think my life resembles a rollercoaster. In this I have a choice: I can just hang on or I can choose to enjoy the ride! But one more metaphor, life is a battleground. Like babies born in Poland in 1942, we were born into a raging world war. Oh, not one of flesh and blood but one much more sinister and evil, for the war I am speaking of, and of which Jesus taught extensively, is a spiritual war for the souls of men!

> For we wrestle not against flesh and blood, but against principalities, against powers, against the rulers of the darkness of this world, against spiritual wickedness in high places.
> Ephesians 6:12

If this doesn't sound menacing, I'm not sure what does! The forces of evil apparently have a hierarchy much like a modern military. There are principalities, i.e., branches of service like the Army, Navy, etc. Powers, e.g., missiles, tanks, and F-16s. They have rulers. We would say, generals, colonels, as well as the commander-in-chief. And they are spiritually wicked in high places. That means they are well placed in all of the great places of our world. Politics, for sure, education, business, entertainment, of course. And, most ominously, they are well-positioned in the religious systems of the world. This is the world in which we live. Paul rightly calls Satan the god of this world (2 Corinthians 4:4). When I don't see this with spiritual eyes, I can easily be taken in. Unfortunately, most people are being wiped out due to their lack of this understanding. The forces of evil want nothing more than for humans to think they are not real, that they are a joke and a fantasy. When the real war is not comprehended, then, whenever strife occurs, we souls tend to blame the wrong entity. It's the government's fault, it's my wife's fault, it's the pastor's fault. No, no, no, it is spiritual, it is always transcendent.

So, given that Satan has temporary control of our world (temporary, for we know the end of the story), it is not surprising that our Lord might mention attacks, He might mention persecutions. For the Devil hates you more than you can imagine. He wants to steal from you, kill and destroy you (John10:10). But, since you are God's, he can only steal from you and kill you, he cannot destroy you, i.e., send you to Hell. Obviously, I don't want him stealing from me or killing me, either. Thus, I definitely do not want to linger in the back of the pack, so to speak. I want to be engaged, I want to be close to the Lord, I want to be strong in the Lord (Ephesians 6:10), then I will be protected from his thievery and murder.

> Yea, all that live godly in Christ Jesus shall suffer persecution.
> 2 Timothy 3:12

So, as to not be taken in, the Bible tells us that persecution will be the lot of the believer's life. I should not be surprised. In fact, I should be glad! You may be thinking, "Why would you say that?" Because, as I am persecuted for righteousness' sake, it shows I belong to Him. It reveals that the Captain of the host of the Lord (Joshua 5:14) is in my heart. Soon, He will take out the rulers of the darkness of this world but, for now, the Lord is allowing them a role to play for purposes that are above my pay grade to explain.

So, what should I do when persecuted? Well, realizing where the attack of persecution is coming from, I need to reverse the battle. Every good general knows that, when attacked, he must weather the initial assault, then counterattack. I need to do the same. I need to go on the offensive. Jesus died, not to keep me safe, but to make me dangerous! I'm hazardous to Satan and the world's system. My debt has been paid, yes, but I'm also filled with His righteousness. I have Christ in me, I'm a little Christ walking around filled with His Spirit and knocking down walls that Satan has erected against others.

Practically, I can pray for others when attacked. Prayer unleashes the forces of heaven. Obviously, when the Devil's henchmen see me praying for others, they will think twice the next time they attack. Praising my Lord when disrespected is another strategy I employ in this fight. Did you know that, before Satan fell, he was called Lucifer and the Bible hints that he was the praise leader in Heaven (Ezekiel 28:11-19)? So, after falling, my Adversary hates to hear praise going up to Jesus. It reminds him what he lost when his pride took him out, when it took him down!

In summary, realize the unseen battle raging all around and enlist in this war. Remember, we are fighting from a position of victory because God is greater than our enemies and He obtained full rights to you by His death on the Cross.

Next, we will look at the last of the Bill of Rights. That of the blessing of suffering persecution for being a Jesus follower!

> Blessed are you, when men shall revile you, and persecute you, and say all manner of evil against you falsely, for my sake. Rejoice and be exceedingly glad: For great is your reward in heaven.
> Matthew 5:11-12

Jesus isn't pulling any punches here. Not *if* men shall revile, but *when* men shall do these evil things to us. No sugar-coating by Jesus. Things in this war are going to heat up. We must expect conflict, expect pushback from men, remembering always the spiritual source from where all of this struggle is coming from.

This topic of suffering at the hands of unbelievers is frequently spoken of by our Lord, as well as by others. Wonderfully, almost every time it is, we see a promise of future joy and glory linked. In this case, we can rejoice and be overflowingly happy as great rewards await His followers who are persecuted in His name.

> These things I have spoken unto you, that in me you might have peace, in the world you shall have tribulation: But be of good cheer; I have overcome the world.
> John 16:33

> Beloved, think it not strange concerning the fiery trial which is to try you, as though some strange thing happened to you: But rejoice, inasmuch as you are partakers of Christ's sufferings; that, when His glory shall be revealed, you may be glad with exceeding joy. If you are

> reproached for the name of Christ, happy are you; for the spirit of glory and of God rests upon you.
> 1 Peter 4:12-14

> We are troubled on every side, yet not distressed; we are perplexed, but not in despair: Persecuted, but not forsaken, cast down, but not destroyed; always bearing about in the body the dying of the Lord Jesus Christ, that the life also of Jesus might be made manifest in our body. For we which live are always delivered unto death for Jesus' sake...For which cause we faint not; but though our outward man perish, yet the inward man is renewed day by day. For our light affliction, which is but for a moment, worketh for us a far more exceeding and eternal weight of glory.
> 2 Corinthians 4:8-11, 16-17

> For I reckon that the sufferings of this present time are not worthy to be compared with the glory which shall be revealed in us.
> Romans 8:18

Obviously, there is a tension between the wheat and the tares, between light and darkness, between people living by the flesh and those walking in the spirit. Solomon poetically speaks with these words:

> An unjust man is an abomination to the just:

> And he that is upright in his way is an abomination to the wicked.
> Proverbs 29:27

> He that justifies the wicked, and he that condemns the just, even they both are abomination to the Lord.
> Proverbs 17:15

So, persecutions and false accusations are going to occur and we can rejoice for the blessing we will receive in the future because of our stand for Jesus, but what can we do now, in the midst of the trial? For one, remember that the name of Jesus has power. "Wherefore God hath highly exalted Him, and given Him a name which is above every name" (Philippians 2:9). In fact, the Name has unlimited power to bless and protect. Speak audibly to Him when attacked, praying "Jesus, help me."

Also, I can bring heaven down to me now. How do I do that? By praising Him. The Bible teaches that God inhabits the praises of His people (Psalm 22:3). As I praise him, my attitude changes, my perspective alters and I am refreshed and renewed. No, the conditions may not have changed, but now I am above them. As has been said, "Life is 10% circumstances and 90% attitude."

When I see others suffering, many times I cannot stop the attack they are in the midst of, but I can remind them of Heaven. Speaking of the reality of our next life, dwelling in glory with Jesus, truly is medicine for a sufferer's soul.

Okay, so we will be happy in the future. What about now? Any benefits of persecutions in the name of Christ?

> For we would not, brethren, have you ignorant of our trouble which came to us in Asia,

> that we were pressed out of measure, above strength, insomuch that we despaired even of life: But we had the sentence of death in ourselves, that we should not trust in ourselves, but in God which raises the dead.
> 2 Corinthians 1:8-9

You see, difficulties lead me to trust in God over self. They pull me away from the idolatry of self-reliance. "He that puts his trust in the Lord shall be made fat, but he that trusts in his own heart is a fool" (Proverbs 28:25-26).

Struggles also help me to mature, to become the man I want to be, and importantly, to become the man He wants me to be. Let me show you:

> My brethren, count it all joy when you fall into different temptations; knowing this, that the trying of your faith worketh patience. But let patience have her perfect work, that you may be mature and complete, lacking nothing.
> James 1: 2-4

Concluding this topic, we have future glory and joy, and we can have present comfort and growth but, best of all, suffering for the name of our Savior makes one great! Look at the Book of Job. In it, we see that the curtain is pulled back on heaven and eternity. Every man, every woman, has only a few chances at greatness in their lives. No one would remember Job if nothing bad had ever happened. But he was refined in his trials and came out the other side as one of the great men of history. I want to be in good company like that and I'll bet you do, too.

Or Shadrach, Meshach, and Abednego, found in the Book of Daniel. Those young men refused to worship the golden statue, facing the wrath of Nebuchadnezzar and risking being thrown into the midst of the burning fiery furnace. The words they spoke indeed were faithful words, words that revealed their greatness. They are words I pray I would speak if called upon in a similar setting.

> O Nebuchadnezzar, our God whom we serve is able to deliver us from the burning fiery furnace, and He will deliver us out of thine hand, O king. But if not, be it known unto thee, O king, that we will not serve thy gods, nor worship the golden image which thou hast set up. Daniel 3:17-18

Those brave men chose obedience over outcome. They certainly believed in God's ability to deliver them but understood that that same deliverance may not be His will for them. So, they submitted to His sovereignty. These words, under the pressure they were beneath, are what made them so great! This is the kind of faith that displays God and His power for all to see. And we know what happened, too. Nebuchadnezzar became enraged at their audacity and had the furnace heated seven times hotter. Into the furnace the three believers in Jehovah were thrown and nothing happened to them except their ropes were loosed. And a fourth One, who appeared as the Son of God, was seen walking with them in the midst of the fire. Indeed, the God of Israel was exalted to the king and the people because of the three believers' incredible stand for Him.

So, Jesus ends His Bill of Rights with the greatest article of all. Walk strong in the face of conflict for him. Those soldiers in this war for the Kingdom will receive eternal blessing as they stand for their Commander. They truly are the greatest generation, wearing medals for all time that make the Medal of Honor look like a boy's tin sheriff's star in comparison.

Summary:

1. The Constitution of the Kingdom of Heaven is found in the Sermon on the Mount.
2. People who are poor in spirit are happy because they realize they need God.
3. God promises to turn sorrow into joy.
4. Meekness is strength under control in God's economy.
5. Extending mercy over judgment is glorious.
6. A pure heart comes from confessing the Savior and forsaking sin.
7. Peacemakers resemble their Father.
8. Resist the Devil when attacked by praying for others and praising God.
9. Persecutions and troubles help one trust in God over self.
10. Standing for Christ honors Him to the world.

For Further Study:

1. How is being poor in spirit related to pride?
2. What is a Bible paradox? Are any of the Beatitudes such?
3. Why is faith in God more rational than unbelief in him?
4. How does one discern whether wisdom is from above or below?

The Kingdom of Heaven: Its Constitution; Part One

The Sermon on the Mount, found in Matthew 5-7 and repeated in part in the Sermon on the Plain, found in Luke 6, is the template, the standard, indeed, it is the constitution for the kingdom Jesus initiated two thousand years ago and will completely inaugurate in the future when He comes back as King of Kings and Lord of Lords (Revelation 19:16). It is far different, as we have discussed, from governmental articles of nations of our world in this day, as it turns upside-down so much conventional wisdom that operates the way we live and interact. We must remind ourselves that in our day the world feels that we humans are running the show but those with eyes to see understand that Satan, the god of this world (2 Corinthians 4:4), is actually in charge. When our Lord returns, that will change. The Devil and his followers will be ousted and the planet will enter a time of peace and prosperity unlike any time our home has ever known. This constitution will be our basis for government. It will be a rule where relationships between men are emphasized and regulations are present only as road signs to keep men going in the proper direction.

Also, as we have mentioned previously, the sermon has been misunderstood by many since it was given. Some have missed the main point of Jesus' words, believing that indeed they were able to completely keep the standard He put forth. In fact, exactly the opposite is in play. This constitution should put an end to all legalism as no bar would be high enough. The sermon reveals to us what God is like, and He is far different than we are! It shows that we all desperately need God's grace. Indeed, grace is found in our Lord's words e.g., "Blessed are the poor and the meek," "Forgive us our debts," etc., but often we miss the grace as we trip over the ideals. Let's not let that happen. As we look at the constitution, we must remember that it is the map to God's heart and righteousness, something we strive for, but realizing always that we fall short, and thanking Him for His grace which He has extended toward us. As has been said:

G-R-A-C-E, God's Riches At Christ's Expense.

Salt and Light

> You are the salt of the earth.
> Matthew 5:13

Of the many gifts the Creator has bestowed on mankind, salt is one of His greatest. Salt adds enjoyment to our meals as it draws out the flavor of food like nothing else. Along with adding to taste, salt produces thirst. Salting our food calls for water to quench the thirst produced. A third property of salt is its preservative feature. Before the days of abundant ice and refrigeration, salt allowed meat to be stored for later consumption, allowing men and women time for other activities than just gathering food. Salt freed up men for higher pursuits as the basic need of food acquisition could be moved back somewhat in importance. Salt has been used as currency in many places and, lastly, salt was used in times past in covenant ceremonies. Specifically, when two parties would contractually agree, they would seal the bond with the so-called covenant of salt.

With this background, one can bring alive Jesus' proclamation that His disciples are to be the salt of the earth, that we are to affect our world like salt. As a follower of Jesus, I want to add flavor to people's lives. To be winsome, positive, and encouraging is my desire. My wish is that, when men and women encounter me, they are blessed, encouraged, and elevated (Colossians 4:5-6). Along with that, we want folks to seek what we have when they come alongside. We have Christ in us (Colossians 1:27) and our hope is that our lovely disposition will create a thirst for others to acquire the Lord in their hearts also. Of course, Jesus is found in God's Word (Romans 10:17), which in many places is likened to the water that we desire when we thirst. We preserve our world when, through the Holy Spirit residing in our hearts, we push back against the schemes and wiles of the Devil. We remind mankind that killing babies is not moral, that family is important, that greed is inherently bad, and that generosity is glorious. Like currency, we want to bring worth and value to people's lives, and, lastly, like the covenant of salt, we want to introduce others to our Lord and see in them a bond with Him which cannot be broken.

> You are the Light of the World. A city that is set on a hill cannot be hid. Neither do men light a candle, and put it under a bushel, but on a candlestick; and it gives light unto all that are in the house. Let your light so shine before men, that they may see your good works, and glorify your Father which is in heaven.
> Matthew 5:14-16

We believers are the Light of the World. What an awesome privilege! We get to illuminate our little spheres so that others can see clearly to move about. For, without light, our friends, neighbors, and people of the world will stumble about, bump into things, and ultimately fall down. But along with that privilege comes responsibility. That is, we can choose to show forth our light or we can hide it, as Jesus' words suggest. How silly is it to put a cover over a candle? Likewise, how pointless it is to conceal our light. Unfortunately, often I do just that! The best example I can think of showing how this happens is with an eclipse of the moon. The light from the sun (picturing Jesus as our Source) is shining upon the moon (us in the analogy) and reflected upon the earth (the people of the world). But, when the earth comes between the sun and the moon, our satellite is cast into darkness, no longer reflecting the light of the sun. Likewise, when I let the things of the world come between me and my Lord, I too stop reflecting His light to others. In contrast, Jesus points out that, when we display our light, when we light the path of others, the Father will be glorified. Ultimately, that is what we were created for. All creation sings His praises and, when we are lighting the way, so do we.

Thus, we are the light that reflects the true light. Jesus is called the Light of the World (John 8:12). He is the true light (John 1:9) that came into the world. He is the Source. He is the light that came down and lightens every man. We are the reflection of the light, not the generators of it. As the Bible says, "I am the vine and you are the branches...without me, you can do nothing" (John 15:5). As we stay close to Him, His light reflects off of us onto others. An Old Testament picture of this is clearly seen in the life of Moses. After spending forty days in God's presence on Mount Sinai, we are told that his face glowed brightly to the children of Israel. That's what we want, too. As we spend time with God, meditating on His Word, praying to Him in secret, and singing to Him in psalms and hymns and spiritual songs, we will shine forth brightly to others without even knowing it, just as Moses did in the presence of his people. All for the glory of the Father!

The Law's Fulfilment

> Think not that I am come to destroy the law, or
> the prophets:
> Matthew 5:17a

Jesus included this statement in His constitution because the Pharisees, scribes, and teachers actually did feel the Rabbi from Nazareth was attempting to dismantle the law. On the surface, one might wonder if some truth to their view was correct because Jesus seemed to go out of His way to stir up controversy with the leaders. For example, many of Jesus' miracles of healing were done on the Sabbath, with the frequent result of enraging the religious authorities. He had His disciples glean corn on the Sabbath to satisfy their hunger, again angering the priests. Of course, when He overthrew the money changers' tables in the temple, many in authority felt the Law had been violated. But, a closer look at all of Jesus' actions reveals He did not breach the Law and the Prophets, the actual God-inspired scriptures. What Jesus often came against was the written and the oral traditions of the teachers and scribes. In particular, the Sabbath, which was given to men and found in Exodus 20, noting the blessing of taking a day off from work. It was expanded greatly by the Jews to codify what work was or wasn't allowed. What originally was a Law of blessing was legislated to a law of the letter, only it wasn't God's law but the traditions of men. This is what Jesus continually was "calling them out" on. The leaders had gotten so far from God's heart, teaching as doctrine what were the commandments of men.

> I am not come to destroy, but to fulfill.
> Matthew 5:17b

"It is finished" is what Jesus cried as He died on the Cross. What was finished? Certainly, the payment for the sins of the world was completed but, along with that, this statement concerning the Law and the Prophets was now fulfilled. The Law had been satisfied in the beautiful life of our Savior. Jesus, the second Adam, lived a perfect life and thus realized the standard that God first gave to Adam in the Garden of Eden and later to Moses on Mount Sinai. "For He hath made Him to be sin for us, who knew no sin; that we might be made the righteousness of God in Him" (2 Corinthians 5:21). Now, with the Law fulfilled, God, through His apostles and prophets, could reveal the primary purpose of the Law, which is to drive us to the realization of our need for a Savior as well as to act as boundaries keeping those who deny the Lord's saving sacrifice in check as they live their ungodly and otherwise lawless lives. Let me show you:

> Wherefore then serves the law? It was added because of transgressions, till the seed should come to whom the promises were made...the law was our schoolmaster to bring us to Christ, that we might be justified by faith.
> Galatians 3:19, 24

> Knowing this, that the law is not made for a righteous man, but for the lawless and disobedient, for the ungodly and sinners, for unholy and profane.
> 1 Timothy 1:9

Now, with the Law being fulfilled by Jesus, His next statement concerning the need to be more righteous than the scribes and Pharisees to enter the Kingdom of Heaven (Matthew 5:20) makes perfect sense. For indeed, faith in Jesus confers His righteousness upon us, making us more righteous than even the scribes and the Pharisees. As Paul points out in his great treatise on faith in the Epistle to the Romans:

> O the depth of the riches both the wisdom and knowledge of God! How unsearchable are His judgments, and His ways past finding out! For who has known the mind of the Lord? Or who has been His counselor?
> Romans 11:33-34

Anger and Reconciliation

After learning that, to enter the Kingdom of Heaven, one must be more righteous than the religious expert, Jesus steps on the gas with His next few statements concerning inward attitudes. If anyone thought they could be more righteous than the scribes and Pharisees, that thought should vanish with Jesus' following words.

> You have heard it said by them in old time, thou shalt not kill (*Exodus 20:13);* and whosoever shall kill (*murder)* shall be in danger of the judgment: But I say to you, that whosoever is angry with His brother without a cause shall be in danger of the judgment: And whosoever shall say to His brother, Raca (*empty-headed or fool*), shall be in danger of the council: But

> whosoever shall say, thou fool, shall be in danger of hellfire.
> Matthew 5:21-22 (italics added)

In God's economy, unrighteous anger is equal to murder. That's because to our Father, all sin is missing the mark. Compared to His holiness, majesty, and glory, all sin is essentially the same size. Think of it this way: The Himalayan Mountain Range is massive when viewed from Katmandu but, when observed from outer space, it does not stand out at all. So it is with our sin. Sins are all the same to our God. Murder is the same as anger. It is no coincidence to God that, in English, anger is closely related to d*anger*!

One of the points to these words of our Lord is that I don't want to be angry with people at all. We wrestle not against flesh and blood but against the evil powers of the darkness of this world. I must channel righteous anger toward the demonic forces behind the fool! I can do this by waging war with prayer, the Word, fasting, and praise. Jesus' brother correctly points out that we disciples need to be quick to listen, but slow to speak and slow to wrath (James 1:19). He goes on to say that the wrath of man worketh not the righteousness of God. What does result in the righteousness of God is love. Instead of the danger of anger, I want to be a lover of men and women. The way to do this is to see them as the Father looks upon them. He is love, and His heart is for all of mankind, saint and sinner. He is fond of us all and is not willing that any should perish but that all should come to repentance (2 Peter 3:9).

> Therefore, if you bring your gift to the altar, and there remember that your brother has aught (*a disagreement*) against you. Leave there your gift before the altar, and go your

> way, first be reconciled to your brother, and then come and offer your gift.
> Matthew 5:23-24 (italics added)

"At the altar" means to do what the spirit leads. If God puts in my heart to reconcile with a brother, to pray for a sister, to meet a need of a friend, in the Kingdom mentality I should immediately do it. Don't delay. To walk in the spirit is to instantly obey. Of course, I talk big! Seldom do I actually do what I have just written. But that's the goal!

> Agree with your adversary quickly, while you are in the way with him; lest at any time the adversary deliver you to the judge, and the judge deliver you to the officer, and you be cast into prison. Truly I say unto thee, you shall by no means come out until thou hast paid the uttermost farthing (*the last penny*).
> Matthew 5:25-26 (italics added)

The point from these words is, in humility, to get things right quickly with a person I have wronged before it becomes a big deal later. Why do I have a problem doing this? Maybe you, too. Because of pride. My flesh hates to apologize. It would be, oh, so much better if the problem would just go away. Jesus says that's not going to happen. The fact is, it only going to get worse. These words of His are so good!

Also, when I consider the Teacher's words about an Adversary, I immediately think of our ultimate Adversary, Satan. Peter cautions us to be sober and vigilant as our Adversary, the Devil, is as a roaring lion, seeking whom he may devour (1 Peter 5:8). Applying Jesus' words to the Devil, it is a good idea to agree with Him when He accuses me. In fact, what He says about me is only the half of it. He can only see my actions, can't read my mind. My heart is actually worse than what He accuses me of. When demons seek to condemn me of sins I commit, it's okay to agree in this setting. In the next breath, though, I can remind that Tempter that my sins are blotted out by the blood of the Lamb.

> And I heard a loud voice saying in heaven, now is come salvation, and strength, and the kingdom of our God, and the power of His Christ: For the accuser of our brethren is cast down, which accused them before our God day and night. And they overcame him by the blood of the Lamb, and the word of their testimony; and they loved not their lives unto the death.
> Revelation 12:10-11

Three things make me an overcomer. First, the blood of the Lamb cleanses me of sin, making me white as snow (Isaiah 1:18). The word of their testimony means I get to share what Christ has done for me, how He has rescued me and set me free, not by my works but by His grace. Lastly, they loved not their lives unto the death can be understood that I overcome by dying to self, by not thinking about myself, not living for my agenda and my little kingdom but by going all in for His agenda, His kingdom.

Lust and Divorce

> You have heard that it was said by them of old time, thou shalt not commit adultery: But I say unto you, that whosoever looks on a woman

> to lust after her has committed adultery with
> her already in his heart.
> Matthew 5:27-28

Keeping the Seventh Commandment, that about committing adultery, has always been hard for men and women, as, from the very beginning, God hard-wired us to be attracted to the opposite sex. In our fallen nature and with the help of Satan and his henchmen, we are easily taken out by the attraction of an encounter with a man or a woman with whom we are not married. That's because God's original intent for the sexual experience was to cement a covenant bond between the couple. In God's words, the two become one flesh (Genesis 2:24). God made it remarkable and wonderful due to the immensity of His plan for marriage and the family. But Satan hates families and he hates marriages. He knows that the bond between a man and a woman picture the relationship between Christ and the Church and he understands that families are a type of the link between the Father and His children, so one of the Devil's major battlefronts is to attack marriages and families.

Jesus also recognizes this. Thus, adding a corollary, if you will, to the seventh commandment, our Lord says not only to avoid the act of adultery but stay away from even the thought of it. Initially, this seems like He is piling on! We already have problems with the seventh commandment, now we are in trouble even if we are bothered by it! But that's the point. By moving the fence away from the alligator, the little boy is less likely to stick his hand through the opening and have it snatched off! Jesus is actually in love helping us men who want to live holy, by posting a sign on the side of the road saying "dead end," literally! (Proverbs 6:24-32)

So, what to do when a lustful thought pops into my mind. First of all, realize that no sin has yet occurred. It's only when I consider and rehash the lustful scenario that sin is conceived. One can't always stop the temptation. But, we can mitigate the temptations we receive by not putting ourselves in places where they inevitably are slung at us. David, who had some issues with women, knows wherewith I speak as he penned in Psalm 101:3, "I will set no wicked thing before mine eyes." Of course, this statement is bigger than looking at women with lust, but it can certainly be a starting point for many of us.

Therefore, after a fiery dart is shot in my direction, as I have preached earlier, I want to go on the offensive with prayer and the Word. Specifically, I like to pray for other men when attacked by my flesh to lust after another. I pray for them to be protected from evil thoughts and images. I suspect the Devil hates it when I remember to do that! Also, I attack the spiritual wickedness in high places with particular sections of scripture. Verses like 1 Corinthians 6:20, 1 Peter 2:11, 2 Corinthians 5:14-15, Psalm 29:2, and Romans 6:6 likely drive my Adversary crazy when I claim them!

> And if thy right eye offend thee, pluck it out, and cast it from thee: For it is profitable for thee that one of thy members should perish, and not that thy whole body be cast into hell. And if thy right hand offend thee, cut it off, and cast it from thee: For it is profitable for thee that one of thy members should perish, and not that thy whole body be cast into hell.
> Matthew 5:29-30

Wow, this sounds super-harsh! But remember, Jesus' tone is important. Two thousand years after these words were spoken, they can read like an e-mail or text message. We don't see our Lord's body language, we don't see the twinkle of His eye or the tear welling up. Recall, He is love, so this cannot be literal. It would not be loving to tell someone to pluck out their eye or cut off their hand...unless He knows something that we don't! You see, Jesus understands the reality of Hell. He recognizes that separation for eternity from His Father will be darkness, evil, and death as God is light, love, and life, so the absence of those qualities pretty much defines Hell! So, once again, Jesus is lovingly emphasizing the importance that sin will do nothing but wipe us out. Scholars explain that the Teacher is using a rhetorical device called "an extreme statement" to emphasize His point. This is something we will see again and again when Jesus preaches about issues about which He is passionate. In this case, the Master is saying I must deal violently with things causing me to sin. Extending this past lust for women, I need to act aggressively against activities, hobbies, entertainment, and even my schedule if they are causing me to sin.

> It has been said, whosoever shall put away his wife, let him give her a writing of divorcement (*Deuteronomy 24:1*): But I say unto you, that whosoever shall put away his wife, saving for the cause of fornication, causes her to commit adultery: And whosoever shall marry her that is divorced commits adultery.
> Matthew 5:31-32 (italics added)

Once again, another corollary to the seventh commandment. But think with me, what is this one pointing out? Why, to take marriage seriously. It should not be like a Hollywood marriage that ends six months after the movie shoot is over. It's for life! Not for convenience. But why is the Lord making things so hard? Moses said a bill of divorcement was okay if a wife did not please her husband. Later, when challenged on this, Jesus clarified that Moses' words were due to the hardness of men's hearts (Matthew 19:8), not God's original intent. You see, sin is not bad because God forbids it; God forbids it because sin is bad. In this case, divorce always affects others. I suspect that children of divorce seldom come out unscathed!

But another point of marriage is that, as I said earlier, it is a picture of Christ and the Church. We become more Christ-like in a marriage relationship as the couple must learn to love like He does, i.e., sacrificially. As has been said, a single person can do things for Christ, but a married person becomes like Christ!

So, while we are becoming like Christ, our flesh and the Tempter will swoop in with the "grass is greener on the other side of the fence" enticement. Don't fall for that one, dear believer. It's not! Our world is littered with men and women who have learned this lesson the hard way. Hear from them. You know, experience is the best teacher but it doesn't have to be your experience!

Truth Telling

> Again, you have heard that it has been said by them of old time, thou shall not forswear thyself, but shall perform unto the Lord your oaths: But I say unto you, swear not at all; neither by heaven; for it is God's throne: Nor by the earth, for it is His footstool: Neither by Jerusalem; for it is the city of the great King.

> Neither shall you swear by your head, because you cannot make one hair white or black. But let your communication be, Yes, yes; No, no: For whatsoever is more than these comes from evil.
> Matthew 5:33-37

This article implies a powerful principle of the Kingdom of God, which is that a man's word must be his bond. There is no need to make an oath, calling upon God or religious icons for support, as truth is to be the norm, not the exception. Of course, when Jesus spoke these words, and to our day today, men prefer lies and half-truths over the integrity of being completely honest. Convenience, fear of men, and pride often propel us toward lying. Before, when we were outside of the Kingdom and under the rule of Satan, lying came naturally as we imitated the god of this world's approach to the truth. But now that the Kingdom is here, truth, complete truth, disruptive truth, is the order of the day. As Solomon so profoundly stated, "the lip of truth shall be established forever, but a lying tongue is but for a moment" (Proverbs12:19).

So, in a culture that has a history of frequent lying, or a person who suffers from the inability to completely tell the truth, we must swear and take oaths to have our words accepted. But even when we make a vow, God tells us in His Word that we cannot always be trusted.

> If a woman also vow a vow unto the Lord, and bind herself by a bond...and her husband hears it, and holds his peace at her in the day that he hears it, then her vow shall stand. But if her husband disallows her on that day that he

> hears it, then he shall make her vow of none effect.
> Numbers 30:3, 7-8

We are the bride of Christ and Jesus is our husband. God in His grace makes a provision for us when we promise things that we cannot deliver. He understands that we are weak, that we say things that we don't really intend to do, and He lovingly releases us from these misguided promises. For example, on the night our Lord was betrayed, Peter told Him that he would follow Him to the death if need be. Jesus disallowed that foolish vow because He knew Peter would not be able to carry that oath to its completion. He lovingly told Peter that would not happen, but then said that He had prayed for him, knowing that he would recover. The same holds for you and me. We want to be truthful, we want to live with integrity but often fall short. Thank God that He knows our frame and takes pity on us. And I thank Him that, in the age to come, truth-telling will be as natural as breathing and our "Yes" will be "Yes" and our "No" will be "No."

Passive Resistance

> You have heard that it has been said, an eye for an eye, and a tooth for a tooth (*Exodus 21:24*): But I say unto you, that you resist not evil: But whosoever shall smite thee on thy right cheek, turn to him the other also. And if any man shall sue you at law, and take away your coat, let him have your cloke also. And whosoever shall compel you to go a mile, go with him two. Give to him that asks you, and from him that would borrow of you turn not you away.

Matthew 5:38-42 (italics added)

We are seeing a theme here. Jesus quotes a precept in the law and then gives an even better way of living. Don't commit murder, but don't get angry either. Don't sleep with another man's wife, but don't even look at her with lust in your heart. Divorce laws are for the hard-hearted, stay together unless infidelity has occurred. No need to take an oath because truth must be the norm and next our Lord says that the best way to resist evil is by doing the opposite of what our flesh tells us to do. We want to actively fight. When hit on the cheek, we swing back. When sued, we mount a vigorous defense and, certainly, if we lose in the courtroom, we don't offer the plaintiff more than the judge awarded. When a law enforcement agent lords his power over us, we are reluctant and slow to comply, and many times it is difficult to have our default setting on "Yes" instead of "No" when asked for a favor by an acquaintance. But Jesus points out that this unnatural way of resisting is actually the best. The reason is that passive resistance puts you, the one being wronged, so to speak, in control. You now have the power. If you doubt this, just look at history. Men who have employed Jesus' Kingdom teaching about passive resistance were the victors. Just ask Mahatma Gandhi and Martin Luther King Jr. if you doubt the veracity of this precept. Turning the other cheek breaks the enemy's will for conflict. Yes, there is short-term pain in not actively fighting back, but long-term gain.

Next, we come to the most radical article of them all...bless them that curse you, do good to them that hate you!

Love Your Enemies

> You have heard that it has been said, thou shalt love thy neighbor, and hate thine enemy. But I say unto you, love your enemies, bless them that curse you, do good to them that hate you, and pray for them which despitefully use you and persecute you.
> Matthew 5:43-44

Once again, Jesus is turning human nature upside-down. Do the opposite of my fleshly inclinations. An enemy typically doesn't love me. No matter, love him anyway. A foe might curse me. No mind, bless her. A rival may hate me; again, do good to that person. And somebody who actually hurts me won't be praying for me; nonetheless, pray for that person!

Four disciplines I must consciously choose when dealing with difficult people, love, bless, do good, and pray.

You see, the kind of love that Jesus is talking about is a verb. Agape love, sacrificial love, is not feelings and goosebumps, it's decisions and efforts. It's action! Love does. It is broken down into its components in the most famous chapter in the Bible.

> Love is patient and is kind, love envies not, love vaunts not itself, nor is puffed up. Does not behave itself unseemly, seeks not her own, is not easily provoked, thinks no evil. Rejoices not in iniquity, but rejoices in the truth. Bears all things, believes all things, hopes all things, endures all things. Love never fails.
> 1 Corinthians 13:4-8a

Look at these attributes: They are all action words and phrases, not feelings and emotions. Patience is the receiving form of love and kindness is the giving aspect. Love doesn't vaunt itself, is not puffed up. We would say it is humble. Does not behave unseemly. That means it is polite. Seeks not her own, i.e., selfless, she is good to competitors! Not easily provoked, that's why we don't see temper tantrums associated with love. Thinks no evil. Seeing the best in people. We call that living without guile. Rejoices not in iniquity but rejoices in the truth, that's sincerity. Bearing, believing, hoping, and enduring all things are the things that make love alive. It is like a living organism. No wonder another name for God is Love! As we love like this, we become imitators of God. Read the breakdown of love again but put Jesus' name in place of love. Still works! How about when I put my name in its place or if you put yours. Does it still fit?

What is the motivator for this kind of love?

> For when we were enemies, we were reconciled to God by the death of His Son.
> Romans 5:10

Why, Jesus is our reason! We were His enemies and yet He loved, blessed, did good to us, yes, even prayed for us. He is our example. He is what drives me. This is why the Savior can say love, bless, do good, and pray for your enemies. It's what He already did!

Look at the result of His sacrificial love. We now belong to Him. We have been reconciled back to God. That is what this type of love does. It sets the stage for possible restitution with my opponent. As I love people when they least expect it and least deserve it, that type of love will change their lives. It is so radical, so like Jesus and unlike me!

Not only do sacrificial love, blessing, doing, and praying change others but they heal me. I lose the bitterness I had been harboring against my antagonist. No longer am I defined by a moment of hurt. That only gives it immortality! No, I can be defined by my deliverance, not my dysfunction!

> That you may be children of your Father which is in heaven: For He makes His sun to rise on the evil and on the good, and sends rain on the just and on the unjust. For if you love them which love you, what reward have you? And if you salute your brothers only, what do you more than others?
> Matthew 5:45-47 (excerpts)

I want to love with abandon, not waiting for others to love me first. I want to talk to people like they are already saved. Doing that may just love them right into the Kingdom! I want to see people as they could be, not as they are. Again, I want to see them as the Lord sees them, glorified and beautiful in His presence.

We learn in Ephesians that Jesus has broken down the middle wall of separation between us (Ephesians 2:14). The application is that we should tear down walls that we have erected against people and groups because of sin. He died for all sins, ours and theirs. The way we tear down walls? Why, with love. The secret is love!

Lastly, loving like this shows the colors of our faith. James tells us that faith without works is dead (James 2:19). As we have established, love is a verb, it is a decision, it is work. Paul preaches, "for in Jesus Christ neither circumcision avails anything or uncircumcision, but faith which works by love" (Galatians 5:6).

The work of faith is love! Love is the evidence of my faith. Dear brothers and sisters, do not forget this. Love is the evidence of your faith!

> Be ye therefore perfect, even as your Father
> which is in heaven is perfect.
> Matthew 5:48

So, we end this first part of the Constitution of the Kingdom of Heaven as we began it. We must not fool ourselves! We can't even begin to meet this standard. Earlier we were told we must be more righteous than the scribes and the Pharisees. Now we learn we must be perfect. Never going to happen! But, thanks to Jesus, we are perfect...perfectly forgiven!

Therefore, in light of that, we are free to work out these truths in our lives, living out the Kingdom mentality with His help as best we can, waiting for the redemption of our fallen world; waiting for the time when these truths will be self-evident!

Summary:

1. The Sermon on the Mount is the constitution, if you will, for the Kingdom still to come.
2. The teachings here should put an end to all legalism as no bar would be high enough.
3. As we stay close to the Lord, His light reflects off of us onto others, for the glory of the Father.
4. The primary purpose of the Law is to reveal our need for a Savior.
5. Anger is related to danger, for the wrath of man worketh not the righteousness of God.

6. When our Adversary condemns us of sin, we must remind him that they were blotted out by the blood of the Lamb.
7. Jesus' extreme statement about injuring our bodies should motivate us to aggressively act against anything that causes us to sin.
8. Our lying natures are fueled by convenience, fear of men, and pride.
9. Love is a verb. It is the evidence of your faith!
10. Loving your enemy is what Christ did to and for us, makes it possible for your enemy to become your friend, and heals your bitterness toward that enemy.

For Further Study:

1. What is your favorite characteristic of salt? Why? How can you be more like that to others?
2. Why was Jesus continually butting heads with the Jewish teachers of the Law?
3. To walk in the spirit sometimes means to instantly obey. Can you think of a time when you did that?
4. Why do the powers of evil make it a priority to attack marriages and families?
5. What is it about marriage that helps a person become more like Christ?
6. How did David's dealings with King Saul demonstrate passive resistance?

The Kingdom of Heaven: Its Constitution; Part Two

In the last chapter, the Constitution of the Kingdom dealt with inward attitudes, matters of the heart. In this next section, while the heart still drives a man, Jesus will address outward activities.

The Lesser and Greater Reward

> Take heed that you do not your alms before men, to be seen of them: Otherwise, you have no reward of your Father which is in heaven. Therefore, when you give your alms, do not sound a trumpet before thee, as the hypocrites do in the synagogues and in the streets, that they may have glory of men. Truly I say unto you, they have their reward. But when you give alms, let not thy left hand know what your right hand is doing: That your alms may be in secret: And your Father which sees in secret himself shall reward thee openly.
> Matthew 6:1-4

Jesus will talk about three spiritual disciplines in these next articles of the constitution, giving, praying, and fasting. The key statement He makes in all three examples is "to be seen of men." If my motivator in my Christian walk is to be appreciated by men, then that's my reward. The momentary pleasure from the acknowledgment and praise of others is all the reward I will receive. A better way is to stay in the background when giving. Keep your gifts between you, God, and any person you are blessing. Don't show off your generosity to third parties. Jesus equates that type of giving as hypocritical.

Now a word about hypocrisy. Jesus has much to say on the subject. So much so, I will devote a chapter later just to His teachings and parables concerning this mask-like behavior. But one important concept for our present discussion needs to be brought forth. The world defines a hypocrite as a moral person who has noticeable flaws. Jesus' definition is importantly different. In His usage (obviously, the correct one) a hypocrite is a religious person who keeps others away from the truth, i.e., away from Him. To the secular person, all Christians are hypocrites, as we all have flaws. But the correct view of a hypocrite is religiosity that keeps a seeker from the truth. In Jesus' day, the religious leaders were placing a trip on others by intimating by their trumpeting that giving alms was a path to God. Clearly, this was not what Jesus taught. Therefore, He called them hypocrites, not because they were sinners like everyone else, but because they were veiling the truth concerning the way of salvation.

Back to giving. The primary reward of generosity is that I become an imitator of God. He is a giver; He gave everything, in fact, when He died for you and me. So, as I give, I become more like Him. But there are rewards associated with liberality, but those rewards only come into play when I have a giving heart, not expecting to receive in return.

> And whatsoever you do, do it heartily, as to the Lord, and not unto men: Knowing that of the Lord you shall receive the reward of the inheritance: For you serve the Lord Christ.
> Colossians 3:23-24

Everything belongs to God (1 Corinthians 10:26). He doesn't owe anybody anything.

That is the proper perspective to maintain. Everything I possess is on loan from Him. As I give, I am just passing around blessings that I have been stewarding. This is the attitude I want; this is the "sweet spot" that will lead a person to be openly acknowledged by the Father!

Next, the Teacher will address prayer:

> And when thou pray, you shall not be as the hypocrites are; for they love to pray standing in the synagogues and in the corners of the streets, that they may be seen of men. Truly I say unto you, they have their reward. But you, when you pray, enter into your closet, and when you have shut the door, pray to your Father which is in secret; and your Father which sees in secret shall reward you openly. But when you pray, use not vain repetitions, as the heathen do: For they think they will be heard for their much speaking. Be not you therefore like unto them: For your Father knows what things you have need of, before you ask him.
> Matthew 6:5-8

Personal prayer is a private matter between a soul and the Father. It is intimate frank dialogue with the Almighty. He is not honored by vague prayers. They should be specific, so He receives the glory when they are answered. Effective prayer includes questioning, praising, confessing, thanking, and petitioning. Jesus points out it should be done in private, away from distractions and interruptions. At other times, it will still be personal and private, but it could be in the midst of a large gathering or in the middle of a difficult project. This type of prayer is the moment-by-moment muttering that Paul spoke of when he taught "to pray without ceasing" (1 Thessalonians 5:17).

Corporate prayer is done in a group setting with a common goal to the prayers which ascend to God. Unlike the hypocritical prayers Jesus was speaking against, where the charlatan was only praying to be seen and to supposedly impress others, all of the members of the community group prayer are involved and engaged.

In Jesus' day and on into our day in Eastern religions, many will pray repetitive, mantra-type prayers. Our Lord dismissed this type of praying saying the Father knows the need before He is asked. Extending this thought, since the Father already knows the need, why is petitionary prayer even necessary? The answer to that question is that prayer isn't so much to urge God to move but to get the person praying to line up with what God is already doing! Often when I pray, I may come to my Maker with anxiety and consternation, bewilderment and questions only to leave with peace and joy as meeting with Him has reset my puny little brain to be in harmony with His purposes.

Obviously, when the hypocrite is praying just to be showy, his prayers will not be heard. But are there times when our genuine requests will not be heard? The Bible says that there are and they are related to unconfessed sin, among other things.

> Behold, the Lord's hand is not shortened, that He cannot save; neither His ear heavy, that it cannot hear: But your iniquities have separated between you and your God, and your sins have hid His face from you, that He will not hear.
> Isaiah 59:1-2

As far as I can tell there are six ways I can short-circuit my prayers. Unconfessed sin (1 John 1:9), failure to ask (James 4:1-3), asking out of lust (James 4:1-3), a man's failure to honor his wife (1 Peter 3:7), failure to forgive (Matthew 6:14-15), and failure to read the Word (Proverbs 28:9).

So, when my prayer life is not seeing results, if none of these inhibitors are in play, I want to keep asking, keep seeking, keep knocking (Matthew 7:7). Patience is important, though. Often, the Lord will not immediately answer my prayer. His timing is always best, though. Also, factors such as a spiritual stronghold may be in play. Daniel Chapter 10 reveals to us that unseen spiritual battles occur at times when we pray, affecting the timing of the heavenly response.

It is important to remember that we don't always know what is best for us and others, even when we think we do. As Garth Brooks sings, "I thank God for unanswered prayers." A better way to pray in light of this is the "reporting for duty" prayer ("What would you have me to do, Lord?"), instead of the so-called "name it and claim it" type of prayer. I want to tell the Father my concerns and requests but I always end my prayer with "Your will be done." John tells us that, when I pray according to His will, He will hear me and I can bank on that prayer being answered (1 John 5:14-15).

Lastly, before we leave this tenet, the Rabbi promised that humble personal prayer will be heard and rewarded by the Father. But our Lord's half-brother adds that it must be in faith:

> But let him ask in faith, nothing doubting. For he that doubts is like a wave of the sea driven with the wind and tossed. For let not that man think that he shall receive anything of the Lord. A double-minded man is unstable in all his ways.
> James 1: 6-8

To doubt is to waver between two opinions. I'm talking to the God of the Universe. No need for doubt in my prayers. Thus, I can pray in faith knowing that He hears my petitions. They are to be simple, secret prayers, and I can be confident that, if it is something good for me, He will not withhold it (Psalm 84:11-12).

Next, we come to the greatest of all prayers, for it is the one our Friend taught us to pray. It is a beautiful sixty-five-word sacrament of the Father's person, purpose, provision, pardon, protection, and preeminence.

The Lord's Prayer

> After this manner therefore pray ye: Our Father which art in heaven, hallowed be thy name.
> Matthew 6:9

The person of the Father is described succinctly. He is *our* Father. He upholds the entire community of believers as only a committed parent can. And the word Father is better translated as "Daddy" or "Papa."

His name is to be hallowed. Awesome was a word in the past, reserved only for Him. He is terrible, He is untamed, He is a consuming fire! He is our shield and our exceeding great reward (Genesis 15:1). He is the "I AM." He is everything we need.

When I consider that His name is to be hallowed, my mind moves to the words of the psalmist, "Be still....and know that I am God" (Psalm 46:10).

> Thy kingdom come, thy will be done in earth,
> as it is in heaven.
> Matthew 6:10

Here, the purpose of the Father is described. "Not my will, but your will be done" is what Jesus prayed on that fateful night in the Garden of Gethsemane. You see, today in our world, God's will is often overridden by the will of man. God has allowed us the free will to choose our own path, which often is opposed to what He would prefer. When we pray, "bring the Kingdom," we are asking for the rule of Jesus to return. When we petition, "Thy will be done in earth as it is in heaven" we are asking heaven to come down to earth. This statement can be both corporate, for the whole world, but also individual, bring heaven to my heart today, Lord!

> Give us this day our daily bread.
> Matthew 6:11

God's provision is seven words. "Give us." As I pray for my needs, I can also pray for others, as we all have similar needs. "Daily bread." Jesus points out to pray this prayer every day because God *is* our daily bread as well as providing it. Of course, the Lord's Table of communion is embedded in this statement.

> And forgive us our debts, as we forgive our debtors.
> Matthew 6:12

The Father's pardon, through the Son, is the uniqueness of Christianity! But look, after we have been forgiven, we remember how beautiful it is to forgive. As Solomon so poignantly stated, "it is a man's glory to pass over a transgression" (Proverbs 19:11).

> And lead us not into temptation, but deliver us from evil:
> Matthew 6:13a

We pray for protection, for it is pride to ask for testing. Often a strong man will succumb in the very area he is stoutest because that's when his guard is down and he is not trusting in the Lord's unlimited strength. We have this treasure in earthen vessels (2 Corinthians 4:7) and it's in our weakness and frailty that God is glorified as we move in His power. Praying for protection is the only wise thing to do in our fallen state. Protection from the evil desires of our old man and the world's system, but also praying for protection from the Evil One!

> For thine is the kingdom, and the power, and the glory, forever. Amen.
> Matthew 6:13b

This great prayer ends with the preeminence of the Father on display. His is the kingdom, the power, and the glory. Presently, we get glimpses of His power and glory in His Creation. To look up at the night stars, to view a majestic waterfall, to observe a cheetah run, these dimly point to the authenticity of His majesty but can be missed by those without eyes that see beyond the visible. But someday, this will surely be our reality. Now we pray in faith, but soon we will talk to Him as a man does to His friend.

> For if you forgive men their trespasses, your Heavenly Father will also forgive you: But if you forgive not men their trespasses, neither will you Heavenly Father forgive your trespasses.
> Matthew 6:14-15

A major key to the release from bondage in one's life is to forgive his or her debtor. To forgive just means to release a debt. There is no requirement for the trespasser to apologize for forgiveness to occur. The Bible teaches "that while we were yet sinners, Christ died for us" (Romans 5:8). Forgiveness is what He did when we were far from Him. Forgiveness releases the forgiver from the bitterness that otherwise would remain. Of course, if the trespasser does ask for forgiveness, well, then the stage is set for restitution.

Another aspect of forgiveness is that it is not the same as forgetting. It might even be considered foolish if, after forgiving a person who has wronged me without seeking restitution, I go ahead and forget the injustice. That just sets the stage for the same abuse to occur again. As has been said, fool me once, shame on you; fool me twice, shame on me!

Lastly, in considering this somewhat difficult passage, we need to discuss how it has been wrongly interpreted as out of the flow of other statements on forgiveness. That's because it seems to say that a prerequisite for God's forgiveness is to forgive our debtor. We understand that this is not the case. We are forgiven completely and only by the blood of the Lamb. The work was finished. What this verse says is that, as we forgive, yes, we receive forgiveness, but if we do not forgive, it is our trespasses, not our souls, that are not forgiven. The trespasses remain and will dog us due to our lack of being able to forgive. Brothers and sisters, it is a healthy thing to bury the hatchet!

The Lessor and Greater Reward (continued)

> Moreover, when ye fast (*Jesus apparently assumes that fasting is part of His followers' lives!*), be not, as the hypocrites, of a sad countenance: For they disfigure their faces, that they may appear unto men to fast. Truly I say unto you, they have their reward. But thou, when you fast, anoint thine head, and wash your face: That you appear not unto men to fast, but unto your Father which is in secret: And your Father, which sees in secret, shall reward you openly.
> Matthew 6:16-18 (italics added)

Jesus considered fasting to be part of a believer's life. In our day, this is not so common, much to our detriment. Looking into the Bible, we see men fasting for both direction from God and liberation from temptation. Fasting is a key to spiritual swiftness. Do you want a breakthrough in a certain area of your life? Your marriage? Your kids? Consider fasting. It demonstrates to God and self that you are serious. God leans in when a person fasts. Abstaining from food, technology, TV, etc., is a spiritual discipline that weakens the flesh. It exercises the "No" muscle. When I say "No" to one thing, I am saying "Yes" to another and vice versa.

Also, fasting quickens your ears to God's voice. As my flesh tells me to eat, I find myself aware of my Maker much more acutely than when full and satisfied.

Lastly, we remember we are in a spiritual battle. Opportunities come my way daily to make Jesus famous or to free a person from oppression. But our enemies are strong. If I'm out of shape, so to speak, I'm not as effective as I would be compared to if I were trim and fit spiritually. Fasting helps keep me ready for the battle. In that light, fasting really should be a way of life. As Francis Chan has said, "the world needs more Christians who don't tolerate the complacency of their own lives." Why would I want to be a justified saint when I could be a sanctified disciple?

In concluding Jesus' comments on the lesser and greater rewards of giving, praying, and fasting, we see that our example is emphasizing the heart. These three areas of spiritual life can be a wild blessing or an awful bummer, all depending upon my attitude. It's a heart issue in the final analysis. Why am I giving, praying, and/or fasting? If it is to be seen of men, manipulate God, or assuage my guilt, then, as our Lord taught, my reward is minimal, if anything at all. But, if I give, pray and fast without regard to men but to be an imitator of God, to converse with Him and to lean in to Him, then the blessing is unlimited.

Heavenly Treasure

> Lay not up for yourselves treasures upon earth, where moth and rust does corrupt, and where thieves break through and steal: But lay up for yourselves treasures in heaven, where neither moth nor rust corrupts, and where thieves do

> not break through nor steal: For where your treasure is, there your heart will be also.
> Matthew 6:19-21

God has blessed all of the souls of the world, both the just and the unjust, with many good gifts. This next section of the constitution speaks of the dark side, though, of those good favors, of the possessions He has bestowed. It speaks of the black side of money, called the love of money, and even the spiritual forces behind that love.

This section also is pointing our eyes up, it is pointing us toward heaven and reminding us that treasure here on this earth is fleeting, as well as temporary. For instance, I am writing this portion of this book in 2020 during the midst of the Coronavirus outbreak. Recently, the stock market lost over 30% of its value in just a few days when "social distancing" and "stay at home orders" were instituted. Wealth that Americans had accumulated over years of investing, just evaporated, just as Jesus said would happen. I'm reminded of an alliterative proverb as I consider the Provider's words:

> Labor not to be rich: Cease from thine own wisdom.
> Will thou set thine eyes on that which is not?
> For riches certainly make themselves wings;
> they fly away as an eagle toward heaven.
> Proverbs 23:4-5

Trusting in money is foolish! It will fly away. Or, as the prophet proclaimed to the Jews of Jerusalem in 500 BC who were busy working on their own houses instead of the Lord's, "he that earns wages earns wages to put it into a bag with holes" (Haggai 1:6).

Also trusting in my treasure, my possessions, my money in this life is foolish because life is so short! Think of it this way. Let's say I have a job in Butte, Montana, for a month. I'm going to unpack my suitcase, hang up my shirts, and put my underclothes into the drawer of the Holiday Inn, but it would sort of be silly to decorate my room with my life savings! But this is exactly what so many of us are doing. We use the treasure (money) the Lord has given us to enrichen our little kingdoms ever forgetting that tomorrow we could reach the end of our stay, so to speak. Our lives, even if eighty or ninety years, are but a moment in comparison to eternity.

No, Jesus gives the better way. Lay up for myself treasure in heaven. There, it won't be ripped off by thieves, there it won't decay with time. As He famously stated, where my treasure is, there my heart will be also. My heart, that is, my innermost emotions, the things I value the most, will follow where I've put my treasure. Thus, it is important to remember that heaven is my home, is my destiny. That will take the emphasis off "living the dream" here and now. I want to focus, not on my pleasure here, but my treasure there!

So, how does one lay up treasure in heaven? Easy: Determine what is temporal and what is eternal. Then put your treasure (money, time, and talent) toward the everlasting bucket. What is eternal in our world today? Why, people, of course! (And my dogs, too, I hope!) Everything else will not last but people go on into eternity. As Levi Lusko has taught, humans are immortals heading toward majesty or misery, so I want to use my treasure to help people toward the Light. I want to extinguish some of the darkness with my money, with my time, with my talents, with my treasure. You see, I can't take my money with me, but I can send it on ahead!

Let me give you a little reminder of what we are speeding toward, a little incentive to stay the course:

> And I heard a great voice out of heaven saying, behold, the tabernacle of God is with men, and He will dwell with them, and they shall be His people, and God himself shall be with them, and be their God. And God shall wipe away all tears from their eyes; and there shall be no more death, neither sorrow, nor crying, neither shall there be any more pain: For the former things are passed away. And He that sat upon the throne said, behold, I make all things new.
> Revelation 21:3-5a

What a future we have as we live for and move toward the majesty He has promised! Continuing with Jesus' words:

> The light of the body is the eye: If therefore your eye be single, your whole body shall be full of light. But if your eye be evil, your whole body shall be full of darkness. If therefore the light that is in you be darkness, how great is that darkness!
> Matthew 6:22-23

A single eye is an Oriental way of saying that a person is trusting in God. In contrast, a person with an evil eye is trusting in money and possessions. That person is in the dark and ultimately may be taken out eternally because of his or her trust in things that have no eternal consequence.

> He that hastens to be rich has an evil eye, and considers not that poverty shall come upon him.
> Proverbs 22:28

Next, we will discuss the spiritual force behind greed, selfishness, and covetousness. The spirit of Mammon!

> No man can serve two masters: For either he will hate the one, and love the other; or else he will hold to the one, and despise the other. You cannot serve God and Mammon.
> Matthew 6:24

Paul taught that the love of money is the root of all evil (1 Timothy 6:10). That love is driven by a powerful spirit called Mammon. This spirit, which is from the pit of Hell, influences men to trust in money and possessions over trusting God. It is contrary to the spirit of the Lord, which seeks to have us trust in Him, to walk by faith, over trusting in our paychecks and 401K's. Jesus teaches that is it impossible to have faith in both, for one will be hated and the other loved. I cannot waver between two opinions! Additionally, the spirit of Mammon is more than just money, it's all created things. If I idolize my sports team, my spouse, or my BMW, to the point that it is my "go-to" place in the day of trouble, well, then I've got a problem. Obviously, the spirit of Mammon won't save in that same dark day, only my Lord can do that!

Our Lord is not saying we cannot use and enjoy the gifts we have been given, including money, but He is saying these things need to be in their proper place. The keyword in this famous statement of His is "serve." I must not serve Mammon, I want to serve God, keep everything under His authority. You see, what defines our lives are the things we hold onto tightly. The main symptom of being ruled by Mammon is having much fear about money. Ask yourself, do I fear God or do I fear losing my retirement plan? Make the proper adjustment in prayer to our Savior if it is the latter. Mammon can be a master, much like a religion, while in actuality it is but a "house of cards." It looks beautiful and ornate, but oh how fragile it can be. A little puff of wind and down it goes, taking all who idolize it with them. Flee away from this spirit dear believer. It is loud and strong but ultimately cannot save! "Trust in the Lord with all thine heart, and lean not upon thine own understanding. In all thy ways acknowledge Him, and He shall direct thy paths" (Proverbs 3:5-6).

O Ye of Little Faith

> Therefore, I say to you, take no thought for your life, what you shall eat, or what you shall drink; nor yet for your body, what you shall put on. Is not life more than meat, and the body more than raiment? Behold the fowls of the air: For they sow not, neither do they reap, nor gather into barns; yet your Heavenly Father feeds them. Are you not much better than they? Which of you by taking thought can add one cubit unto his stature? And why take thought for raiment? Consider the lilies of the field, how they grow; they toil not,

> neither do they spin: And yet I say to you, that even Solomon in all of his glory was not arrayed like one of these. Wherefore, if God so clothe the grass of the field, which today is, and tomorrow is cast into the oven, shall He not much more clothe you, O ye of little faith? Therefore, take no thought, saying, what shall we eat? Or, what shall we drink? Or, wherewithal shall we be clothed? (For after these things do the Gentiles seek). For your Heavenly Father knows you have need of these things.
> Matthew 6:25-32

Three times the Lord says to take no thought. We would say take no worry. Don't be anxious about your basic daily needs. God will take care of you. Don't be like the Gentiles. In today's verbiage, He is saying, don't be like unbelievers. You belong to the Father, have faith! He uses three examples about which so many of us worry: food, drink, and clothing. Will we have enough money left over at the end of the month to feed the kids, to get them clothes for school? Jesus says don't worry about these things; your Father is faithful. As David penned, "I have been young, and now am old; yet have I not seen the righteous forsaken, nor His seed begging bread" (Psalm 37:25).

You see, worry makes problems bigger and does not accomplish anything. Jesus points out that worry is unnatural. Look at the birds, God takes care of them. You are valued even more than they, is our Father's heart. Be carefree people like the lilies. Don't get all worked up. Better is to cast our worries to God in prayer with thanksgiving (Philippians 4:6).

Besides making our problems bigger, worry, which leads to fear, delights our Adversary. This is not what I want! I want to delight my Father by walking in faith. And Satan really likes to get me going about the future. What will come to pass, etc. When I find myself fearing some future scenario, I try to remember that fear is not the opposite of faith but an occasion for faith. I want to use my fear to call out to God in faith. Actually, the future is a phantom the Devil uses to spook me! It almost never turns out to be the way I envisioned. A trick I learned from Sarah Young's daily devotional is to imagine Jesus with me in that troublesome future and then bring my mind back to the present. I want to live for eternity and the present, not the past or the future. The Amplified Bible version gives a wonderful rendering of Hebrews 11:1 that I find helpful: "Faith is the assurance of things hoped for, perceiving as real fact what is not revealed to the senses." Faith goes outside of the five senses. It sees into the unseen spiritual world that God inhabits (Isaiah 57:15a). Much like accepting radio waves and x-rays as real, faith understands that there is much swirling around that is out of reach of my senses but nonetheless real and in play.

Finally, this self-talk that I tell myself about myself is related to fear and faith. Fear establishes the limits of my life while faith breaks them!

> But seek ye first the Kingdom of God, and His righteousness; and all these things shall be added unto you. Take therefore no thought for the morrow: For the morrow shall take thought for the things of itself. Sufficient unto the day is the evil thereof.
> Matthew 6:33-34

Along with faith in God, trusting in the Father, Jesus concludes this portion of the Sermon on the Mount by reminding us to seek the things of the Kingdom, to strive for His Kingdom, to continually pursue the eternal over the temporal, over my little kingdom. That means to seek the Lord's agenda, His rule. Ultimately my little world will be meaningless and worthless without hitching my wagon to His. I want to hold onto His hand tightly like a little boy would hold onto his father's hand when crossing over a river on a fallen tree trunk. The Psalms hold a promise that speaks to this relationship:

> Nevertheless, I am continually with thee: Thou hast held me by my right hand.
> Thou shall guide me with thy counsel, and afterward receive me to glory.
> Psalm 73:23-24

So I don't want to worry about tomorrow. It won't be like I imagine anyway. I want to live in the present, enjoying the journey as much as the destination. And I certainly don't want to rehearse my troubles. The only thing that will do is let me experience them multiple times. No, the Kingdom mentality calls me to trust totally in my Father's provision and protection. To be dependent on Him over trusting in my limited abilities and resources. To eat from the Tree of Life over eating from the Tree of the Knowledge of Good and Evil.

Summary:

1. Giving, praying, and fasting are not to be done to be seen of men.
2. A primary purpose of prayer is to get the petitioner's will to line up with God's.
3. The Lord's Prayer speaks of the Father's person, purpose, provision, pardon, protection and preeminence.

4. In the Bible, we see fasting employed for direction from God and liberation from temptation.
5. To lay up treasure in heaven, determine what is eternal, then put a portion of your time, talent, and money toward those things.
6. Worry for the child of God is unnatural and leads to fear. Trust pleases the Father and leads to peace.

For Further Study:

1. What is your primary motivator for giving? Is tithing relevant for the New Testament believer?
2. How can your prayers be hindered?
3. When you forgive, what benefit do you receive? Is restoration with your offender required to forgive?
4. What would be a benefit of making fasting a way of life?
5. Why is the love of money the root of all evil? To which of the seven deadly sins is the love of money related?
6. When worry strikes, do you have a Bible verse or two with which to respond? Hint: See Philippians 4:6-7 and Proverbs 3:5-6

The Kingdom of Heaven: Its Constitution; Part Three

A method of teaching that most great communicators use is that of repetition (2 Peter 1:12). Jesus is no exception. Comparing the four gospel accounts, we see portions of this constitution given in Luke Chapter 6, the so-called Sermon on the Plain, as well as Luke Chapter 11. In this next section, we will draw from the Teacher's words, not only found in the Gospel of Matthew but as He repeats these important truths at various sites and to differing audiences.

Judgment and Insight

> Judge not, that you be not judged. For with what judgment you judge, you shall be judged: And with what measure you use, it shall be measured to you again. And why do you behold the mote (*splinter*) that is in your brother's eye, but consider not the beam (*larger splinter*) that is in your own eye? Or will you say to your brother, let me pull out the mote out of your eye; and, behold, a beam is in your own eye? You hypocrite, first cast out the beam out

> of your own eye; and then shall you see clearly
> to cast out the mote of your brother's eye.
> Matthew 7:1-5 (italics added)

We humans are especially good at judging others. We've got that one down pat. We put labels on almost everyone. He's a Democrat, she's a gossip. He talks too much, she's a holy roller. On and on it goes! Jesus says not to do that! As I've heard Pastor Jon Courson preach, it is better to love people and let God do the judging. So often we have that one backward. It is more natural in our present earthly state to judge people and leave the loving to our Maker!

But you see, He has all knowledge about people, their motives, their life experiences, what makes them do the things they do, and I don't. When I label and judge people based on my limited information about them, well, I'm really just displaying my foolishness. Best not to judge, best not to label. Instead, just love, love, love!

Now the type of judging our Lord is speaking of is judgment unto condemnation. Later in this discussion, we will see that it is actually important to evaluate, to judge, for identification (Romans 16:17). We need to be able to discern between right and wrong, between good and evil, between fruit and poison!

After imploring us not to judge others, our Leader gives us a motivator for good behavior. That is, however we judge will be the measure with which we are judged! No, God won't judge me to condemnation, as I'm positioned in Christ, but people will. If I spew judgment around, that is what I can expect to receive from others. We've all witnessed this. That harsh person in your family or group is not the one you want to spend much time with.

In Luke's reporting of Jesus' later Sermon on the Plain, Jesus extends the boomerang effect of judgment to also include mercy, forgiveness, and giving.

> Be ye therefore merciful, as your Father also is merciful. Judge not, and you shall not be judged: Condemn not, and you shall not be condemned: Forgive, and you shall be forgiven: Give, and it shall be given unto you: Good measure, pressed down, and shaken together, and running over, shall men give unto your bosom. For with the same measure that you mete withal (*give out*) it shall be measured to you again.
> Luke 6:36-38 (italics added)

This is huge! Life is one big garden. As I plant crops, whether they be potatoes, carrots, or tomatoes, later a harvest will come forth of those same vegetables. Likewise, as I sow mercy or judgment, forgiveness or condemnation, bounty or leftovers, these are what I can expect in return. Friends, choose the good; you will receive the good in great measure!

Before leaving this article of the constitution, Jesus cautions those of us who often feel the urge to help others who have a problem. Those who want to help others who have the so-called splinter in their eye. I must do it in the spirit of meekness, realizing that I too have splinters, have blind spots, that if not acknowledged, only reveal my hypocrisy. Jesus added in the Sermon on the Plain the fallacy of restoration without meekness. "And He spoke a parable to them, can the blind lead the blind? Shall they both not fall into the ditch?" (Luke 6:39)

> Give not that which is holy unto the dogs, neither cast your pearls before swine, lest they trample them under their feet, and turn again and rend you.
> Matthew 7:6

Here we see an example of judging for identification. In this case, foolish and scornful souls are compared to dogs (a common term in Jesus' day for Gentiles) and swine (a common term for non-practicing Jews). Jesus preaches to be wary of with whom you share your treasure (Proverbs 9:8, 14:7, and 23:9). In His day, those two groups were generally not open to the things of God and actively persecuted true believers. In our day, dogs would be lawless pseudo-Christians who have turned the grace of God into lasciviousness and swine are the legalists who say Christ is okay but you really have to sacrifice to reach God (2 Peter 2:22). Remember, in the context of the constitution, holy things and pearls are the treasure that I store in Heaven. The time, talent, and money I offer to advance things eternal, to help people into the Kingdom by calling upon the salvation offered in Christ. Jesus teaches that identification is important in deciding to whom to share the gospel. In the next verses, He tells us the *how* of witnessing truth.

> Ask, and it shall be given you: seek, and you shall find; knock, and it shall be opened unto you: For every one that asks receives; and he that seeks finds; and to him that knocks it shall be opened. Or what man is there of you, whom if his son ask bread, will give him a stone? Or if he asks a fish, will give him a serpent? If you then, being evil, know how to give good gifts

> unto your children, how much more shall your Father which is in heaven give good things to them that ask him?
> Matthew 6:7-11

In Luke's account, Jesus points to the best gift of all which we can ask for from the Father.

> ...If you then, being evil, know how to give good gifts to your children: How much more shall your Heavenly Father give the Holy Spirit to them that ask him?
> Luke 11:13

The *how* of sharing truth is to ask for the Holy Spirit to give guidance when to speak and with whom to share. As I walk in the spirit, I want to listen for nudges from His Spirit speaking to me and then act upon those impressions. This is effective kingdom ministry. Without the spirit, I may share with an open person but at the wrong time. It's four-dimensional. The who and when of speaking truth. Our prayer is for the tongue of the learned.

> The Lord God hath given me the tongue of the learned, that I should know how to speak a word in season to him that is weary: He wakens morning by morning, He wakens mine ear to hear as the learned.
> Isaiah 50:4

The Law and the Prophets

> Therefore, all things whatsoever you would that men should do to you, do you even so to them: For this is the Law and the Prophets. Matthew 7:12

Here we have the Golden Rule our parents taught us when we were little. "Do unto others as you would have them do unto you." And this famous statement, which even the most spiritually unschooled has heard of, is preceded by the word "therefore." When we see the word, therefore, we must always ask, "What is it there for?" In this case, in light of our Lord's preaching about the need to avoid judgment unto condemnation, restoring a person in the spirit of meekness and asking him with whom he wants us to share truth, we are to flip the switch. That is, we are to interact with all people in the way we would like them to relate with us. Kindness, mercy, generosity, forgiveness are the things that come to my mind that I like to receive from others. These are just some of the components of love. What I want is love from others. That is what I must dole out, with the help of His Spirit, of course. Jesus taught here that love is the sum of the Law and the Prophets.

This was a revelation to His listeners. Still is to us today. All of the teachings of the Torah and the prophetical writings can be summed up in love. This is a different way than most read the Bible. We often see rules and regulations, rebellion and stubbornness in the words and stories and sort of get mixed up, distracted, and off track. Jesus wants to bring His followers back to center. It's all about love!

> Then one of them, which was a lawyer, asked Him a question, tempting Him, and saying, Master, which is the great commandment of the Law? Jesus said unto him, thou shall love the Lord thy God with all your heart, and with all your soul, and with all your mind. This is the first and great commandment. And the second is like unto it, thou shall love your neighbor as thyself. On these two commandments hang all of the Law and the Prophets.
> Matthew 22:35-40

The entire Bible hangs on, hinges on these two commandments...love God and love your neighbor. Live a life of love. No walls, no pretense, no masks! Obviously, I can only do this with the help of His Spirit. But this should be my mission statement. Love everybody, just as I want to be loved. Treat people just as I want to be treated.

Paul echoes this same concept to the Galatians:

> For all the law is fulfilled in one word, even this; thou shall love thy neighbor as thyself.
> Galatians 5:14

This makes all of the difference in my life, but also in my reading of the Word of God. You see, when I read the Bible, it is reading me. I often see only what I want to see. And at times, it may not be lovely. I might use God's Word to justify harshness and judgmentalism. Or possibly to rationalize lasciviousness or divorce. But Jesus said, "On these two commandments hang all of the Law and the Prophets," so, the question is, "Do I love more after reading His Word?" That's what I need to be getting out of my devotional time in reading. If it's not love, then my understanding is flawed. For all of the Law and the Prophets is summed up by and in love. Indeed, Love did hang. He hung on the Cross!

The Strait Gate

> Enter you in at the strait gate: For wide is the gate, and broad is the way, that leads to destruction, and many there be which go in through it: Because strait is the gate, and narrow is the way, which leads unto life, and few there be that find it.
> Matthew 7:13

Here near the end of the Sermon on the Mount Jesus circles back to the beginning; that is, we need a Savior. Just like His statement calling for righteousness which exceeds the scribes and the Pharisees, now our Lord insists that those who would find life will enter in at the strait gate. The strait gate would be clearly understood by His listeners. You see, in Jerusalem, there are two types of gates, each with differing purposes. The strait gates were narrow and reserved for nobility. Herod's Gate, the Lion's Gate, and the Eastern Gate were examples of strait gates. The masses entered the city from gates called Fish, Dung, Tanner's, and Fountain, among others. These gates were known as wide gates.

So gates were doors into the city. Jesus, using a metaphor, calls for those who would find life to enter in by the narrow opening. What does this mean? Well, comparing scripture with scripture, we see that Jesus is equating Himself with the strait gate (John 3:14-16, 10:7 and Revelation 3:20). He is the entrance into life. He is the Way (John 14:6). When we come to the chapter entitled "The New Birth," these scriptures will be discussed more fully.

But we must speak of one important concept now. Really, this is a principle that is far above my pay grade though. As you read the upcoming discussion, realize that God is the ultimate arbitrator of the meaning of the strait gate.

> Thomas saith unto him, Lord, we know not where you are going; and how can we know the way? Jesus said unto him, I am the way, the truth, and the life: No man comes unto the Father, but by me.
> John 14:6

Here we come to the great Christian truth that seemingly causes many unbelievers to stumble over Christ. He is the way, the truth, and the life and no one, absolutely no one can come to the Father except by Him. The answer to the question above my reach is summarized by two terms: Christian exclusivism and Christian inclusivism. You see, it is clear that Jesus died for the sins of the entire world (John 3:16). It is also clear that, if a man or a woman, a boy or a girl, confesses Jesus as Lord and believes that God raised Him from the dead, they are saved (Romans 10:9 and 13), they are heaven-bound, and going to be with the Father. Christian exclusivism says that these are the redeemed. Those who believe in Christ's atoning work, the narrow way, the strait gate, and no one else.

But what about those who have never heard the gospel or have never heard a cogent presentation of the gospel. Are they damned? Christian inclusivism says, not necessarily. This impression of John 14:6 says that Jesus indeed died for the sins of the world but the choice of salvation rests with God instead of the sinner. That is, God, who sees into the heart of men and women is free to give salvation to those who would have called upon the name of His Son had they been given an adequate chance and choice. This understanding would allow those poor souls brought up and steeped in the wrong doctrine of Eastern religions, etc., to be offered eternal life from God should they in sincerity seek after God. This type of heart can be summarized by two statements people can make. "Thy will be done" or "My will be done." In Christian inclusivism, those meek of the world can also enter in by the strait gate at God's discretion.

To summarize, the only difference between the two is that, in Christian exclusivism, the sinner chooses Jesus. In Christian inclusivism, Jesus chooses the sinner! Which is correct? I have no idea. We will have to wait and see. But this I do know: God, who sees all and knows all, will make the proper determination. We will all say on that day, "True and righteous are thy judgments" to the Lord (Revelation 16:7).

On a baser level though, why not just choose Jesus? That bypasses this entire argument. By choosing Him, I enter through the strait gate into the Father's presence. Those masses in the West who have heard the gospel but refused to repent and believe wouldn't be included in the second interpretation anyway because they have heard but rejected the good news. For, indeed, it is also clear that the definition of an unbeliever or an unsaved person is one who will not repent, one who persists in saying, "My will be done."

Constitutional Warnings

Lastly, we come to three landmines on the road to the Kingdom of Heaven. Three groups of people who may feel they will be included in the Lord's kingdom but tragically will not be.

False prophets, those who call on Jesus for the wrong reasons, and those who hear the Word but do not act upon it. As Paul cautions all of us who are walking by faith, "Wherefore my beloved, as you have always obeyed, not in my presence only, but now much more in my absence, work out your own salvation with fear and trembling" (Philippians 2:12). We must make our calling and election sure in the fear of the Lord.

> Wherefore we receive a kingdom which cannot be moved, let us have grace, whereby we may serve God acceptably with reverence and godly fear: For our God is a consuming fire.
> Hebrews 12:28

Clarifying, the fear of the Lord is not being afraid of Him, no, it is being terrified at the prospect of being separated from Him, of being away from Him, of disappointing Him. The fear of the Lord is a wonderful thing because it causes a man or a woman to hate and depart from evil (Proverbs 8:13 and 16:6).

> Beware of false prophets, which come to you in sheep's clothing, but inwardly they are ravening wolves. You shall know them by their fruits. Do men gather grapes of thorns, or figs of thistles? Even so every good tree brings forth good fruit; but a corrupt tree brings forth evil fruit. A good tree cannot bring forth evil fruit, neither can a corrupt tree bring forth good fruit. Every tree that brings not forth good fruit is hewn down, and cast into the fire. Wherefore by their fruits you shall know them.
> Matthew 7:15-20

Once again, Jesus tells us to judge for identification. We are to be fruit inspectors! Is the man of God, the prophet, sowing love, peace, gentleness, kindness, etc., or is strife, anxiety, discontent, and discord the crop coming forth? We must look at the fruit, not the person. For the person may be gifted and charismatic. He may look like one of the sheep, but inwardly, as Jesus points out, he or she is a wolf! And what do wolves do? They eat the sheep! Remember, Satan himself can transform his appearance into an angel of light.

The New Testament, as far as I can tell, gives five characteristics of false prophets. First, they seek to draw men to themselves versus pointing the sheep to the Shepherd (Acts 20:29-30). They also will seek your money (2 Peter 2:3a). They twist and turn the grace of God to allow, teach, and preach that lasciviousness (sexual immorality) is acceptable (Jude 4). They speak doctrines of devils, i.e., they question God's Word forbidding things God has allowed (1 Timothy 4:1-5). And lastly, they have a form of godliness, but deny the power; they ever learn but do not come to the knowledge of the truth, and they seduce and deceive themselves and others (2 Timothy 3:1-13). This last evil fruit is what makes this so sad. That is, they deceive even themselves! They are often not even aware that they are living a lie. Of course, we have seen this in past historical figures. The religious leaders of Jesus' day, including Paul before he was converted, as well as the historical leadership of the Catholic Church in the Middle Ages, come to mind. They led men away from the truth while many times believing they were in God's will. Let that not happen to us. I must walk in the spirit, judging the prophets, not blindly following.

> Not every soul that says unto me, Lord, Lord, shall enter into the kingdom of heaven; but

> he that does the will of my Father which is in heaven. Many will say to me in that day, Lord, Lord, have we not prophesied in your name? And in your name have cast out devils? And in your name done many wonderful works? And then I will profess unto them, I never knew you: Depart from me, you that work iniquity. Matthew 7:21-23

Here we have the second group of people who miss the straight gate. Those who come to the Lord for the wrong reasons! That is, they did not do the will of the Father.

This is important! What does the Bible say is the will of the Father? For in making my calling and election sure, this is what I want to be doing. Here is what it says...Christ is to be the center (Ephesians 1:9-10), we are to be thankful (1 Thessalonians 5:18), we are to avoid sexual immorality (1 Thessalonians 4:3-4) and we are to live well (1 Peter 2:15).

Those who did not do the will of the Father on that day will have three faulty arguments. They prophesied, cast out demons, and did good works in the Lord's name. How could this be if they don't know him? Well, they could be lying, they could be operating in demon power, they could be used by God despite their unbelief, e.g., Ballam, Caiaphas, and Saul, or they could have followed Jesus for the wrong reason, such as personal gain, like Judas.

Heartbreakingly, the Lord will tell those workers of iniquity to depart, as He never knew them. A better rendering of workers of iniquity is those who practice lawlessness, those who are not submitted to God. Fortunately for us, Paul gives a promise that allows us not to fear these warnings from Jesus as we work out our salvation. "But if any man love God, the same is known of him" (1 Corinthians 8:3). The Old Testament prophet Nahum also has words of comfort. "The Lord is good, a stronghold in the day of trouble; and He knows them that trust in him" (Nahum 1:7).

> Therefore, whosoever hears these saying of mine, and does them, I will liken him unto a wise man which built his house upon a rock: And the rain descended, and the floods came, and the winds blew, and beat upon the house; and it fell not: For it was founded upon a rock. And every soul that hears these saying of mine, and does them not, shall be likened to a foolish man, which built his house on the sand: And the rain descended, and the floods came, and the winds blew, and beat upon that house; and it fell: And great was the fall of it.
> Matthew 7:24-27

The third group of unfortunate souls are the foolish ones of the world who hear His message but fail to act. As in the movie, *Twenty Feet from Stardom*, they are so close yet miss it all. They watched the game but failed to get off of the couch! You see, the wise man not only hears the Word, but he does the Word. It's not enough to agree if I don't live it out. Moses' words to Joshua before he was commissioned should be underlined in all of our Bibles.

> The book of the law shall not depart out of your mouth; but you shall meditate therein day and night, that you may observe to do according to all that is written therein: For then you shall

> make your way prosperous, and then you shall
> have good success.
> Joshua 1:8

The key word is DO! Life is a verb, it is action, it is motion. No sitting still. It is running through the tape, it is finishing strong.

In the case of the Sermon on the Mount, it is coming to the right conclusions concerning the Savior, that is, realizing that I need a Redeemer, that I need the Lord. For I have a choice. There are two gates, wide and narrow. There are two foundations, sand and rock. For the rains will fall, the floods will come and the wind will blow. We all will die. But before that day, I need to choose, not from the Tree of the Knowledge of Good and Evil, but from the Tree of Life!

So, we end Jesus' formal words concerning His kingdom principles. The kingdom life that we can live even now while we wait for Him to return and formally establish that wonderful reign. We saw that what the world values and esteems is often contrary to His ways. We can seek peace, righteousness, purity, mercy, and meekness. We want to be salt and light. We want to deal violently with our own sin while always being truthful and loving, even to our enemies. We must not be showy but forgiving and we want to store up our time, money, and talents in heaven as we support and build up eternal things, i.e., people. We are not to judge for condemnation but only for identification and we are to live the Golden Rule, loving God and people as ourselves. In so doing, we fulfill all of the Law and the Prophets. Lastly, we want to build our house on the Rock, that is, the Rock we know as Jesus the Christ.

Next, we will look at a few parables that Jesus spoke illustrating in living color the nature of His Kingdom.

Summary:

1. The measure I use in judgment, mercy, forgiveness, etc., will be the measure others use for me.
2. The Word of God is anchored on the two great commandments, love God and love your neighbor.
3. The strait gate is Jesus. He is the Way. No one comes to the Father except by Him.
4. False prophets can be discerned by looking at the fruit they produce.
5. It is not only important to mentally ascent to God's Word, but also to act upon it.

For Further Study:

1. What does "casting your pearls before swine" mean to you? How do you know a swine when you see one?
2. Would you consider composing a personal mission statement that includes the two great commandments?
3. Do you have an opinion on whether Christian inclusivism or exclusivism is the correct interpretation of John 14:6?
4. What does the term "the fear of the Lord" mean to you?

Illustrations of the Kingdom of Heaven

We believers in Jesus Christ today are living between His two advents. He personally invaded our planet over two thousand years ago and accomplished His prophesized mission of becoming the spotless suffering servant, the Lamb of God. He took away the sins of the world and redeemed our planet back from the clutches of the god of this world, Satan. Unknown to His friends at that time, part of that mission was to be rejected as the King from heaven by His brothers, the Jews. Thus, His physical presence left the building, so to speak, as He ascended back to the Father. But, sending His Spirit, His transcendent presence, remains with us. As Paul so poignantly stated, "the Kingdom of God is righteousness, peace, and joy in the Holy Ghost" (Romans 14:7). Before Jesus left, He set up His Kingdom principles, which we have been studying, and He also pictured through parables for us how His kingdom would look and function during the interim before His second advent. It will be on that great day, He will return in power and great glory as the King of Kings and the Lord of Lords!

The Parables of the Treasure, the Pearl and the Fish

> ...the kingdom of heaven is like unto treasure hid in a field; the which when a man found, He hid, and for the joy thereof went and sold all that He had, and bought the field.
>
> Again, the kingdom of heaven is like unto a merchant man, seeking goodly pearls: Who, when He had found one pearl of great price, went and sold all that He had, and bought it.
>
> Again, the kingdom of heaven is like a net, that was cast into the sea, and gathered every kind: Which when it was full, they drew to shore, and sat down, and gathered the good into vessels, but cast the bad away. So shall it be at the end of the world: The angels shall come forth, and sever the wicked from among the just...
> Matthew 13:44-49

Jesus pictured the Kingdom of Heaven as a field full of treasure, as a pearl of great price, and as net full of both good and bad fish. Of course, all of us see ourselves as the man buying the field to get the treasure, the merchant purchasing the goodly pearl, and the angler catching the good fish. The treasure, pearl, and good fish are of course pictures of Jesus and His kingdom for which we are giving everything away, putting all else behind, so we can pursue our wonderful Lord. I've even heard these parables preached this way from the pulpit. Aren't we something! Going "all in" for Jesus!

Nothing could be further from the truth! Jesus' intent in these three parables is not to show our need to give all to receive His Kingdom. No, He is showing what HE did to establish His Kingdom! Jesus our Savior is the man who bought the field with everything He had, for He gave everything for you and me on the Cross. He is the merchant who cashed in all to purchase the pearl of great price. He is the fisherman who casts His net out into the sea catching both good and bad fish. We are the treasure, the pearl, and the good fish. How crazy is that? We are beautiful in His sight, we are valuable to Him, so prized that He would do the outrageous thing that we know He did.

> ...who for the joy that was set before Him endured the cross, despising the shame, and is setdown at the right hand of the throne of God.
>
> Hebrews 12:2b

We are the joy! Being with fallen humans for eternity is what motivated Him to sell all and buy the field and the pearl.

An application is screaming at me to share as I consider how our Lord views us. If Jesus sold everything to buy the field and the pearl, and He did, I need to see all people as the treasure He gave everything for. I need to appreciate all humans as image-bearers of God, as immortals, as more important than anything else! For this, indeed, is how He looks upon us!

Now, these three parables are actually one. Like a cluster on the vine, they are individual grapes, yet one cluster. So, too, these parables are intimately related. Let me show you. In the Bible, when the land is pictured or illustrated, the Author is talking about Israel. When the sea is brought forth in type, God is speaking of the Gentile nations. In this parable, the field with the treasure in it is the nation of Israel. Jesus saw His chosen people as a treasure and sold everything to buy them back. Our Lord saw us Gentile believers as the pearl of great price coming up from the sea and likewise He went "all in" to purchase us to him. So, we have Jews and Gentiles, making up the Church of Christ, as the treasure and the pearl. These two gems have populated the kingdom up until this time as we are waiting for the King to return. But what about the third portion of this parable? Who are the good and bad fish? They are the souls who are present at the end of the world, as His parable states. They are the people of the Tribulation age found in the Book of Revelation. As Jesus taught, the angels will come forth and sever the wicked from the just. Those who called upon Jesus during those dark days, the good fish, and those who denied him, calling instead upon Antichrist, the bad fish.

Next, we will examine in parabolic form the two kingdoms that have populated the world for the past two thousand years, the Kingdoms of Darkness and of Light.

The Parable of the Wheat and Tares

> Another parable put He forth unto them, saying, the kingdom of heaven is like unto a man which sowed good seed in His field: But while He slept, His enemy came and sowed tares among the wheat, and went his way. But when the blade was sprung up, and brought forth fruit, then appeared the tares also. So the servants of the householder came and said unto him, Sir, did not you sow good seed in your field? From where then has it tares? He said unto them, an enemy has done this.

> The servants said unto him, will you then that we go and gather them up? But He said, no; lest while you gather up the tares, you root up also the wheat with them. Let both grow together until the harvest: And at the time of the harvest I will say to the reapers, gather you together first the tares, and bind them in bundles to burn them: But gather the wheat into my barn.
> Matthew 13:24-30

Here we see the story of the last two thousand years. Wheat and tares have been growing together in the field, one plant producing fruit while the other only took nutrients from the earth. Interestingly, when the blade first appears, they both look similar. And so it is in our world as we interface and interact with the wheat and tares of this day. They are hard to tell apart until fruit is produced. Thus, as we have discussed previously, we must not judge too quickly for identification. Could it be possible that, when looking for fruit in a person's life, I may be evaluating that soul in a time before the fruit comes forth? Only God sees the big picture of a person's life. He knows who ultimately will be wheat and who are the tares. It's not for us to decide! Think back to yourself. You were not always bearing fruit like you are now. You could have been mistaken for a tare in your earlier days. Me too! I thank God for His patience with me. Indeed, He is ever so gracious toward us.

Let's break down this parable, which contains so much still future information, with Jesus as our guide.

> Then Jesus sent the multitude away, and went into the house: And His disciples came unto

> him, saying, declare unto us the parable of the tares of the field. He answered and said unto them, He that sows the good seed is the Son of man; the field is the world; the good seed are the children of the kingdom; but the tares are the children of the Wicked One: The enemy that sowed them is the Devil; the harvest is the end of the world; and the reapers are the angels. As therefore the tares are gathered and burned in the fire; so shall it be in the end of the world. The Son of man shall send forth His angels, and they shall gather out of His kingdom all things that offend, and them which do iniquity; and shall cast them into a furnace of fire: There shall be wailing and gnashing of teeth. Then shall the righteous shine forth as the sun in the kingdom of their Father. Who has ears to hear, let him hear.
> Matthew 13: 36-43

We see that Jesus and the Devil both are sowing seed in the earth, which is pictured as the field. The wheat represents those who are God's children, those who have called upon Jesus as Lord and Savior. The tares are those who have not. We see that, denying Jesus as Lord, stepping over His dead body, so to speak, trampling over His sacrifice for the sins of the world, leads to a person being called a child of the Wicked One! As a digression, I suspect that if I told an unbeliever that, in his present state, he was at risk of being Satan's offspring, he might be just a little offended! Nonetheless, that is what our Lord reveals.

Continuing, harvest time is the end of the world. By that, Jesus means the end of this present age. The time when the god of this world will be judged and cast into the abyss for a thousand years (Revelation 20:1-3). It will be the day when Jesus returns as King of Kings and Lord of Lords (Revelation 19:11-16). We see the angels as reapers, gathering up both the wheat and the tares (Revelation 14:14-19). The tares are cast away, receiving their wish of existence apart from their Creator, and the wheat shines forth brightly in the Kingdom of God.

All of this is spelled in greater detail in the Revelation given to John, as cited above. But before we leave this teaching of our Lord, a couple of points need to be gleaned.

First, the tares choose their destiny; it is not forced upon them. When a person says, "My will be done" over "Thy will be done," they are making the same mistake Lucifer initially made. They are saying, I am the god of my world, not the Almighty. What leads to that poor conclusion? Why the greatest of the seven deadly sins...pride! A person's pride can blind him from seeing his need for a Savior. How sad that is!

Secondly, the harvest times of Israel picture prophetically some of God's plan for our age. You see, in biblical Israel we comprehend two harvests, one in the spring and one in the fall. The first harvest was the barley harvest, which came in very early, around the time of Passover. Pertinent to this discussion, the Sunday after the Passover sacrifice was the celebration of the firstfruits (Exodus 23:16), the time when the first of the barley harvest was dedicated to God with the promise that He would then bless the rest of that harvest. Later, at the end of the growing season, in autumn, the much larger wheat harvest would be reaped. Now, putting this together, the barley harvest represents the first resurrection. That is, the resurrection of Jesus Christ and several hundred other believers on the Sunday after Passover (Matthew 27:52-53). Paul in his writings describes Jesus' resurrection as the firstfruits (1 Corinthians 15:23), i.e., the barley harvest. Fittingly, Easter Sunday occurred on the Sunday after Passover, i.e., the Feast of Firstfruits! Here in our present parable, we see Jesus equating the Hebrew wheat harvest at the end of the growing year with the gathering of believers at the end of this age. Just as farmers would harvest their wheat in the fall, the angels will be sent forth and gather those who have called upon Jesus as Lord and Savior during the dark days at the end of the Tribulation time frame as referenced above from the Revelation.

Since our Lord was talking to a Jewish audience when He preached this parable, He did not include the fate of the subsequent Church of God. Those Jews and Gentiles who have called upon Jesus in our day will be resurrected a short time before that great day Jesus is speaking of in this parable. That resurrection, called the Rapture, is spoken of by Paul in great detail in his letters to the Thessalonians and Corinthians (1 Thessalonians 4:13-18, 2 Thessalonians 2:1-9, 1 Corinthians 15:51-57).

Continuing with another illustration of His kingdom, let's consider how the wheat will be granted entrance into the kingdom. For they will become like children!

Jesus and the Little Children

> And they (*parents*) brought unto Him also infants, that He would touch them: But when His disciples saw it, they rebuked them. But Jesus called them unto him, and said, suffer little children to come unto me, and forbid them not: For of such is the Kingdom of God. Truly I say unto you, whosoever shall not receive the Kingdom of God as a little child shall in no wise enter therein.
> Luke 18:15-17 (italics added)

To say this is an important parable would be an understatement! The entrance to the Kingdom is opened by this door: I must receive the kingdom as a little child. What does this mean?

A couple of thoughts for your consideration. First of all, children do not yet work. Their parents care for them and they for the most part happily receive and are grateful for their parent's attention and gifts to them. So it is with us. Our Heavenly Father attends to us without regard to any work or effort we add. Entering the Kingdom of God as a child means receiving it as a child. As a gift, not something to be earned.

A second, related way of looking at this statement of our Lord's is to come to the Father as a child. How does that look? Well, children are humble, trusting, teachable, and dependent. They do not think evil against other people and they do not seek distinction or authority. Lastly, children are curious and creative. These are the characteristics Jesus is alluding to when telling us adults that childlike faith is the way!

Look over the above list. How is your humility? Little children, for the most part, do not suffer from the pride of their accomplishments. Do you realize everything you have done has been enabled by God? No room for pride in our hearts when you think about it. How about your trusting? Is it, "I can do all things" alternating with "I can't do anything" or is it "I can do all things through Christ which strengthens me" (Philippians 4:13)? What about teachability? Here are two Proverbs to consider when evaluating your teachability. "He that refuses instruction despises his own soul" (Proverbs 15:32). Are you often bothered when your spouse tells you how to do things? How about, "He that obtains wisdom loves his own soul: He that keeps understanding shall find good" (Proverbs 19:8). Are you seeking wisdom?

Are you dependent or independent? One of the hallmarks of leaving adolescence and moving to adulthood is that we become independent of our parents. That being true, we are always children in relation to our Heavenly Father. It's a big mistake to distance ourselves from Him in a pathetic effort to be free of His guidance. Think of it this way: Do you like leaving home without your hand-held device? Of course not. You feel as if something is missing. To an infinite degree, this is what it is like for any created being to try and become independent from his or her Maker. No access to information, no power, no peace! I quote Robert Morris from his book *Truly Free*. "To be capable, one must be dependent."

Children do not think evil of others. The reason is partially due to the other two characteristics it is grouped with; that is, they are not climbing over each other in an effort to be noticed or to lead. They don't seek distinction or authority. Neither should I. Better to accept where the King has placed me, realizing that it is only what I do for His glory that has any lasting value anyway. Nothing I do to elevate myself and my little kingdom will ever succeed eternally. So, I would be foolish to attempt to live that way. Once again, like the Beatitudes before, Jesus' words, which on the surface seem simplistic and impractical, are really the best way to live.

Lastly, children are curious and creative. Unfortunately, these two beautiful characteristics of our kids are so often lost as we "grow up." What a shame! It is the curious nature of a child that allows her to seek the Lord while He can be found. So often, souls come to the Lord in faith at a relatively young age. How rare it is for a grownup to find Jesus. One reason is that his curiosity has left. Also, like their Father, children love to create. The joy obtained from a pre-school project or drawing is one of the reasons children resemble their Creator and will feel very comfortable in that future day in His presence.

Now, before I leave childlike faith, two points to make. First, I want to be childlike, but not childish. Childish behavior is dominated by selfishness. Its antonym is love and must be learned. Unfortunately, some never grow out of their childish tendencies.

Secondly, I must discuss some tension that is present because children are so trusting. That is, in their simplicity they can easily be taken out by false doctrine. Thus, it is important for the child of God to incorporate the flip side to childlike faith, which is to be as wise as serpents but as harmless as doves (Matthew 10:16). Don't be stupid. Satan is on the prowl and he uses religion if he can to trip up God's kids. This is the thing that really upsets our Lord. Look at His warning to those who would endeavor to stumble one of the little ones who have come unto him:

> But whosoever shall offend one of these little ones which believe in me, it were better for him that a millstone were hanged about his neck, and that he were drowned in the depth of the sea.
> Matthew 18:6

Interesting to me, Jesus prayed for forgiveness for those who were crucifying Him (Luke 23:34) but He is ready to condemn the one who would keep others from knowing Him. An important understanding: I don't want to be the cause of anyone losing their faith!

Next, leaving childlike faith, we should discuss the gifts of talent and time, which God has given us, in light of eternity.

The Parables of the Talents and of the Pounds

The Christian experience can be characterized by the word "done." "It is finished" is what Jesus cried from the Cross immediately before His death for our sins. At that moment, the veil in the Temple separating the Holy Place from the Holy of Holies was torn in two from top to bottom. Jesus had opened the way for us to enter into the throne room of grace by His sacrifice in our place (Hebrews 4:16). No longer did worshippers of God have to do anything. The work had been, and continues to be, done!

But the finished work is so contrary to just about everything else we humans encounter in the world we live in. We are told by Mom and Dad to work hard to succeed. We are graded in school against our peers and certainly every sport I ever participated in involved besting my opponent. No free passes in much of our day-to-day work-week. Some of you are so indoctrinated by this "matrix" of competition and exertion that we are living in that the Christian message of "finished" seems a little far-fetched, just a little too easy. If that is the case, then this section is for you! For we will see in these parables that Jesus expects us to do something. Specifically, He expects us to do good works. He desires that, in appreciation for the justifying sacrifice which He accomplished on our behalf, we will desire to offer back good works to Him and for His glory. No, we definitely are not saved by good works, but we are saved FOR good works.

> For by grace are you saved through faith; and
> that not of yourselves: It is the gift of God:
> Not of works, lest any man should boast.
> For we are God's workmanship, created in
> Christ Jesus unto good works, which God has
> before ordained that we should walk in them.

> Ephesians 2:8-10

We have the choice to do, or not do, the good works God has planned for us. But we don't have to, we "get to." And, along with getting to respond to God's love and generosity by walking in service, we are told by Paul and our Lord that heavenly rewards await as we follow His lead.

> For we must all appear before the judgment seat of Christ: That every one may receive the things done in his body, according to that he has done, whether it be good or bad.
> 2 Corinthians 5:10

The Judgment Seat was called the Bema Seat in ancient Greece. It was the awards platform that winning athletes stood upon to receive their Olympic garlands. There they received glory for their accomplishments of hard work and dedication.

Continuing with the athletic allegory: If I am on the Super Bowl-winning team, I will get a beautiful ring that I will wear proudly for the rest of my life, even if I was injured and didn't play. But, if I scored the winning touchdown, well then, I get the glory, too! So, too, believers in Christ get eternal life, but the stars who shone brightly for Him in this life get the glory!

> You are God's building. According to the grace of God which is given unto me, as a wise master builder, I have laid the foundation, and another builds thereon. But let every man take heed how he builds thereupon. For other foundation can no man lay that is laid, which is Jesus Christ. Now if any man build upon this

> foundation gold, silver, precious stones, wood, hay, stubble; every man's work shall be made manifest: For the day shall declare it, because it shall be revealed by fire; and the fire shall try every man's work of what sort it is. If any man's work abide which he has built thereupon, he shall receive a reward. if any man's work shall be burned, he shall suffer loss: But he himself shall be saved; yet so as by fire.
> 1 Corinthians 3:9b-15

The foundation is Jesus Christ and Him crucified, buried, and resurrected (1 Corinthians 15:3-4). But, after that, we build upon that foundation works which may or may not abide the fire of the Bema Seat. Paul has taught us that three things will abide, faith, hope, and love (1 Corinthians 13:13). The things we did in this life out of faith, hope, and/or love are the gold, silver, and precious stones and they will abide and result in our reward. Things not done in this light are wood, hay, and stubble and will not carry forward. For some, rewards will be minimal as jewels were not used on the foundation. Oh, they will be saved as they have called upon Jesus, but I can't help but think that regrets will also lead to some tears on that day when crowns are awarded by our King. Those crowns, which are better than the garlands of the Olympic champions, are called the Crown of Rejoicing (1 Thessalonians 2:19), Crown of Righteousness (2 Timothy 4:8), Crown of Life (James 1:12), Crown of Glory (1 Peter 5:4), and Crown of Incorruption (1 Corinthians 9:24-25).

As an application: As I look back upon my life, I initially regret the things I did that were wrong. But, as time passes, what I regret more are the things I didn't do that were right! In the short term, we regret the things we did. In the long term, we regret the things we didn't do. What if I was more concerned with missing opportunities than making mistakes? I want to count the cost, for sure. But, also, I should count the opportunity cost of not doing something! Don't fear failure in God's economy. Better to "go for it" than not to try. And, unlike the world, where failure is often disciplined by a culture of shame, failure in the spiritual realm will never be if my efforts were born out of initiative and innovation. As Jonathan said to his armor-bearer when considering taking on the Philistine garrison, "It may be that the Lord will work for us: For there is no restraint to the Lord to save by many or by few" (1 Samuel 14:6). Indeed, He did, and a great victory was obtained because of Jonathan's willingness to engage.

With that introduction, let's consider Jesus' words:

> For the kingdom of heaven is as a man traveling into a far country, who called his own servants and delivered unto them his goods.
> Matthew 25:14

Indeed, for the last two thousand years the man, Jesus, has traveled far away, to heaven. We, His servants, both true and false followers of Him were given the goods. We were all given gifts and abilities of differing degrees. Some are wonderful musicians, others teachers and preachers. Some are very intelligent and others are gifted with a beautiful appearance or impressive physical strength. Some have multiple gifts and others only a few. We will see subsequently that all of these gifts, called talents, are given at the discretion of the man, i.e., Jesus.

> And to one he gave five talents, to another two, and to another one; to every man according to his several ability; and straightway took

> his journey. Then he that received the five talents went and traded with the same, and made them other five talents.
> Matthew 25:15-16

Good for him! He used his God-given gifts and abilities and saw a nice return for his master. That's what I long to do. A key to doing this effectively is in busy times to use my gifts moment by moment and in quiet times I want to use my abilities on bigger projects (1 Kings 5:4-5). Another strategy, as we will soon see, to gain future rewards in Heaven, is to do something, anything, just get going! Often, I can be paralyzed into inactivity as I look at all of the mixed motives for my actions. That's silly! Only if I were perfect would I not have mixed motives. I want to trust God to separate the precious from the vile (Jeremiah 15:19). He won't throw out the baby with the bathwater! I don't want to bury my talents.

> And likewise, he that had received two, he also gained other two.
> Matthew 25:17

Note that, while the first man gained five and the second man only two, they both saw a 100% return on the investment entrusted to them. They both did well! One saw the greater, but he was given more. We will see that, when the accolades are given by the master, the reward is the same for both.

> But he that received one went and dug in the earth, and hid his lord's money. After a long time, the lord of those servants came and reckoned with them. And so, he that received five

> talents came and brought other five talents, saying, Lord, you delivered unto me five talents: Behold, I have gained beside them five talents more. His lord said unto him, Well done, thou good and faithful servant: You have been faithful over a few things, I will make you ruler over many things: Enter thou into the joy of thy lord. He also that had received two talents came and said, Lord, you delivered unto me two talents: Behold, I have gained two other talents besides them. His lord said unto him, Well done, good and faithful servant; you have been faithful over a few things, I will make you ruler over many things: Enter you into the joy of thy lord.
>
> Matthew 25:18-23

This is galactic! This is going to be reality, it's not just a nice allegory. Jesus started this parable by saying that it pictures activity in the Kingdom of Heaven! The Lord is telling me not to sit on my talents! God has chosen to partner with people, with me, to see His will accomplished. I need to take this very seriously! This also shows me that, while I can't change how much God loves me because that's a constant, I can change how much He is pleased with me (Psalm 16:11). Again, I want to do the works He has called me to do, the works that He has foreordained for me to walk into (Ephesians 2:10).

> Then he which had received the one talent came and said, Lord, I knew that you are a hard man, reaping where you have not sown, and gathering where you had not strawed: And

> I was afraid, and went and hid your talent in the earth: Lo, have thou what is yours. His lord answered and said unto him, you wicked and slothful servant, you knew that I reap where I sowed not, and gather where I have not strawed: You should have therefore put my money to the exchangers, and then at my coming I should have received mine own with usury.
> Matthew 25:24-27

The master was not buying the servant's excuse of fear. He saw through that argument, noting that it was his wickedness and laziness that led to his inability to receive a return for his master. Notice also that the master agreed that he expected a return with interest, that he reaped where he did not sow. But he did not go along with the assessment of the servant that he was a hard man. Indeed, Jesus is anything but a hard man! He is the most compassionate person who has ever lived. As we have mentioned previously, in the gospel narrative, sometimes the tone of our Lord's remarks can be missed. We should picture the master having misty eyes as he is talking to this third servant, for that is the true nature of our Savior, (2 Peter 3:9).

Next, we come to what I call the "law of responding." It is a quote given in the gospels, four times to my count, which demonstrates that the Lord will add to my account when I give of my talents or share the word, but will subtract from my account when I don't do those things.

> Take therefore the talent from him, and give it unto him which has ten talents. For unto every one that hath shall be given, and he shall have

> in abundance: But from him that hath not shall be taken away even that which he has.
> Matthew 25:28-29

We see that the servant who had gained the most was given even more! This isn't preached much, but it should be. These are Jesus' words; they are alive with meaning! This is a secret of life. To whoever responds, more shall be given. Whoever does not respond, well, even what he has will be taken away. Put in practical terms, God is not going to entrust abilities to people who won't use them for His glory. They will fade away while the responder will only grow larger in ability. In another parable, Jesus uses this same law to show that he who hears and shares the word, metes it out, will receive more revelation, will receive more insights, while the one who does not hear and share will lose even what he once understood. Let me show you:

> And He said unto them, take heed what you hear (*how you hear*): With what measure you mete (*give out*), it shall be measured to you: And unto you that hear shall more be given. For he that hath (*hears and shares*), *to him shall be given:* And he that hath not *(hears and shares not)*, from him shall be taken even that which he has.
> Mark 4:24-25 (italics added)

These words of Jesus come on the heels of His teaching of the sower and the seed. He is talking about His Word. If I want to receive revelation from Him, I need to pass it forward!

Now, for the sad ending to Jesus' parable of the talents:

> And cast ye the unprofitable servant into outer darkness: There shall be weeping and gnashing of teeth.
> Matthew 25:30

This servant is a type of an unsaved person, of an unbeliever. We understand this because he is sent to the place Jesus uses in other scriptures to describe Hell. By definition, a saved person will respond to God's goodness with at least a modicum of good works (James 2:19 and Galatians 5:6), for he has the Holy Spirit dwelling within, while the unsaved servant, by nature of being spiritually dead, cannot really do anything of lasting value: "For apart from me you can do nothing" (John 15:5). This sounds similar to Paul's description of the Bema Seat and the one who only had wood, hay, and stubble on the foundation. But the key difference is that that servant is saved because he has the foundation, he has Jesus and Him crucified. So, while that servant is saved, he will be a pauper in heaven, as he did not store up any treasure there during his life. This servant, being wicked and slothful, apparently rejects the Lord's offer of salvation and thus is sent away from Him.

Next, let's uncover truths from Jesus' similar-sounding, yet different parable of the pounds.

> He said therefore, a certain nobleman went into a far country to receive for himself a kingdom, and to return. And he called ten servants, and delivered them ten pounds, and said unto them, occupy till I come...And it came to pass, that when he returned, having received the kingdom, then he commanded these servants to be called unto him, to whom he had given

> the money, that he might know how much every man had made by trading. Then came the first, saying, Lord, your pound has gained ten pounds.
> Luke 19:12-13, 15-16

These two parables are both spoken during the last week of our Lord's life. The first was given on the Mount of Olives to His disciples after they asked Him about the times around His future coming. This latter parable was given a few days earlier when the Teacher was in Jericho on His way up to Jerusalem for that fateful last week. We see in this parable that, unlike the parable of the talents, where the servants were given differing amounts, these servants are all given the same. In this distinction is a great understanding. The talents of Jesus' first parable represent the differing gifts and abilities that all people receive from the Creator. But the pounds in this parable represent something very singular. Since they are equivalent, they represent the equality of opportunity, things that everybody is given by God that are exactly alike, such as time. We all are given twenty-four hours each day to work with. Such as the tithe: We all are told to offer the first 10% of our increase back to the Provider regardless of whether we are rich or poor. Such as the gospel message: It is the same gospel message we are all entrusted to proclaim. We see that the first servant made excellent use of his equal opportunity as he saw a ten-fold increase of his master's pound. Let's see how he fares. You can imagine that it will be good!

> And he said unto him, well, thou good servant: Because you have been faithful in a very little, have thou authority over ten cities. And the second came, saying, Lord, your pound has

> gained five pounds. And He said likewise to him, Be thou also over five cities. And another came, saying, Lord, behold, here is your pound, which I have kept laid up in a napkin: For I feared you, because you are an austere man: You take up that which you laid not down, and reap that which you did not sow. And he said to him, out of your own mouth will I judge you, thou wicked servant. You knew that I was an austere man, taking up that which I laid not down, and reaping that I did not sow. Wherefore then gave not your money into the bank, that at my coming I might have required my own with usury? And he said unto them that stood by, take from him the pound, and give it to him that has ten pounds...For I say unto you, that unto every one which has (*responds*) shall be given; and from him that hath not (*responds not*), even that which he has shall be taken away from him.
> Luke 19:17-24, 26-27. (italics added)

We see that the first servant was praised and given great authority in the nobleman's kingdom. The second servant was given the exact same praise from the master but was given less authority. I suspect that the responsibilities given to the two were commensurate with their prior work ethic. Unfortunately, the third servant, the one who hid his pound, is noted again to be wicked, like the third servant in the parable of the talents. And like that other servant, he too loses what little he had and saw it given to the servant who produced the ten-fold return of the nobleman's investment. Once again, the law of responding is in play regarding how we use our opportunities of equal time, etc.

These two parables should move us! They should inspire us to do everything we can to make our lives count. We want to be relevant. We want to add to the Kingdom. We want to make a difference. A few thoughts to help...Do for somebody what you would like to do for everyone. Like Elisha and the Shunammite woman and her son (2 Kings 4:8-37): He couldn't minister to everyone in Israel as he did with them. But I want to have a circle of people that I really give out to as much as possible. In other words, minister by the spirit and say "Yes" often! Don't be like the world and have "No" as your default setting.

Also, take seriously the opportunity to help people and don't let your limited abilities stop you. Remember the story of the five loaves and two fish. Meager supplies mean nothing to the Lord. Do whatever you can, wherever you are, with whatever is in your hand. This really speaks to me loudly when I consider the servant given only one talent. Unfortunately, people with limited gifts sort of "check out" thinking they cannot make a difference. The drop-in-the-bucket phenomenon comes into play. That is a lie from Hell! Even folks who are handicapped, elderly, or otherwise incapacitated physically can make a difference, for they can pray! As I've heard Pastor Jon Courson tell of advice which he gave to his ninety-year-old father-in-law who was lamenting the inability to finish strong in his present state: "You are there, in that chair, for the purpose of prayer." Intercessory prayer is a ministry all of us can partake in.

So I hope I have inspired some of you to use your time, talent, and finances to further the Kingdom. You won't be sorry!

Next, let's look at another aspect of the present Kingdom, which, if understood and applied, will help you to succeed in the things of which we have just spoken.

The Parable of the Sower and the Seed

> Behold, a sower went forth to sow: and when he sowed, some seeds fell by the wayside, and the fowls came and devoured them up: Some fell upon stony places, where they had not much earth: And forthwith they sprung up, because they had no deepness of earth: And when the sun was up, they were scorched; and because they had no root, they withered away. And some fell among thorns; and the thorns sprung up, and choked them: But some fell into good ground, and brought forth fruit, some a hundredfold, some sixty, some thirty-fold. Who hath ears to hear, let him hear.
> Matthew 13:3-9

In this, we have one of the best-known of all of Jesus' parables and teachings. This story is found in Matthew, Mark, and Luke, and in all three we are told that it was the first parable in which Jesus explained the mysteries of the Kingdom of Heaven. We see four types of soil, each with differing capacities to incorporate the seed that the sower spreads. We will see that these four represent different people groups but also can represent four different stages of an individual's heart in regards to its receptivity to receive the seed at any given time.

The disciples did not really understand the meaning of this parable and rightly asked the Teacher for amplification. Here is His reply:

> Now the parable is this: The seed is the word of God

Luke 8:11

Indeed, the Word of God is the seed, which, when planted, will produce the saving knowledge of our Savior. "Being born again, not of corruptible seed, but of incorruptible, by the word of God" (1 Peter 1:23). Along this line, Paul teaches that saving faith comes by hearing the word of God (Romans 10:17). Unfortunately, the first type of soil doesn't incorporate the seed because it is hard and trodden down, not at all prepared to receive the seed.

> Those by the wayside are they that hear, then comes the Devil, and takes away the word out of their hearts, lest they should believe and be saved.
> Luke 8:12

Remember, we are living in the middle of a war. Sometimes people can't believe because the hounds of Hell are closing their minds. It is always important to pray for release of the captives whenever sharing the seed, whenever speaking the word to a person. Also, hard ground needs to be plowed before seed will grow in it. The spiritual equivalent of plowing the field is to make folks aware of their sin and their subsequent need for a Savior. People need to understand that the wages of sin is death (Romans 6:23) before they comprehend their need for a Redeemer.

> But he that received the seed into stony places, the same is he that hears the word, and initially with joy receives it: Yet hath he no root in himself, but continues for a while: For when tribulation or persecution arises because of the word, by and by he is offended.

Matthew 13:20-21

This second type of soil initially receives the seed. In fact, since the stones in the ground generate heat, these seeds sprout quickly. This is a type of young believer whom we sometimes see going "all in" initially but, unfortunately, he has no grounding in the word, no roots, and thus tends to fall back when the heat of the summer sun arrives. That is, when the invariable tough times of life occur, this believer can fall away. The problem isn't the heat of the sun but the lack of roots going down to where the water in the deeper soil is located. The antidote for this baby in the faith is to not protect him from the sun but to encourage him to go deep into the Word. He needs roots. For the trials of life do one of two things to any person: They either cause a withering if roots are not deep or produce growth if those same roots are established. Thus, it is very important to encourage a new follower of Jesus to press into God's Word from the very beginning.

We see that this person becomes offended by the word he initially received when trials come. An offended person has forgotten what our Lord did for him. He has lost sight of the sacrifice Jesus made to bring him into the Kingdom. The saving gospel message always needs to be front and center when I under-shepherd any new believer because of this common people reaction in our fallen world.

> And these are they which are sown among thorns; such as hear the word, and the cares of this world, and the deceitfulness of riches, and the lusts of other things entering in, choke the word, and it becomes unfruitful.
> Mark 4:18-19

This third group also hear the word but, instead of withering, they are choked and produce no fruit. Like the rocky soil, they initially receive the word, they are saved if you will, but they end up like the carnal Christian described by Paul as only having wood, hay, and stubble to show for their lives. We see three thorny things that choke out the word sown in this soil. Cares, deceitfulness of riches, and lusts. Cares can certainly be distracting. They produce anxiety and threaten a person's faith. Many times, cares take the form of financial pressure. They attack people considered less well off. Contrast that with the deceitfulness of riches. This idol is seen more commonly, but not exclusively, in wealthy people. And we understand that it's not riches but the lure of riches that is the problem. The last thorn hits all people, rich and poor alike, that being lust. We recognize lust to be the passionate desire for something without regard to the harm that will come with obtaining it. By definition, lust is something shiny and attractive but ultimately harmful.

How do we help these people? The answer is to get them to look up! The thorns have placed their eyes here in this world. We want them to get the vision of Heaven. The choked believer needs to grasp the reality of heaven and realize that it is not that far away. As has been said: "If heaven is real, and it is, then that's all that matters. If heaven isn't real, then nothing matters at all!" Talk about heaven often to the carnal Christian who's living with one foot in the world.

Next, we get to the good part of this story...the soil that produces much fruit!

> But he that received the seed into the good ground is he that hears the word, and understands it: Which also bears fruit, and brings

> forth, some a hundredfold, some sixty, some
> thirty.
> Matthew 13:23

Here we see that the one who produces great fruit not only hears the word, but he understands it. He does not let trials and cares distract him from pressing into God's Word. He takes seriously Paul's admonition to young Timothy to study to show himself approved unto God, a workman who needs not to be ashamed rightly dividing the word of truth (2 Timothy 2:15). You see, the Devil can't take the believer to Hell, but he can prevent him or her from living for Heaven! The tricks he uses are always the same, distraction and delay. It's easy to see that distraction can take my eye off the ball, but how does delay work? Delay is saying, "I'll get to that later." Guess what? Later never comes! When the Spirit nudges you to spend time with Him, to read the Word, to share with someone a blessing or a gift, don't delay. Remember, instant obedience is the way to live. As I said earlier, I don't do this that well, but that's the goal!

We see that the one who hears and understands the Word produces varying degrees of fruit. Fruit is a Bible word loaded with meaning. Spiritual fruit is what Jesus is speaking of. As far as I can tell, the New Testament has six references to different types of fruit which the hearer and assimilator can produce. Soul winning (Romans 1:13), holiness (Romans 6:22), financial giving (Romans 15:28), fruit of the spirit (Galatians 5:22-23), good works (Colossians 1:10), and praise and thanksgiving to God (Hebrews 13:15).

Now you may be saying, "I don't see that much fruit in my life." Well, in Luke's rendering of this parable, the fruit is brought forth with patience (Luke 8:15). That is, it's a growth process. The Word doesn't spring up overnight. Hang in there, keep plugging away and what has been sown, like a garden, will sprout up in due season.

Let me give you some tips about how to be soil that is receptive to God's Word.

First, realize that the seed, the Word, is, in reality, another name for Jesus Christ (John 1:1) and (Revelation 19:13). When I take in the Word, I'm taking in Jesus, I'm getting to know Jesus, I'm becoming like Jesus. Not only am I becoming like my Lord, but I am liking Him, too! I see how beautiful He is as I take in and treasure His Word. As the Song of Solomon sings:

> My beloved is white and ruddy, the chief among ten thousand.
> His head is as most fine gold, His locks are bushy, and black as a raven...
> His cheeks are a bed of spices, as sweet as flowers:
> His lips like lilies, dropping sweet smelling myrrh...
> His legs are as pillars of marble, set upon sockets of fine gold:
> His countenance is as Lebanon, excellent as the cedars.
> His mouth is most sweet: Yea, He is altogether lovely.
> This is my beloved, and this is my friend, O daughters of Jerusalem.
> Song of Solomon 5:10-16

Indeed, He is all together and He is altogether lovely! When we get this, when we perceive how our Husband will appear when we see Him, well, it should make our hearts leap in anticipated joy!

Next, read the word often and read it expectantly and conversationally. By this I mean, expect God to talk to you every time you read or hear His Word. That means, have your device or pen and paper ready. Write down your impressions so you can meditate later on things He is saying to you. And converse with Him. Stop often and speak your heart to Him about what you are reading. And be real with Him. He can take it!

Some of you may be thinking, "How can I be sure that the Bible is the same seed of which Jesus is speaking? Doesn't it have errors and contradictions?" Actually, it's the differences in the accounts that reveal that collusion did not take place. If all of the gospel writers, for instance, had exactly the same perspectives, one would know that some funny business took place in "revising" Jesus' story. Also, the scholar of the scriptures notes that there is unity among books and authors. We don't see radically different ideas in the men who faithfully wrote as they were inspired by the Holy Spirit (2 Timothy 3:16). Archeology over time has, again and again, backed up the scriptures and is well documented elsewhere. Prophecy is found in nearly one-third of the Word. We serve a God who challenges others to prove Him in the area of predicting the future. No god except the true and living God dares to do such a thing (Isaiah 46:10). My favorite argument for the veracity of the Bible is that my Lord quoted the hard-to-understand portions. Jesus talked about Adam and Eve as if they were real persons and not just representatives of mankind. He spoke of Noah and the Flood as well as Jonah and the whale who swallowed him. No, Jesus is the center and, if He believed the scriptures, so should I.

Another strategy to see fruit produced in your life is to memorize verses of scripture that impress your heart and then speak forth those words to others exactly as they are written in the Word. Then watch what happens! Power will be released. The Word of God is like a lion in a cage. When you let it out, it will go wild! You and everyone who hears it will be blessed, exhorted, and encouraged. Now know, though, if you do this, the other team will try and trick you by saying you are unworthy, for indeed you are. We all are. But it's the message, not the messenger that is important. In fact, the less polished the presentation, the more glory reflects back to the Father when the Word hits its target. Think of it like the FedEx man, he is only delivering the package, it's about the parcel and not about him. So, go for it for a blessing!

Lastly, before leaving this parable, fruit will be produced as you meditate upon God's Word. To meditate means to chew the cud, to cogitate, to mull over and deeply consider what is being said. As I actively and intentionally rehearse the scriptures, they become part of me with the result that I receive "the mind of Christ" (1 Corinthians 2:16).

> Blessed is the man that walks not in the counsel of the ungodly, nor stands in the way of sinners, nor sits in the seat of the scornful.
> But his delight is in the law of the Lord; and in His law does he meditate day and night.
> And he shall be like a tree planted by the rivers of water, that brings forth his fruit in his season; his leaf shall not wither; and whatsoever he does shall prosper.
> Psalm 1:1-3

Next, let's consider a parable that presents the flip side of the Kingdom of God. Instead of emphasizing works we can do for His glory, this parable is all about God's grace, all about His unmerited, undeserved, and unearned favor which He bestows upon us all.

The Parable of the Workers in the Vineyard

> For the kingdom of heaven is like unto a man that is a householder, which went out early in the morning to hire laborers into his vineyard. And when he had agreed with the laborers for a penny a day, he sent them into the vineyard. And he went out about the third hour, and saw others standing idle in the marketplace, and said unto them; go you also into the vineyard, and whatsoever is right I will give you. And they went their way. Again, he went out about the sixth and ninth hour, and did likewise. And about the eleventh hour he went out, and found others standing idle, and said unto them, why stand you here all day idle? They said unto him, because no man has hired us. He said to them, go you also into the vineyard; and whatsoever is right, that you shall receive. So, when evening was come, the lord of the vineyard said unto his steward, call the laborers, and give them their hire, beginning from the last unto the first. And when they came that were hired about the eleventh hour, they received every man a penny. But when the first came, they supposed that they should have received more; and they likewise received a penny. And when they had received it, they murmured against the goodman of the house.

> Saying, these last have worked but one hour, and you have made them equal with us, which have borne the burden of the heat of the day. But he answered them one of them, and said, friend, I do you no wrong: Did you not agree with me for a penny? Take what yours is, and go your way: I will give unto the last, even as unto you. Is it not lawful for me to do what I will with mine own? Is your eye evil, because I am good? So, the last shall be first, and the first last: For many be called, but few chosen. Matthew 20:1-16

What a story! Most of us, like the listeners in Jesus' audience on first impression, do not feel this is very fair. The workers who labored for the entire twelve-hour workday received exactly the same as the ones who barely had time to pick any grapes at all! Sort of a raw deal, even though that was the arrangement they had negotiated. And that's the point. One of the ideas of this parable is that it is all about God's grace. And grace by definition is not fair! It is unmerited, undeserved, unearned favor and thus cannot be earned. It is totally up to the discretion of the giver of grace to determine what He is bestowing.

So it is very important for us to not compare blessings with other people. Grace is not level or equal. The householder told the other workers that whatsoever was right, they would receive. Thus, without a specific contract, they were in a position to be joyful when the goodman settled things with them at the end of the day. You see, the laborers all needed what the householder was offering. They all needed work. Likewise, we laborers here in this world all need what the Father is offering, that is, we need salvation! All of the workers except the first group recognized the offer as a gift because no contract was really initiated. The first group had an agreement, though. If they worked all day, they would get a penny. This pictures the Law. If a man or woman obeyed the entire Law, then he or she would obtain salvation without God's grace being needed, so another level of this parable is that it typifies the nation of Israel. As holders of God's covenant, they are the first workers hired and the only ones with a contract. In Bible typology, a vineyard always has an embedded meaning to Israel. The other workers are the Gentiles who come in later, some very late, and yet receive the same blessing, a penny. Or, in the allegory Jesus is presenting, all receive salvation. Like the Prodigal Son's older brother, whom we will discuss later, the first workers murmured and complained to the goodman. This is all because they "supposed" they would receive more after seeing the gifts given to the later workers. Indeed, that would have been the case if works instead of grace were in play. Of course, they were reprimanded for their jealously because the householder correctly pointed out that it was completely his discretion as to what he conferred.

We are introduced to another Bible paradox when we are told that the first shall be last and the last shall be first. This certainly has been true for the nation of Israel because we have seen Israel shrink back since they for the most part rejected Messiah and the Gentiles, having embraced him, became the blessed group. At the end of the present age, though, Israel will recognize Jesus as Lord and, as Paul preaches, "all Israel will be saved" (Romans 11:26). But on a personal level, this also holds true. So often, in God's economy of grace, we see the late comer receiving a blessing out of proportion to his effort or station. Again, this is because grace is not a contract. It's a gift. The key for the believer is not to despise the grace of God when it is bestowed on another who may seem less worthy than you. I want to remember what Jesus did for me, in saving me from destruction, and not worry about anything He does for other undeserving people I may know. As I read in God's Word, it is clear that the Giver of Gifts does not like murmuring from His kids, and why should He? We don't like it in our children, either! I want to stay away from complaining and just remember how good He has been to me. I want to recognize that every new day is a gift of God's grace to me. I want to unwrap it, I want to embrace it, I want to savor it!

Next, let's look at two parables of the Kingdom which speak of the Church of Christ and its manifestation in the world over the last two thousand years.

The Parables of the Mustard Seed and of Leaven

> Then said he, unto what is the Kingdom of God like? And whereunto shall I resemble it? It is like a grain of mustard seed, which a man took, and cast into his garden; and it grew, and waxed a great tree; and the fowls of the air lodged in the branches of it. And again He said, whereunto shall I liken the Kingdom of God? It is like leaven, which a woman took and hid in three measures of meal, till the whole lump was leavened.
> Luke 13:18-21

These two parables were given by the Lord when He was challenged by the ruler of the synagogue after He healed a woman on the Sabbath. Jesus noted his hypocrisy, charging that the ruler certainly would lead his animals out for water on the Sabbath, so why shouldn't He heal a daughter of Abraham who had been bound by Satan for eighteen years on the Sabbath? Of course, the head of the synagogue had no rebuttal to this logical observation. Our Lord then gave these two parables, which are related, so we, His followers, will not be surprised when we look at the kingdom being established. Jesus said it would start small, like a mustard seed, but would grow into a great tree. As we have noted over the past two thousand years, the kingdom, also called the church, started like a mustard seed. Only Jesus and the twelve. Later, disciples and women were added so that near the day of Pentecost one hundred and twenty were present (Acts 1:15). Then on Pentecost, three thousand were added and the growth has never really stopped. Today, three billion souls on our planet call Jesus their Lord. But, along with this prophesized explosive growth of the Church, Jesus is pointing out something else that is relevant in the context of His recent attack by the ruler of the synagogue. You see, nowhere does a mustard plant, which is an herb, grow into a tree. On the contrary, it grows into a five- to eight-foot plant, not a large tree big enough to have birds nest in it, so we see unusual growth to the Church and we learn that fowls will be at home in it. Birds (except doves and eagles) in Bible typology are nearly always types of evil. Here is no exception. Jesus is teaching that evil will take up roost in the Church. Same with the second parable. Just as birds picture sin, so does leaven. It too infiltrates throughout the whole lump just as sin has permeated the entirety of the Church. Paul, Peter, and Jude among others write in their various epistles of the need to watch out for false teachers propagating evil (1 Timothy 4:1-3, 2 Timothy 3:12-13, 2 Peter 2:1-2, Jude 4), for they, too, warned of this relationship. The history of the Church is riddled with corruption. We can look at the Catholic Church of the Middle Ages and its dishonest leadership or the present-day lukewarm church and its prosperity and "culturally correct" gospel and see this to be true. So Jesus is teaching that we should not be surprised when this happens.

Matthew reports that these two parables were given by Jesus on a second occasion, immediately on the heels of His parable of the wheat and the tares. We remember in that parable, good and bad also traveled through life together, side by side, until the reapers (angels) were instructed to gather them separately at the end of the age, which is still to come. So, along with not being startled by hypocrisy in the Kingdom, we should instead celebrate the good in the Church, for, as Jesus said to the churches of Revelation 2 and 3 (The sum of which picture the Church in its entirety,) "for I walk in the midst of the seven golden candlesticks (churches)" (Revelation 1:20-2:1). The Church is where Jesus is today. The Church is where the message of salvation is shouted forth. The Church is where hospitals, relief agencies, and schools have flourished. The Church, where the Comforter resides, is why the god of this world has been held back, as there is much evil that he would love to inflict, but cannot. When that spirit and the Church depart, at the end of the age, we will see a time when evil will be unleashed to a degree never before realized (2 Thessalonians 2:1-4).

The Old Testament contains a picture that is relevant to how we should look at the Church, despite its many flaws.

> When you shall besiege a city a long time, in making war against it to take it, you shall not destroy the trees there by forcing an axe against them: For you may eat of them, you shall not cut them down...Only the trees shall you cut down which be not trees for fruit.
> Deuteronomy 20:19-20

Fruit-bearing trees were not to be cut down. Only trees without fruit were to be used in a siege. Likewise, I should not cut down other denominations that seem strange and possibly wrong on some doctrines, when fruit is being produced. We learn from Paul that the Church is the body of Christ (1 Corinthians 12:12-14); it is a living organism. And like the body, some parts will be sore and sick from time to time. When this happens, I nurture that part of my body, I don't cut it off. So too, we should give tolerance to the Church of Christ while we are waiting for it to be perfected, in the age to come!

Lastly in this chapter, we will talk about the parable of the ten virgins and the need for us to be watching and ready during this preamble. This time when the Kingdom of Heaven is among us as righteousness, peace, and joy in the Holy Spirit but still awaiting the return of the King. In that day, all will be made right. For then, will be the era when the earth shall be full of the knowledge of the Lord as waters cover the sea (Isaiah 11:9).

The Parable of the Ten Virgins

> Then shall the kingdom of heaven be likened unto ten virgins, which took their lamps and went forth to meet the bridegroom.
> Matthew 25:1

This parable was given as part of Jesus' Olivet discourse after His disciples asked him about the signs surrounding His return as King of King and Lord of Lords at the end of the age. The context of this parable, as well as the one of the talents, which we have already discussed, is to be watching and ready. As Peter so poignantly teaches, we are to give diligence to make our calling and election sure (2 Peter 1:10). In other words, if how I live my life for the next week determined my income for the next ten years, I certainly would be intentional about my actions and not leave things to chance. So too, this life and how I live and what I believe are clearly related to future rewards, not to mention personal salvation. Thus, I need to pay attention to what Jesus is saying here as my future destiny hangs in the balance of my choices.

> And five of them were wise, and five were foolish. They that were foolish took their lamps, and took no oil with them: But the wise took oil in their vessels with their lamps.
> Matthew 25:2-4

This parable is talking about individual salvation. Oil is a picture of the Holy Spirit. Paul adds that those who hear the gospel of salvation through belief in Christ are sealed with the Holy Spirit as the earnest, or proof, of our inheritance until that heritage is fully realized in heaven (Ephesians 1:13-14). These words are a sober warning by Jesus, to all, not to delay. For the words He said to His disciples, He says to all, "Who say you that I am?" (Matthew 16:15)

> While the bridegroom tarried, they all slumbered and slept. And at midnight there was a cry made, behold, the bridegroom comes; go you out to meet him. Then all the virgins arose, and trimmed their lamps. And the foolish said unto the wise, give us of your oil; for our lamps are gone out.
> Matthew 25:5-8

This perfectly pictures the Jewish wedding ceremony. At a time known only by the father of the groom, he would send his son with a friend through the streets of the city with a cry and a trumpet sound to announce he was coming for his bride. The bride, of course, would be waiting and ready, for she knew not the day or the hour the bridegroom would appear. Some of you no doubt are tracking with me; this also is a picture of the Rapture of the Church, for the believers in Jesus are the Bride of Christ. Paul teaches that the Lord will descend from heaven with a shout, with the voice of the archangel, and with the trump of God and we will be caught up to be with the Lord (1 Thessalonians 4:16-17). Indeed, one understanding of this parable is its relationship to the saved of the world meeting the Lord on that awesome day!

> But the wise answered, saying, not so; lest there be not enough for us and you: But go you rather to them that sell, and buy for yourselves.
> Matthew 25:9

Herein is a great truth. Salvation is not inherited or conferred. I must obtain it myself by correctly answering that great question of his, "Who do you say I am?" God has children, but He does not have grandchildren.

> And while they went to buy, the bridegroom came; and they that were ready went in with Him to the marriage:
> Matthew 25:10

How wonderful this will be. I want you to see this. If you are ready, and you will be if you call Jesus Lord, then you will go into the marriage ceremony. You are the Bride of Christ. The intimacy you will experience I cannot even begin to describe! David was blown away when the Lord told him he would be related to Messiah (1 Chronicles 17:16-27). How much greater will this be? We are going to be married to him!

> Afterward came the other virgins, saying, Lord, Lord, open to us. But He answered and said, truly I say unto you, I know you not. Watch therefore, for you know neither the day nor the hour wherein the Son of man comes.
> Matthew 25;11-13

This is so sad to me. For it clearly suggests that, once we see him, it is too late to decide our fate. We must choose before that terrible day. We have discussed this before, haven't we? God makes His presence veiled to a great degree so as to provide us a choice to love Him or not. Upon seeing Him in all of His glory, choice flies out the window as the blinding light of His presence would preclude any ability to love Him by our own free will. Dear soul, today is the day of salvation, choose Jesus. It is the best decision you will ever make. One you will never regret.

So we end our discussion of many of the parables concerning the Kingdom of Heaven. In them we saw Jesus selling everything, giving His all to buy us back to him, both Jews and Gentiles. We learned that the children of God and the children of the Devil will coexist together until the end of the present age. Jesus emphasized the need to come to Him as a little child and we saw that how we use our time and talent determines rewards we will receive on that great day. Our response to God's Word, the seed sown, is how we produce fruit to His glory and we were given a lesson in how God's grace is doled out. We learned that the Kingdom as manifested by the Church will grow like a living organism and become sick and injured from time to time, needing tending from Jesus, the head. The parable of the ten virgins reminds us that God only has children, not grandchildren. And lastly, we also were given a vision of our future marriage feast to the Lord as we contemplate our position as the Bride of Christ.

In our next section, we will visit the words of the Apostle John as he faithfully reports to us those great words Jesus spoke that evening to Nicodemus, "You must be born again."

Summary:

1. The parables of the man who bought the field with the treasure and the merchant who purchased the pearl of great price are speaking about Jesus and what He did to purchase us to Himself.
2. The parable of the wheat and the tares reveals that God has allowed His children and those of the Devil to live together so that those destined to become His children will be given every opportunity to do so.
3. We come to Jesus as a child in humility, trust, teachability, and dependence. Along with that, as we mature, we leave our childish tendency toward selfishness and learn love.
4. We are not saved by good works but we are saved for good works.
5. Jesus taught that future responsibilities and rewards in Heaven will be determined by how we use our time and talent in this life.
6. The law of responding states that, whenever you respond to God, whether in word or deed, you will receive more.

But, when you don't respond to God, even what you have will be lost.

7. When it comes to ministry opportunities, "If you don't know, get up and go." Say "Yes" often. When it comes to worldly activities, "If in doubt, opt out."
8. The parable of the sower and the seed speaks of four different people groups but also of four different ways my heart can be in responding to God's Word. I want to guard my heart to keep it fruitful ground, ready to receive, as much as possible.
9. The parable of the workers in the vineyard shows us that God's grace is not a contract, not earned, and not even fair. It goes above and beyond fair!
10. The Parables of the Mustard Seed and of the Leaven predicted the growth of the Kingdom of God as manifested by the Church of Christ. They also foretold that evil and sin would intermingle with the good. Nevertheless, Jesus is present in His Church and will cleanse her on that day, not very far away!

For Further Study:

1. Since Jesus gave it all to purchase humanity, how should I view other people?
2. What does coming to God as a little child look like?
3. What is your greatest regret? Something you did which you shouldn't have or something you didn't do but wish you had?
4. What are some things you can do with your time and talent to make an eternal difference in your world?
5. What is some fruit you have seen in your life as you have responded to the seed, God's Word?

6. What tips would you give others to help them see fruit produced in their lives?

Jesus and the New Birth

"Are you born again?" This is one of those catch-phrases that the people of the world toss around, sort of mockingly, when they think of fundamentalist Christians. Unknowingly to them, this phrase is the heart of Jesus' message. When the respected and learned Pharisee, Nicodemus visited Jesus at night, this is what he heard...words that are applicable to all.

> Truly, truly I say unto you, except a man be born again, he cannot see the Kingdom of God.
> John 3:3

Understand, a "born-again Christian" isn't a type of Christian, like a Methodist or a Presbyterian, it is the way one becomes a Christian! Thus, the god of this world, the Devil (2 Corinthians 4:4), wants to do all he can to discredit this message as he knows that in it, is the power of life and death.

Let's look into what Jesus is saying about this most famous Christian sound bite, "born again."

> Nicodemus said unto him, how can a man be born when he is old? Can he enter the second time into his mother's womb, and be born?
> John 3:4

"You must be born again, Nicodemus. It's all about regeneration, getting a new heart and a new spirit, not just cleaning up. What you are doing, sir, is not going to work!"

The religious leader's reply is telling... "How can a man be born when He is old?" But Jesus immediately understood what Nicodemus was saying: "How can I start over? I've been doing this Pharisee thing for a very long time. It's part of me now."

> Jesus answered, truly, truly, I say unto thee, except a man be born of water and of the Spirit, he cannot enter into the Kingdom of God. That which is born of the flesh is flesh: and that which is born of the Spirit is spirit. Marvel not that I said unto you, you must be born again.
> John 3:5-7

"You must have a physical and a spiritual birth, Nicodemus. You see, flesh begets flesh and spirit begets spirit. When your mother birthed you, that was flesh begetting flesh, and fleshy works only produce more of the flesh. But when you are born of God's Spirit, that's the spiritual birth, that's the new birth I am speaking of."

You see, a born-again Christian has been crucified with Christ (Galatians 2:20). He has died to the Law (Romans 7:4) and he is born into the faith of Jesus Christ. It is finished. That new believer goes from the Old Covenant, the pact of the Law, to the New Covenant, a contract of grace involving spiritual indwelling. The one who is born again has two birthdays, his physical one and his spiritual one.

This response of Jesus also speaks of the Word of God. In Bible typology, water is a type of the Word (John 15:3 and

Ephesians 5:26, among others). A person must be born again by hearing the Word (Romans 10:17) and by a move of the Spirit in his life.

> The wind blows where it blows, and you hear the sound thereof, but cannot tell where it comes from, and where it is going: So is every one that is born of the Spirit.
> John 3:8

It's not fabricated when the Spirit moves. It is spontaneous, it is quick and it can be subtle! There is no formula or even a prayer that, if recited, brings the spirit, it is a work of God in a person's heart, plain and simple!

> Nicodemus answered and said unto him, how can these things be? Jesus answered and said unto him, are you a master of Israel, and know not these things?
> John 3:9-10

"Incredible, Nicodemus, you're the great teacher in Israel and you don't understand what I am saying!" Jesus was quoting well-known scripture from Ezekiel as well as Jeremiah concerning the Spirit, i.e., the dry bones prophecy found in Ezekiel 37 and the New Covenant prophecy found in Jeremiah 31. He expected Nicodemus to also recall the following from the priest and prophet Ezekiel:

> Cast away from you all your transgressions, whereby you have transgressed; and make you a new heart and a new spirit: For why will you

> die, O house of Israel? For I have no pleasure in the death of him that dies, says the Lord God: Wherefore turn yourselves, and live.
> Ezekiel 18:31-32

Jesus expected Nicodemus to recall God's message found later in Ezekiel's prophecy:

> Then will I sprinkle clean water upon you, and you shall be clean: From all of your filthiness, and from all your idols, will I cleanse you. A new heart also will I give you, and a new spirit will I put within you: And I will take away the stony heart out of your flesh...And I will put my spirit within you.
> Ezekiel 36:25-27

God will sprinkle clean water by His Spirit. And it will move like the wind, wherever it will. In other words, it is all by His Spirit, even the grace to believe. And it's absolutely not by works. This discourse shows the utter need for a Savior. Works won't save!

> Truly, truly, I say unto you, we speak that we do know, and testify that we have seen; and you (*the Jewish leaders*) receive not our witness. If I have told you earthly things, and you believe not, how shall you believe, if I tell you heavenly things? And no man has ascended up to heaven, but He that came down from heaven, even the Son of man which is in heaven.
> John 3: 11-13 (italics added)

"Being born again is basic, Nicodemus! I'm the one from heaven telling you this. The world will make no sense unless you are born again. To the unsaved, life is a long series of distractions and then you die. But the one who has the spirit, he is the one who realizes the big picture." You see, being born again doesn't have to make complete sense, it just has to work! As Paul stated, the gospel is foolishness to the Gentiles and a stumbling block to the Jews, but to those who believe, it is the power of God unto salvation (1 Corinthians 1:23-24).

> And as Moses lifted up the serpent in the wilderness, even so must the Son of man be lifted up: that whosoever believes in Him should not perish, but have eternal life.
> John 3:14-15

"It's so simple, Nicodemus, just look to me, look to the Son and be saved! And it's all there in Old Testament. Like in Numbers 21, where the people sinned and were plagued by biting serpents. Remember how my Father told Moses to make a fiery serpent and lift it up on a brass pole and have the people look at it? Those who looked were delivered while those who did not suffered and died. This is the same, Nicodemus. I, the Son of man, will be lifted up on a Roman cross so that all who look to me in faith will be saved."

In another encounter with the Pharisees, Jesus told them to "search the scriptures; for in them you think you have eternal life: And they are they which testify of me" (John 5:39). Of course, the only scriptures at that time were what we call the Old Testament, as the New Testament had not yet been written. Jesus said, your very scriptures, the ones you hold in such high esteem, speak of me. Not only was He speaking of the Brazen Serpent, but that statement included the Tree of Life, the Passover sacrifice, the story of Jonah and the whale, the sacrifice of the Red Heifer, and many, many others.

> For God so loved the world, that He gave His only begotten Son, that whosoever believes on Him should not perish, but have everlasting life. For God sent not His Son into the world to condemn the world; but that the world through Him might be saved. He that believes on Him is not condemned:
> John 3:16-18a

Again, we see God's heart, plan, and will in this most famous of all Bible verses! God loved the souls of the world, He gave His Son for them, i.e., Himself, so they in believing would live.

> But he that believes not is condemned already, because he has not believed in the name of the only begotten Son of God. And this is the condemnation, that light is come into the world, and men loved darkness rather than light, because their deeds were evil. For everyone that does evil hates the light, neither comes into the light, lest his deeds should be reproved.
> John 3:18b-20

The crux of the matter is that some men won't believe so that they can continue to practice their evil lifestyle. As we have discussed previously, for the unsaved it is "My, not thy will be done." Men want to stay in the dark, rejecting the Lord's offer of salvation because they inherently understand that involved in that choice is giving over the control of one's life and forsaking sin as much as is possible. Men want to continue in their idolatry, fornication, lasciviousness, drunkenness, etc. Choosing Jesus sort of throws water on that fire!

The Lord correctly points out that the light reproves the darkness. They are unwise not to see this. As Solomon penned: "Reprove not a scorner, lest he hate you: Rebuke a wise man and he will love you" (Proverbs 9:8). Those destined to be condemned love the darkness and thus will not receive correction, they choose death over life. They fail to understand that God is Light (John 1:9) and Life (John 11:25) and by rejecting the Lord they are choosing to be away from him, away from light and life. Thus, they will inhabit light and life's antonym, that is, darkness and death!

The irony in all of this is that everyone believes deep down in their heart that there is a God (Romans 1:20). They believe in eternity (Ecclesiastes 3:11) and they realize they are sinners destined for judgment (Psalm 14:3). All unsaved souls fear death (Hebrews 2:15) and they are subject to emptiness (Romans 8:20). Lastly, they have all been shined on by the Light (John 1:9) and, as a believer in Christ, they expect something from you. So, don't hold back, afraid of what that unbeliever will think of you. Actually, he will think less of you, knowing you believe in Jesus, if you don't speak of Him!

> But he that does truth comes into the light, that his deeds may be made manifest, that they are wrought in God.
> John 3:21

But the wise man, the one who can say "thy will be done," loves the light, loves the truth, and wants his deeds to line up with his Lord's agenda. Thus, he is willing and desirous to have his deeds be reproved if necessary, to stay in the Light, and to do the works of God.

The gospels have at least three parables that speak of the need for regeneration over reformation, that speak to the need to being made new over just cleaning up.

> And it came to pass, that, as Jesus sat at meat in his house (*the tax collector and future apostle, Matthew's house*), many publicans and sinners sat also together with Jesus and His disciples: For there were many, and they followed him. And when the scribes and Pharisees saw Him eat with publicans and sinners, they said unto His disciples, how is that He eats and drinks with publicans and sinners? When Jesus heard it, He said unto them, they that are whole have no need of a physician, but they that are sick: I came not to call the righteous, but sinners to repentance.
> Mark 2:15-17 (italics added)

We opened this book with this verse, Jesus' mission statement, if you will. The Great Physician came to seek and save the lost, He came to call sinners to repentance! Earlier in this chapter, Jesus demonstrated His power to forgive sins by healing the paralytic man (Mark 2:3-12). In this, the context of His mission statement, we see that all men need their sins forgiven. All need a Savior! The way to that Deliverer is spoken of next:

> No man also sews a piece of new cloth on an old garment: Else the new piece that filled it up takes (*tears*) away from the old, and the rent is made worse.
> Mark 2:21 (italics added)

"I'm doing a new thing here. It is a new covenant, as spoken by Jeremiah (31:31-34). Belief in me, the new, will not fit on the old, the Law. It will soon be finished. The old system cannot be patched up. It will be discarded for a new garment, a new covenant, one where sinners can repent and be forgiven."

> And no man puts new wine into old bottles: Else the new wine does burst the bottles, and the wine is spilled, and the bottles will be marred: But new wine must be put in new bottles.
> Mark 2:22

Men need to be regenerated, made new, not just cleaned up is the analogy here. Again, the second understanding in these words is the New Covenant replacing the Law. Jesus fulfilled the Law and thus paved the way for the new wineskins.

Another parable Jesus put forth demonstrates the futility of cleaning up a person, forsaking evil, without receiving God's Spirit, being made new.

> When the unclean spirit is gone out of a man, he walks through dry places, seeking rest; and finding none, he says, I will return unto my house whence I came out. And when he comes, he finds it swept and garnished. Then

> goes he, and takes to him seven other spirits more wicked than himself; and they enter in, and dwell there: And the last state of that man is worse than the first.
> Luke 11:24-26

Reformation without regeneration is doomed to fail. Through a parable, the Teacher is saying we must catch the fish before we can clean it! A person needs to toss out the bad AND receive the good! That's why Christians don't want to put all of their efforts into cleaning up the problems of the world at the expense of neglecting the good news of Jesus Christ. I can spend all of my time promoting the environment, politics, or even standing against the murder of the innocents, but if Christ is not the center of the conversation, worldlings will not "get it." Paul understood this after powerfully preaching around Jesus in Athens and seeing no fruit to his labor, he changed his tactics when he next traveled south to Corinth. There his words were received as he preached the following message:

> And I, brethren, when I came to you, came not with excellency of speech or of wisdom, declaring unto you the testimony of God. For I determined not to know anything among you, save Jesus Christ, and Him crucified.
> 1 Corinthians 2:1

That's what I want to do also! It's not about how eloquent I speak or how powerfully I command God's Word. It's all about what the Savior did. He died for me. That's what I want to talk about. And I'm not saying social causes are bad; no, not at all! But I want to have the proper perspective. I want to live with eternity's view in mind. In one hundred years, every social problem we have now will be different than today. But the truth about Jesus and our need for His saving grace will remain. Once again, I want to keep the main thing, the main thing. And that is Jesus Christ and Him crucified!

Lastly, I would like to speak of the so-called "Romans Road." Three verses which the Spirit of God will use as water of the Word to move in a person's heart. Three short truths to memorize and share that can usher an unbeliever right into the Kingdom.

> For all have sinned and come short of the glory of God.
> Romans 3:23

> For the wages of sin is death; but the gift of God is eternal life through Jesus Christ our Lord.
> Romans 6:23

> That if you shall confess with your mouth the Lord Jesus, and shall believe in your heart that God has raised Him from the dead, you shall be saved.
> Romans 10:9

All have missed the mark, the sentence of sin is death, but the penalty has been commuted by Jesus Christ. To receive the pardon, one verbally acknowledges Jesus as Lord and believes that He rose from the grave. This is the gospel, the death, burial, and resurrection of Jesus Christ (1 Corinthians 15:1-3), cleansing us of sin and giving us resurrected life in him!

Summary:

1. A born-again Christian isn't a type of Christian, but the way one becomes a Christian.
2. Being born again is a spiritual birth that occurs when the Spirit moves in a person's life and is made possible by hearing and understanding the water of God's Word concerning salvation.
3. Being born again is looking up to (believing, trusting, following) the Son of man who was lifted up on the Cross.
4. Men and women reject the gospel so they can continue to live in darkness.
5. Jesus Christ and Him crucified is the main thing.
6. The "Romans Road" can be a good witnessing tool to help a person come into the Light.

For Further Study:

1. Does a person who is born again choose God or does God choose him?
2. When Jesus marveled that Nicodemus, a master in Israel, did not understand the concept of the new birth, what scriptures was He alluding to that Nicodemus should have connected?
3. Why is the gospel foolishness to the Gentiles and a stumbling block to the Jews?
4. According to Romans 1:20, is it possible for a person to really be an atheist?
5. Why should you not be surprised that people of the world do not understand you?
6. In our day, does it take much faith to believe that Jesus actually rose from the dead?

I AM...

Jesus of Nazareth is much more than a great teacher. More than an inspirational example of excellent living. No, He is the centerpiece of history. He is the decision point of life. All must come to terms with His message, certainly. But all must also decide just who He is. As C.S. Lewis has famously said, "Jesus of Nazareth is either a liar, a lunatic, or He is Lord." There is no middle ground. The things He said, some of which we will discuss in this section, can only be said by God.

The disciple Jesus loved wrote extensively about his master. He opened his gospel by stating that Jesus was from the beginning and that He is God (John 1:1-14). His narrative compliments the first book of the Bible, that of Genesis. In that section of the Torah, given to Moses by God, we learn that in the beginning, God... (Genesis 1:1). There we are introduced to Almighty God and His many names which reveal to mankind His very nature. This is also what John has done for us with the second person of the Godhead. They are both I AM. They are both equally whatever we need!

The Bread of Life

Another name we learn for God, found in Genesis 22, is Jehovah Raphe. That is, God who provides. In that portion of scripture, God proved Abraham's faith in an incredible way when

He asked him to sacrifice his beloved son Isaac as an offering back to Him. Little did Abraham know that God was picturing for all time what He was planning upon doing in sacrificing His beloved Son for the sins of the world. Abraham, with mind-boggling faith to me, believed God and was willing to sacrifice his son. Of course, God called off the offering after Abraham demonstrated his willingness to carry it forth. The Provider then caused a ram to be caught in a thicket nearby and Abraham presented that to God as a substitute. Abraham then worshipped the God of heaven, calling Him Jehovah Raphe, God who provides.

Likewise, in John's gospel, we find seven names Jesus announced to His followers that reveal His equality with God, the I AM, as well as His nature. All seven names are preceded by the Old Testament name of God, I AM. The first of the I Am names also reveals Jesus as the God who provides, as He is the Bread of Life. He is the provision that gives eternal life!

In Chapter 6 of John's gospel, when Passover was nigh (vs 4), Jesus multiplied five loaves of bread and two small fish to feed five thousand men as well as uncounted women and children. The hungry souls were reminded of manna from heaven given to their forefathers centuries prior and desired to make Jesus king upon recognizing the significance of this miracle. This was not the Father's plan for Jesus at that time, thus our Lord departed alone to escape their desire. He sent His disciples across the Sea of Galilee and later rejoined them in a way that should blow our minds if it were not so familiar: He walked on water to reach them. No floatation devices, no jet skis, just walked out to them! The many followers noticed the next day that Jesus did not go with His men, so when He was together with them on the other side of the lake, they were understandably perplexed, wondering how He was able to travel over to the opposite side. Jesus got them back on point with soft reproof to His followers that they were not really seeking miracles, not seeking the power of His ministry, but only because they were hungry and desiring to be filled. He then told them what they really needed. What we all really need...Him.

> Labor not for the meat which perishes, but for that which endures unto everlasting life, which the Son of man shall give unto you: For Him has the Father sealed. Then said they unto Him, what shall we do, that we might work the works of God? Jesus answered and said unto them, this is the work of God, that you believe on Him whom He has sent. They said therefore unto Him, what sign show you then, that we may see, and believe you? What work do you do? Our fathers ate manna in the desert; as it is written, He gave them bread from heaven to eat. Then Jesus said unto them, truly, truly, I say unto you, Moses gave you not that bread from heaven; but my Father gives you the true bread from heaven. For the bread of God is He which comes down from heaven, and gives life unto the world. Then said they unto him, Lord, evermore give us this bread. And Jesus said unto them, I am the bread of life: He that comes to me shall never hunger; and he that believes on me shall never thirst.
> John 6:27-35

Come unto Him and believe and one will never ever hunger or thirst. Belief in Him is the work of God. Jesus is the fulfillment of the manna given in the wilderness. He is the realization of the type given to Abraham on the mount of sacrifice. He is our provision for everlasting life. He is the Bread of Life.

Jesus went on to explain to His listeners that these words of His are spirit and they are life (John 6:63). That is, His Word, God's Word, activates the Spirit in my life. It is what really makes me alive!

Next, let's look at the second I Am statement. That of Light.

The Light of the World

Five months later, Jesus traveled to Jerusalem for the Feast of Tabernacles. During that week-long feast, Josephus writes that the Jews would stoke a raging fire on a high hill nightly to light up the sky. That light could be seen for over sixty miles. They would then extinguish it after the feast ended. So, the morning after the feast concluded, Jesus was again found teaching in the Temple, as was His custom. The Jewish leaders by this point were in the process of rejecting their Messiah and were now in temptation mode, trying to discredit Jesus to the multitudes of common people who had embraced His message. They brought a woman, but curiously not her partner, who was caught in adultery. The penalty for that crime was death to both parties. Would Jesus, the man of compassion agree to this judgment? Of course, He saw through their trap and brilliantly stated, "Yes, stone her, but let him who is without sin throw the first stone." Then, with the finger of God, He wrote in the sand, recalling to our minds the finger of God that wrote the Ten Commandments on the two stone tablets years earlier. Commentators preach that Jesus likely wrote the accounts of the sins of the men holding the rocks, as they left one by one. With no one left to accuse the woman, neither could our Lord, as the Law directed that by the witness of two or more could a person be condemned.

He next gave that great statement to His listeners demonstrating His godly wisdom:

> I am the Light of the World: He that follows me shall not walk in darkness, but shall have the light of life.
> John 8:12

With the bright light on the hill now extinguished, Jesus contrasted His light with their humanly attempt at bringing light to their world. He is the One that brings illumination. He is the One that brings discernment. Earlier in John's gospel, we are told that Jesus is "the true Light, which lights every man that comes into the world" (John 1:9). This is an awesome statement when taken at face value. This is saying that every person who has ever lived has at some time been exposed to His light. No one can really say that there is not a Creator.

Paul picks up this thought as he opens his Epistle to the Romans with this powerful and equally dramatic statement:

> For the invisible things of Him from the creation of the world are clearly seen, being understood by the things that were made, even His eternal power and Godhead; so they are without excuse.
> Romans 1:20

Creation declares the Godhead, declares Jesus.

Well, the Jews did not accept Jesus' testimony of being the Light of the world, of being the source and the illumination they needed, and they attempted to stone Him for what they believed was blasphemy, that of a man making himself God. It was not

Jesus' time and He escaped their attempt. But immediately thereafter, He demonstrated His power over creation by healing a man who was born blind. He took dust from the ground, made clay out of it, and put it in the man's eyes, telling Him to go and wash in the Pool of Siloam (meaning Sent One). Once again, He repeated that heavenly proclamation:

> As long as I am in the world, I am the Light of the World.
> John 9:5

Of course, this miracle points us back to the creation of Adam, when God formed that first man also out of the dust of the ground.

Later, in the Revelation given to John, we see Jesus lighting up the entire planet! Let me show you:

> And the city had no need of the sun, neither of the moon, to shine in it: For the glory of God did lighten it, and the Lamb is the light thereof.
> Revelation 21:23

Indeed, Jesus is the I AM. He is all that we need. In this case, we need light. We need direction, we need warmth, we need wisdom. In concluding this section on the Light of the world, I would be remiss if I did not remind you that Jesus and the Word are also one and the same (John 1:1). Jesus is called the Word of God (Revelation 19:13), so, as I take in the Word, I am taking in Jesus. Let that sink in...if you learn, if you meditate, if you assimilate God's Word, you are intimately partaking of our Lord! You are getting light, wisdom, discernment, and insight. Not a bad deal!

> Thy word is a lamp unto my feet, and a light unto my path.
> Psalm 119:105

Next, let's travel to later that same day and hear our Lord's words to those who would say they see but, in reality, are blind, for they do not see Him as the door.

The Door to the Sheep

After the Light of the World gave sight to the one born blind, the man boldly witnessed the awesome power of God to the unbelieving Jewish leaders, saying:

> Herein is a marvelous thing, that you know not from where He is, and yet He has opened my eyes. Now we know that God hears not sinners: But if any man be a worshipper of God, and does His will, him He hears. Since the world began was it not heard that any man opened the eyes of one that was born blind. If this man were not of God, He could do nothing.
> John 9:30-33

The blinded Jewish leaders cast the man out of Judaism for the audacity of his bold speech to them. No matter, for when Jesus heard that the man was cast out for his stand, He sought him out. The Lord revealed himself more fully to the seeing man as the Messiah. He then spoke another of His many paradoxical statements that reveal God's nature in comparison to man's.

> For judgment I am come into the world, that they which see not might see; and that they which see might be made blind.
> John 9:39

The Pharisees in the audience called Jesus on that statement. (Remember, the Pharisees were considered the ones most likely to inherit eternal life before Jesus' arrival.). They said to Jesus, "Are we blind also?" To that question, the Teacher gave the following answer as well as a parable demonstrating their need to open "the door" to obtain sight.

> If you were blind, you should have no sin: But now you say, we see, therefore your sin remains. Truly, truly, I say unto you, he that enters not by the door into the sheepfold, but climbs up some other way, the same is a thief and a robber. But he that enters in by the door is the shepherd of the sheep. To him the porter opens; and the sheep hears His voice: And He calls His sheep by name, and leads them out...This parable spoke Jesus unto them: But they understood not what things they were which He spoke unto them. Then said Jesus unto them again, truly, truly, I say unto you, I am the door of the sheep. All that ever came before me are thieves and robbers: But the sheep did not hear them. I am the door: By me if any man enter in, he shall be saved, and shall go in and out, and find pasture.
> John 9:41 – 10:1-3, 6-9

Like His proclamation in Matthew's gospel to enter in by the strait gate, Jesus again uses a metaphor that involves an entrance-way. He invoked God's name, I AM, and said He is that door. In a moment, He will add that, in addition to being the door, He is also the Shepherd. In this parable, the sheep of course are believers who follow the shepherd by entering in and going out via the door of Jesus and His sacrifice for us. Other false messiahs and teachers climb over the wall to fleece the sheep. Jesus calls them thieves and robbers but points out that His sheep are not fooled by them.

Immediately on the heels of this I AM statement, Jesus will explain the next one, that of the Good Shepherd. The One the Song of Solomon called the Shepherd King, the one David sang of in Psalm 23, "The Lord is my shepherd."

The Good Shepherd

Did you know that sheep are stupid! They tend to follow blindly, walking single file on the same path day after day. They are clueless and easily freaked out too. They have been known to walk over cliffs, following in step with the animal immediately preceding them. Sometimes they wander off when they are at rest in their pasture. And not only are sheep dumb but they are also defenseless. They are easily scattered and taken out by bears, lions, and wolves. With these characteristics, it is easy to see why humans are likened to sheep throughout the Bible. We too can be pretty stupid. We live day to day, walking in the same paths even when green pastures are within our reach if we would only lift our eyes. We often follow blindly after others to our detriment. We wander away constantly when staying put is the comfortable and safe thing to do. And bears, lions, and wolves (all pictures of the Devil in scripture) can easily scatter us and whip us into a frenzy. Indeed, sheep need a shepherd. Indeed, we need the Good Shepherd. Jesus' next words to His listeners explains why:

> The thief comes not but to steal, kill and destroy: I am come that they might have life, and that they might have it more abundantly.
> John 10:10

The thief, of course, in this parable is the Devil and his hordes of Hell. His agenda toward us is threefold. First, he wants to steal from you. Promises from God given to you, he wants you not to live in. He can't have them, so why should you, is his thinking. A life full of peace and joy is available to you through Jesus. Satan does not want that for you. He can take it from you by enticing you to worry and complain. Anxiety and murmuring are his weapons to steal from you. Don't let him. "Resist the Devil and he will flee from you" (James 4:7). How do you overcome anxiety and complaining? With trust and thankfulness. It's very hard to worry when you are praying words of trust to your Father. And being thankful sends complaining and murmuring back to the place it belongs. Back to its home where the father of lies resides! Secondly, the thief wants to kill you. This speaks of his desire to end your earthly life. Know for a certainty, though, that he cannot do that without the Lord's permission. The two witnesses found in the Revelation could not be killed until they had finished their testimony (Revelation 11:3-7); same for you and me. If you have a testimony that God has for you to share, you won't die until you have accomplished that, whatever it is! This, of course, doesn't mean bad things won't occur in your life along the way but the Lord will redeem those difficult chapters of your life for His glory and as part of your testimony. Now, the lamb who gets caught up and ensnared by the Thief may no longer have a testimony. That is what the Devil wants...to short-circuit your story. That is the person that sometimes can be killed prematurely because he has left his witness behind and is vulnerable to being slain by the thief. Of course, I am not saying that everyone who seemingly dies before old age must have been tripped up. Many times, the greatest testimony for the Lord is realized in death. Lastly, the Devil wants to destroy you. Simply put, this means he wants your soul! He desires you to experience separation from God eternally. He wishes to take you with him to Hell and whatever terrible thing that entails. Thankfully for the believer in Christ, Satan cannot do that. Jesus said, "All that the Father has given me I lose none," (John 18:9). While the thief wants to steal, kill, and destroy, Jesus wants to give us life and that more abundantly. How does He do that? Read on:

> I am the good shepherd: The good shepherd gives His life for the sheep. But he that is a hireling, and not the shepherd, whose own the sheep are not, sees the wolf coming, and leaves the sheep, and flees: And the wolf catches them, and scatters the sheep. The hireling flees, because he is a hireling, and cares not for the sheep. I am the good shepherd, and I know my sheep, and am known of mine. As the Father knows me, even so know I the Father: And I lay down my life for the sheep. And other sheep I have, which are not of this fold: Them also must I bring, as they shall hear my voice; and there shall be one fold, and one shepherd.
> John 10:11-16

The Good Shepherd gave His life for us! The hireling, the poser, doesn't care for the sheep. He will run away and let the sheep be scattered. Of course, in Jesus' parable, this is exactly what has happened and continues to happen when we humans, the sheep, follow after dishonest leaders and false messiahs. We are always scattered and taken out by the wolves. Not so with our Lord, as the Good Shepherd, He gave His life voluntarily for us to buy us back from the Thief. Others, the hirelings, could not or would not do that. The I AM is the only one with the power to save (Revelation 5:1-6).

And His sheep know him, they recognize His voice and they follow Him (John 10:27). Other sheep, those of another fold, will also hear His voice and follow Him. This parabolically speaks of the Gentiles who will hear the gospel message and believe, being brought into the life of the Christian faith, having Christ in them, the hope of glory (Colossians 1:27).

Sometimes though, sheep, in their stupidity, wander off. Jesus spoke to that frequent eventuality with these wonderful words:

> How think you? If a man have a hundred sheep, and one of them be gone astray, does he not leave the ninety and nine, and go into the mountains, and seek that which is gone astray? And if so be that he finds it, truly I say unto you, he rejoices more of that sheep, than of the ninety and nine which went not astray. Even so it is not the will of your Father which is in heaven, that one of these little ones should perish.
> Matthew 18:12-14

This wonderful parable reveals that God's love is unconditional, individual, and emotional! Our Shepherd gives us much worth, not for anything we have done, but because of who He is. He loves us individually and passionately!

Before we leave the Good Shepherd, we must speak of one of the most recognized Psalms of all time, that being Psalm 23.

"The Lord is my shepherd; I shall not want." He purchased me with His blood. So, when my relationship is in order with him, I have no wants, no needs. All is well! Again, He is the I AM, He is whatever I need.

"He makes me to lie down in green pastures: He leads me beside still waters." You know, sometimes I can't get comfortable, I can't rest. Thankfully though, He senses that and makes me to lie down as I walk with Him (Matthew 11:28-30). And He quenches our thirst with the water of His Word (Matthew 5:6).

"He restores my soul: He leads me in the paths of righteousness for His name's sake." Sheep can be tossed. This is called casting. They can become fat or overgrown with wool and roll onto their backs, unable to right themselves. It's easy to see this happen to us. I'm thankful that the Good Shepherd restores my soul! And when I get into the rut of walking the same path day after day, He gives me the direction and motivation to break free of my sheep-like habitual nature.

"Yea, though I walk through the valley of the shadow of death, I will fear no evil: For you are with me; your rod and your staff they comfort me." Death has no substance to the believer. It's only a shadow! Fear leaves me as I walk with my Shepherd, basking in His love (1 John 4:18). His rod keeps the Enemy away and His staff brings me back to Him as I stray. They comfort me!

"You prepare a table before me in the presence of mine enemies: You anoint my head with oil: My cup runs over." Indeed, He has invited me to His table. I can partake of communion with

Him any time I desire. And He has filled me with His Spirit so that His power overflows in my life and walk.

"Surely goodness and mercy shall follow me all the days of my life: And I will dwell in the house of the Lord forever." I don't have to look over my shoulder, afraid of the other shoe dropping, for goodness and mercy are following me. And after my life comes to an end, well, it's really only the beginning as I will dwell in the house of the Lord forever!

Why can we say death is a shadow, for it is appointed unto men once to die (Hebrews 9:27)? That's where the next "I Am" statement comes into play. If I am going to dwell with the Lord forever, and I am, then I need the resurrection and the life!

The Resurrection and the Life

Approximately six months later, during the spring season and before the fateful Passover celebration when our Lord gave His life for the sins of the world, Jesus learned that His friend Lazarus was ill and near death. His sisters were Mary and Martha, two women who consistently supported Jesus' ministry when He traveled in the area. They had a special relationship with Jesus, as their generosity to the Lord was not to be outdone. As an aside, when you and I are generous to others, in the name of the Lord, we too will be blessed over and above the level of our magnanimity (Proverbs 19:17). Well, the two women sent word to Jesus, asking Him to come and minister healing to their brother. Jesus was up north, in Galilee and presumably word did not travel fast in those days. Likely, it was a week or two after the message was sent before it was received by their Lord. Then, curiously at first, Jesus delayed another two days before leaving on the journey to Bethany, a town near Jerusalem which was the home of Mary, Martha, and Lazarus. We don't know how long it took Jesus and

His disciples to travel to Bethany, but we are told that, when He arrived, Lazarus had been dead four days.

This is where we will pick up our story of the resurrection and the life. When Mary learned that Jesus was near, she left her home and went out to meet Him. A wonderful exchange followed when she encountered him:

> Lord, if you had been here, my brother had not died. But I know, that even now, whatever you will ask of God, God will give you.
> John 11:21-22

What wonderful faith Martha is demonstrating. Her paradigm was that Jesus would come and heal Lazarus before His death but she can see past her request to something even better: Jesus bringing her brother back to life! That was something she had not considered when she first sent word to Jesus about the situation. This is what the Lord is looking for from you and me also. We are to think outside of the box for miracles, as God operates outside of the four dimensions we inhabit. He can do anything in any way He desires. We must give Him space when we call out to Him to move in the way He sees best.

Continuing:

> Jesus said to her, your brother shall rise again. Martha said unto him, I know that he shall rise again in the resurrection at the last day.
> John 11:23-24

We will see subsequently that Martha misunderstood what Jesus was saying. She interpreted Jesus' promise for a future date, not that very day. This is often my mistake, too! Jesus gave a promise for that day, for today, but Martha, and I, see it applying to a future dispensation. Often, the Lord's promises are for today but I mistake them for a later time and place. Three errors in her thinking led to this false conclusion. First, in her Jewishness, she may have still seen resurrection as works-related and not a gift from God. Secondly, resurrection is never at a later time; we will soon see that Jesus IS the resurrection. Resurrected life starts immediately when I receive the Lord as my Savior. Lastly, Mary looked at death from her perspective instead of God's. In His eyes, the believer never dies!

Listen:

> Jesus said unto her, I am the resurrection, and the life: He that believes in me, though he were dead, yet shall live: And whosoever lives and believes in me shall never die.
> John 11:25-26

I AM the Resurrection and the Life. Jesus is what she, and Lazarus, needed over anything else. He is what I need over anything else. The Lord is what gives and brings life to my world. Over miracles and promises, it's the Person! As the Father said to Abraham when he was fearful of Canaanite retaliation after he had liberated Lot, "I am thy shield, and thy exceeding great reward" (Genesis:15:1). And, because we have Him, we don't have to fear death. You see, God's definition of death is not the absence of a heartbeat or brain waves but separation from Him. That parting will never happen to you as a believer in Jesus. What the Messiah said to Martha and, by extension, to us, is that the "real you" of His followers, their consciousness, if you will, never dies! Sin is what leads to death (Romans 3:23) and our sins have been blotted out by His sacrifice. Thus, it is possible to be dead while alive and alive while dead. In our case, we will never die, just move to another dimension, to a better place when our body ceases to function. As Paul so poignantly stated, "For me to live is Christ, and to die is gain" (Philippians 1:21). He knew he would be with the Lord the moment that he passed on from this life. So will we!

Next, let us consider the true way to life. The only way to true life.

The Way, the Truth, and the Life

A few days before His death and subsequent departure back to heaven, the Lord gathered His disciples, giving important final teachings for which they would need to have a handle. He knew there would be issues and attacks as they took the gospel to the entire world by the power of the Holy Spirit. Jesus understood that, during times of tribulation, the vision of heaven will carry the believer forward. He also recognized that Satan would continue to attempt to counterfeit the gospel message, thus, His next I Am statement emphatically was made in response to that sure future eventuality as well as to give comfort to His followers.

> Let not your heart be troubled: You believe in
> God, believe also in me.
> John 14:1

Fight for your heart! The implication is that we have power over our hearts. How do we activate that power? By believing in the promises of God. He is for you. He will never leave you. He came to give us abundant life. He has set us free. No good thing does He withhold from you! You see, belief in God and His Son, faith that energizes hope (Hebrews 11:1), is the cure for a troubled heart. For that faith assures us we have a home waiting in heaven. That Jesus will be there. That we can pray in His name. That we have the Comforter abiding with us and that we can have peace.

> In my Father's house are many mansions: If it were not so, I would not have told you. I go to prepare a place for you. And if I go and prepare a place for you, I will come again, and receive you unto myself, that where I am, there you may be also. And where I go you know, and the way you know. Thomas said unto him, Lord, we know not where you are going; and how can we know the way? Jesus said unto him, I am the way, the truth, and the life: No man comes unto the Father, but by me.
> John 14:2-6

Let's all thank Thomas for asking one of the most important questions of all time. What is the way? The answer...He is the Way! Not keeping the commandments, that cannot be done. Not having more good works than bad, for God is holy and we are not. Not disciplining and flagellating our bodies in sacrifice, no amount would be enough! No, He is the way, the only way. Simply put, Jesus is the way to the Father. He is the way to heaven, that place of many mansions, the place of truth and life.

But why would God only make one way of salvation? That's easy when you think about the spiritual battle that rages around us at all times. You see, if God allowed several roads to salvation, Satan would have a much easier time counterfeiting the truth. If there were five paths to heaven, Satan would have ten false passageways for us to stumble thereby. With the Lord being the only way, it is clear. All other roads are not true. All other roads end with a dead-end sign (pardon the pun).

And Jesus is the Truth. Pilate asked, what is truth (John 18:38). That which is aligned with the mind, will, character, and glory of God is truth. Whatever the Almighty says is truth. And without a Supreme Being, well, then, the concept of truth makes no sense at all. There would be no such thing as truth. Everything would be relative. What would be truth for one might not be for another. Obviously, we need a referee to determine truth. Thankfully, we have that in our King. As Mary so wonderfully stated to the servants at the wedding ceremony at Cana, "Whatever He says to you, do it" (John 2:5).

He is the Life. He is our Source. He is the resurrection life we spoke of in our last section. He is our sun and shield (Psalm 84:11). He is the one that holds everything together. Unlearned scientists have unsubstantiated faith in "atomic glue" holding all things jointly; we know better:

> God, who at sundry times and diverse manners spoke in time past unto the fathers by the prophets, has in these last days spoken unto us by His Son, whom He has appointed heir of all things, by whom He made the worlds: Who being the brightness of His glory, and the express image of His person, and upholding all things by the word of His power...
> Hebrews 1:1-3

Jesus upholds everything by His Word. The atomic nucleus, having only positive charges, should not stay together. But it does, not with wishful-thinking atomic glue but by the word of

His power. It's an unbelievably awesome power that He wields in our universe. For He IS the Life!

Lastly, we get to come back to earth and consider our partnership with him. For He is the Vine and we are the branches.

The True Vine

> I am the true vine, and my Father is the husbandman.
> John 15:1

The setting again is during the last week of our Lord's ministry before His crucifixion. He was building up His disciples, for He knew later the Jews would ostracize them. The irony here is that the Jews felt they were the true vine. The Bible does call Israel a vine (as well as an olive tree and a fig tree). Whenever these three plants are mentioned in the Bible, an application for the nation of Israel is present. But the distinction here is the True Vine. That is Jesus. He is the vine that nourishes all of the branches, as we shall see. Being separated from the vine, Israel, as would happen to them, is nothing as long as they stayed attached to the True Vine. In addition, once again He proceeds this truth with the name of God, I AM, but distinguishing himself from the Father in the same breath.

> Every branch in me that bears not fruit He takes away:
> John 15:2a

The Greek for "takes away" is "airo." A better translation is, "He lifts up." Did you know that grape branches are weak, just as are we? Unless they are held up, they fall to the ground and are limited in the amount of fruit they produce. The branches that are attached to the True Vine are lifted up by the husbandman, by the Father.

> And every branch that bears fruit, He purges it,
> that it may bring forth more fruit.
> John 15:2b

It is certain that most readers would see this as the pruning that God will do in our lives from time to time. The cutting away of things that inhibit our growth is well understood as a biblical principle that the Author of Life will use from time to time. But, as we read this in the context of the parable, we see that "purges," or "pruning," is better translated as "cleans." He cleans us after lifting us up. Look with me:

> Now you are clean through the word I have spoken to unto you.
> John 15:3

"Wherewithal shall a young man cleanse His way? By taking heed thereto according to your word" (Psalm 119:9). It is the Word of God that the Father uses to lift me up and to clean me. Have you noticed how good it feels to spend time with the Lord in His Word? Indeed, it is better than the best bubble bath or hot shower you can even imagine.

> Abide in me, and I in you. As the branch cannot bear fruit of itself, except it abide in the vine; no more can you, except you abide in me. I am the vine, you are the branches: He that abides in me, and I in him, the same brings

forth much fruit: For without me you can do
nothing.
John 15:4-5

Just like the branch in relation to the vine, we are totally dependent upon our Lord. And we abide in Him by being in His Word. (Remember, Jesus and the Word are one and the same; John 1:1-2 and Revelation 19:13.). Adam and Eve wanted to be independent of God when they ate of the Tree of the Knowledge of Good and Evil. The second Adam came to make a way for us to abide again with God, to be dependent again with him. For indeed, apart from Him, we can do nothing. Nothing of any eternal value!

We see also that the one who abides in Him, the one staying close to Him by making His Word a priority, by often meditating in His Word, produces much fruit. This reminds me of the parable of the sower and the seed. The seed (the Word) that fell on good ground produced much fruit, some thirty, some sixty, and some a hundredfold. And the fruit He is talking about? Why it's love! Love God and love people. For, as we have discussed, on these two commands hang all of the Law and the Prophets (Matthew 22:40). In agreement with the two great commandments, the fruit of the spirit, mentioned by Paul, is love (Galatians 5:22-23). The aspects of love are the other components mentioned, i.e., joy, peace, patience, gentleness, kindness, faith, meekness, and self-control. Other fruit this promise of abiding includes, as I have cited previously, is fruit unto holiness, soul-winning, praise, and good works.

We have come to the end of Jesus' I AM statements found in the gospel of John, seven statements that reveal various aspects of God. He is the Bread of Life, our Provider, and the Light of the World, our Source of illumination. He is the Door to the Sheep and the Good Shepherd, He leads us in all of our ways. He is the Resurrection and the Life and the Way, the Truth and the Life. He gives us hope for the future. And, lastly, He is the True Vine. Abiding in Him allows us to partner with Him in the world, producing much fruit for His Kingdom.

I hope these words of His have helped you see Jesus in a much bigger way. That of King of the Universe, that of God becoming a man, that of showing us Himself in a way that we can understand, displaying to us the very nature of God!

Summary:

1. Jesus, the Bread of Life, is our provision for everlasting life.
2. Jesus, the Light of the World, has shined light upon every man, according to John 1:9.
3. The Devil wants to steal, kill, and destroy but the Good Shepherd gave His life for the sheep that they might have abundant life.
4. He who believes in Jesus, the Resurrection, and the Life, will live on even after his body dies. He need not fear death.
5. Jesus is the Way of salvation, the Truth that reveals the mind, will, character, and glory of God and the Life that upholds everything in the universe by the awesome word of His power.
6. The Word of God is used by the Father to lift us up and to clean us so that we might bear much fruit.

For Further Study:

1. According to John 6:29, what is the work of God?
2. How does the Lord's Table fit into your thinking of Jesus as the Bread of Life?

3. How is the Word of God related to light? Hint: See John 1:1-4 and Psalm 119:105 and 130.
4. Jesus is the Door into the sheepfold. Can you think of other times the Savior is pictured in the Bible as an entranceway?
5. What are the two "T's" of overcoming anxiety and complaining?
6. What does "thinking outside of the box" for miracles mean to you? Is it better to pray with specificity or to pray "Thy will be done?"
7. Why is there only one way to the Father?
8. What is the fruit you produce as you abide in the Vine?

Traditions of Men

The Jews of Jesus' day had the Law and the Prophets and they followed these sacred writings to a great degree, but they also believed in and obeyed non-inspired teachings of learned elders and rabbis of their Jewish religion. These precepts were often at odds with our Lord and His teachings.

Let's take a look and see how we can apply truths from their experience to our own.

> Then came together unto Him the Pharisees, and certain of the scribes, which came from Jerusalem. And when they saw some of His disciples eat bread with defiled, that is to say, with unwashed hands, they found fault. For the Pharisees, and all the Jews, except they wash their hands often, eat not, holding the tradition of the elders. And when they come from the market, except they wash, they eat not. And many other things there be, which they have received to hold, as the washing of cups, and pots, bronze vessels, and of tables. Then the Pharisees and the scribes asked him, why walk not your disciples according to the tradition of the elders, but eat bread with unwashed hands?

Mark 7:1-5

Understand, this is not the same as we have today with washing our hands before meals. In that day, a formal process, which had little to do with hygiene, was required by all supposed good Jews who wanted to appear to please Jehovah. In reality, as we shall appreciate, these laws were done to be seen by men.

> He answered and said unto them, well has Isaiah prophesied of you hypocrites, as it is written, this people honor me with their lips, but their heart is far from me. Howbeit in vain do they worship me, teaching for doctrines the commandments of men. For laying aside the commandment of God, you hold the tradition of men, as the washing of pots and cups: And many other such like things you do. And He said unto them, full well you reject the commandment of God, that you may keep your own tradition...Making the word of God of none effect through your tradition, which you have delivered: And many such like things do you.
> Mark 7:6-9, 13

Jesus, who sees into the hearts of men, noted the hypocrisy of their traditions and, more importantly, He indicted them for discarding the laws of God to serve their man-made regulations. He called the Jews out for their hypocrisy of showing off their pseudo-holiness to be seen of men as well as their sin of neglecting the commandments of God to keep their own traditions. In addition to rituals of washing, were the Sabbath customs that also were used by the Jews to agitate Jesus as well as by Jesus to shake up the Jews.

In this case of eating with unwashed hands, Jesus puts their hypocrisy down by pointing out the true nature of God's heart and desire for men's lives in this area. Let's listen:

> And when He had called all the people unto him, He said unto them, hearken unto me every one of you, and understand: There is nothing from without a man, that entering into him can defile him: But the things which come out of him, those are they that defile the man. If any man have ears to hear, let him hear.
> Mark 7:14-16

Parabolically, Jesus spoke of spiritual truths, but the listener's ears were dull and they were stuck in the physical realm. To their credit, the disciples asked the Teacher for amplification. Here is His explanation:

> Whatsoever thing from without enters into a man, it cannot defile him: Because it enters not into his heart, but into the belly, and goes out into the draught...that which comes out of the man, that defiles the man. For from within, out of the heart of men, proceeds evil thoughts, adulteries, fornications, murders, thefts, covetousness, wickedness, deceit, lasciviousness, an evil eye, blasphemy, pride, foolishness: All these evil things come from within, and defile the man.
> Mark 7:18-23

Bam! It is not what goes in the mouth but what comes out that reveals a man's heart. The Lord then listed, not the seven deadly sins, but thirteen lethal transgressions that reveal the condition of men's hearts. It is this very list of our common faults, indiscretions, and rebellious acts from which He came to save us. The very things that will separate us from Him for all of eternity, if it were not for His loving sacrifice to cover these terrible "heart issues" that we were born with and possess.

In Luke's gospel, we find the Sermon on the Plain. Similar to the Sermon on the Mount, we hear a parable of Jesus which also speaks to these things we have discussed: That of following godly leaders and teachers and ultimately following Jesus and not after foolish and false teachers preaching the traditions of men.

> And He spoke a parable unto them, can the blind lead the blind? Shall they not both fall into the ditch? The disciple is not above his master: But every one that is perfect (*mature*) shall be as his master.
> Luke 6:39 (italics added)

Jesus preceded this parable with His words on the precepts of the Kingdom. Reading on from the Sermon on the Plain, we see that following blind leaders, those steeped in the traditions of men and not producing good fruit, leads to hypocrisy and judgmentalism (Luke 6:41-45). Ultimately, following Jesus results in building upon the rock where the winds and the rains cannot shake it. But the one who follows what the Lord calls the bramble will see the ruin of his house because he did not build upon the rock of the Word of God (Luke 6:46-49).

What about our day today? Do we have traditions in the church that reject the commandment of God to keep our own tradition? Of course, we do! The Church is made up of sinners saved by grace. Until Jesus physically comes back for us and we live with Him on the restored earth, there will be errors in our thinking and in our responses to Him.

One such tradition which has caused me to pause is the formula for salvation that we hear in the Evangelistic Church today. Sinners come to Jesus, as I have written earlier in this book, by praying and believing the sinner's prayer. Included in that prayer is confession (remorse over sin) as well as assertion of Jesus as the Savior and belief that He died for our sins and rose again from the dead (Romans 10:9). This is all well and good. No, this is fantastic! A soul transformed from death to life by walking the Romans Road (Romans 3:23, 6:23, and 10:9). What I worry about though, is the motivation by which the converted soul is brought into the fold. Often, in my opinion, the benefits of being a Christian are present in the unfolding of the gospel without also instructing the seeking soul about the cost of following Jesus. Fellowship, compassion, grace, and mercy are stressed without explaining that tribulation, attacks, and warfare also await the one who walks with Jesus. Not often have I heard in an evangelistic meeting or in later teaching, for that matter, verses like "All that will live godly in Christ Jesus shall suffer persecution" (2 Timothy 3:12) or "If any man come after me, let him deny himself, and take up his cross, and follow me. For whosoever will save his life shall lose it: And whosoever will lose his life for my sake shall find it" (Matthew 16:24-25). This type of unbalanced gospel feeds the flock but does not warn them. I fear that, in some cases, we may be just fattening up the sheep for the slaughter! For tough times will come upon all of us; Jesus' Parable of the Sower and the Seed speaks to this. Some seed fell upon rocky soil where there was no depth. When the sun came out, the wheat was scorched and withered. This indicts powerfully this uneven gospel where the saved soul falls back into carnality, lasciviousness, and lawlessness, falls back into practicing sin when trouble and pressure arrive.

The antidote for the new Christian and the old one, for that matter, in not falling back into sin, is twofold. First, as we have discussed, we in the church need to teach that being in God's Word is cleansing and keeps us from sin (Psalm 119:9 and 11). We do a good job of this.

The second, not so good. It is the fear of the Lord. This is not spoken of often, much to our detriment. "The fear of the Lord causes men to depart from evil" (Proverbs 16:6). "The fear of the Lord is a fountain of life, to depart from the snares of death" (Proverbs 14:27). "The fear of the Lord, that is wisdom; and to depart from evil is understanding" (Job 28:28).

Conversely, the lack of fear of the Lord can lead to lawlessness.

> Thine own wickedness shall correct you, and your backslidings shall reprove you: Know therefore and see that it is an evil thing and bitter, that you have forsaken the Lord your God, and that my fear is not in you, saith the Lord God of hosts.
> Jeremiah 2:19

Now, the fear of the Lord is not being afraid of Him; it is being terrified of life apart from Him. It's about respect and reverence. It is having that "first love" feeling for God perpetually. The fear of the Lord is to figuratively tremble at His Word. It is to instantly and willingly obey, even when it is painful or not making sense, when compromise or disobedience might seem a better course. When I am in the fear of the Lord, I will choose His presence over my comfort. I embrace His heart, trusting that He will do what is best in all circumstances. The fear of the Lord is to want His will over my own.

The fear of the Lord is seen most clearly in looking at the Redeemer as He sweat blood in the Garden of Gethsemane. As horrible as His upcoming suffering was to be, the thing that really alarmed Him was being apart from the Father. For all of eternity, this had never happened! This is sobering to me. Am I frightened at being away from God, because of my sin, like this? Jesus was scared by what my sin was going to do to Him!

In the Church, for some reason, probably because we like to think of the Lord's love, compassion, mercy, and grace, we gloss over this important part of the gospel. Possibly it's because we aren't comfortable with the Almighty's justice and holiness. These two attributes of His cast us into a bad light and we may even fear that our Adversary will twist them in a way that makes our Father look unloving and harsh. This is unfortunate, as the fear of the Lord, more so than loving the Lord, is the best way to keep from sin. You see, agape love, unconditional love, is a decision, not a feeling. We must decide daily to walk in love. In our fallen state, we are subject to our feelings and emotions, which can derail our love from time to time. But the fear of the Lord is a mindset; it is not as vulnerable to our circumstances, thus it is much harder to shake when the invariable tough times of life roll in upon the believer.

In Ephesians 5, we find the marriage chapter: How husbands and wives are to relate effectively and intimately with each other is spelled out in some detail. Paul then flips his inspired remarks by stating that marriage is really a picture of Christ and His church, of Jesus and His Bride. He concludes by saying, "Nevertheless, let every one of you in particular so love his wife even as himself; and the wife see that she reverence her husband" (Ephesians 5:33). Now track with me here: Jesus is the husband in our relationship, He is to love us. Our job as the wife is to reverence Him, to respect Him, to have His fear in us. It is to live in the fear of the Lord. Loving Him only, without reverencing Him also, is like the wife who does not respect her husband. It ought not to be!

If this were not enough, there are two more great benefits when I regard how astounding is our God. First, the fear of the Lord helps me to finish strong (Psalm 19:9). This is critical! I don't want to live decades serving the Lord and His Kingdom only to crash and burn before the end of my days. It's the fear of the Lord that keeps me from coasting on my past laurels and thus not letting my love grow cold. Secondly, Jehovah promises mercy to the soul that reverences Him.

> For as the heaven is high above the earth, so
> great is His mercy toward them that fear Him.
> Psalm 103:11

> And:

> The Lord takes pleasure in them that fear Him,
> in those that hope in His mercy.
> Psalm 147:11

So, "The fear of the Lord is the beginning of wisdom" (Proverbs (9:10). It's the thing that makes us want to be holy, even in our fallen state, as we wait for the redemption of our bodies. It is being aware of His awesomeness, that He is a consuming fire (Hebrews 12:29), that protects us from evil. Thus, the one-two punch of the gospel message is the jab of the love of God in substitutionarily saving our souls, followed by the left hook of the fear of the Lord which enables us to walk in holiness.

Summary:

1. In God's eyes, heart issues are the important things, not outward activities that are done to impress Him or to be seen of men.
2. What comes out of a person's mouth reveals that person's heart at any given time.
3. Following after godly teachers leads to building upon the rock. Walking after blind leaders results in constructing upon the sand. One can tell the godly from the blind by their fruit.
4. The Christian life is not all roses and butterflies. Part of a balanced gospel presentation includes an understanding of the cost of following the Lord, of eternal judgment, and, along with learning of God's love, mercy, grace, and compassion, His justice and holiness need to be appreciated.
5. The fear of the Lord is not being afraid of Him, but it is being terrified of life apart from Him, even for a moment.
6. The fear of the Lord causes men to depart from evil.
7. Unconditional love is a decision, not a feeling, thus it is more vulnerable to our circumstances than the fear of the Lord. The latter is a mindset or paradigm and much harder to shake when the attacks of life occur. Additionally, a life lived in the fear of the Lord correlates with the respect a wife is admonished to have for her husband.
8. The fear of the Lord helps a person to finish strong in life. To run through the tape!

For Further Study:

1. Why did Jesus call teachers hypocrites who taught as doctrines the commandments of men?

2. Besides the traditions of the Sabbath laws and the washing precepts, what other customs did the Jews hold that Jesus came against?
3. From Mark 7:18-23, with which of the thirteen "heart issues" do you struggle? How can you be delivered from your weakness?
4. What other traditions, besides the one brought forth in this section, are present in the church today? Which ones are based on balanced scripture interpretation and which ones are not?
5. Is there such a thing as a perfect church? Why or why not?
6. What happens to sheep if they are constantly fed but not otherwise tended?
7. From this section, what are two things that help a person not to sin? Can you think of another thing not mentioned which also keeps a person from sin? Hint: See 1 Peter 4.
8. Can advice from someone who does not fear the Lord be eternally helpful?
9. Why should God's attributes of justice and holiness make humans nervous?
10. What are the benefits of a life lived in the fear of the Lord?

Pitfalls of Popularity and Prosperity

In the meantime, when there gathered together an innumerable multitude of people, insomuch that they trod one upon another Luke 12:1a.

In the early days of Jesus' ministry, He indeed was a celebrity that all wanted to see and hear. Wherever He went, the masses followed after, desiring to see the miracles He performed and to hear the marvelous words He spoke. He fed the hungry and spoke with authority, not as the scribes and teachers of the Law. He gave the people hope and they were actually starting to imagine that their yoke of oppression from the Romans would be lifted from their necks by this wonderful prophet from Galilee. They started to dream that He was indeed the very prophesized Messiah who would arrive on the scene and set them free.

Of course, this was not Jesus' mission. Political freedom without spiritual life was of no eternal benefit to men, as Jesus very well knew. Thus, with this background, Jesus felt it most important to temper His disciple's enthusiasm, because of His and their growing popularity, with words of warning about two issues with eternal consequences.

> He began to say unto His disciples, first of all, beware you of the leaven of the Pharisees,

> which is hypocrisy. For there is nothing covered, that shall not be revealed; neither hid, that shall not be known.
> Luke 12:1b-2

The first warning the Teacher gave was a caution of what can happen when the world esteems me, what can occur when I become popular. Hypocrisy can creep into my life like leaven. It is insidious and subtle. It is intoxicating and addictive. And it will always lead to misery as I move the focus to self instead of others.

Hypocrisy is saying one thing and doing another. It is mask-wearing, literally. In the world's definition, it is people of faith who have flaws that result in their not living up to the precepts of their faith, thus giving that faith a "black eye." But remember, Jesus' definition of hypocrisy is religious people who by their words and actions keep others from him! Jesus is telling His men to keep their eye on the ball, to not lose sight of the vision and the mission because of the intoxicant of popularity. It's always about God and His Word, not about me. It's about the message and not the messenger! Popularity can take me out by leading me to wear a mask to keep the party going. You see, hypocrisy is fueled by the desire to have popularity, prestige, power, priority, and/or preeminence. It's ultimately ignited by one of the seven deadly sins, that of lust.

Jesus points out that all will be revealed. The mask will not stay covered. He correctly points out that hypocrisy is irrational because the truth will come out, always!

> Therefore, whatsoever you have spoken in darkness shall be heard in the light; and that which you have spoken in the ear in closets shall be proclaimed upon the housetops.

Luke 12:3

Remember, whenever you see the word "therefore," you must ask, "What it is there for?" In this case, because hypocritical words and actions will always be found out and exposed, it is a good idea to get out in front of this promise. It's wise to confess this mask-wearing, this tendency to elevate self over the Lord. This is certainly true concerning hypocrisy and it's right concerning all manner of sin. I want to confess and move on, otherwise I will be embarrassed later when the truth is revealed for all to see. "He that covers his sins shall not prosper: But whoso confesses and forsakes them shall have mercy" (Proverbs 28:13).

> And I say to you my friends, be not afraid of them that can kill the body, and after that have no more they can do. But I will forewarn you whom you shall fear: Fear Him, which after He has killed has power to cast into hell; yes, I say unto you, fear Him.
> Luke 12:4-5

This is not a "power trip" by Jesus. He is just putting things in perspective. "Just saying" ... "don't fear men, you need to fear God!" Whether they understood at that point, that He was God, I do not know. But we know. Jesus is Lord, He is the Son, He is God and it is Him we revere. Understand, the cause of hypocrisy is fear. But it is fear of the wrong thing. It is the fear of man over the respect of God which we spoke of in the last section. And it's always a snare (Proverbs 29:25). What will people think of me if I go "all in" for the Lord? Jesus lovingly tells us that He is the only one that matters. What anyone else thinks of me is nothing compared to what He knows about me. So, stop worrying about what others think of me, stop wearing a mask, and only be concerned about what the lover of my soul feels about me and sees in me. That all that really counts.

> Are not five sparrows sold for two farthings, and not one of them is forgotten before God? But even the very hairs of your head are all numbered. Fear not therefore: You are of more value than many sparrows.
> Luke 12:6-7

The God who is so big that He cares even about the sparrows, things that we feel are insignificant and trivial, also cares about us. He values us, He knows us, He remembers and watches over us! We have nothing really to fear when you think about it in this light. The God of the Universe loves you and cares about you. This should cause you to pause and bask in this remarkable truth!

> Also, I say unto you, whosoever shall confess me before men, him shall the Son of man also confess before the angels of God:
> Luke 12:8

Going on record and His follower is the cure for hypocrisy. As I confess Jesus before men I lose the need to falsely please others with things that are not true. Whenever I'm in a new environment or setting I want to be quick to somehow convey that I am a Jesus follower. That I'm His man, His agent, His hands and feet!

> But he that denies me before men shall be denied before the angels of God: And who-

> soever shall speak a word against the Son of man, it shall be forgiven him:
> Luke 12:9-10a

The people of the world will try to get you to deny your faith. Don't do it! Again, don't fear men, fear God. Thankfully, when I fall short of our Lord's expectations and lose the courage of my convictions, there is forgiveness. Oh, the grace and mercy of our Friend!

> But unto him that blasphemes against the Holy Ghost it shall not be forgiven.
> Luke 12:10b

This is critical. To blaspheme against the Holy Spirit is to live a life in resistance to and rejection of the love of God in my life. It is to willfully and purposefully walk over the broken body of Christ given as payment for the massive debt of my sin. It is to continually and persistently say "No" to God. The blasphemy of the Holy Spirit is the only unforgivable sin. That is, rejection of the Spirit in wooing the lost soul to faith in Christ is the only unpardonable offense. All other manner of iniquity, including denying Him in fear, e.g., Peter's three denials that night, will be forgiven by our loving Savior.

> And when they bring you unto the synagogues, and unto the magistrates, and powers, take no thought how or what thing you shall answer, or what you shall say: For the Holy Ghost shall teach you in the same hour what you ought to say.
> Luke 12:11-12

"So, you are popular now, but it will not always be this way. The tables will turn. You most certainly will have times of hardship and persecution. I'm telling you this now so, when it occurs you will not be surprised, alarmed, and wiped out because of fear. Just stay close to me and you will always know what to do and what to say."

What wonderful words these are for us. I want to confess Jesus and I will lose the power and the pull that people of the world would otherwise hold over me.

Next, let's look at the second issue of eternal consequence. The pitfall of prosperity.

> And one of the company said unto him, Master, speak to my brother, that he divide the inheritance with me. And He said unto him, man, who made me a judge or a divider over you?
> Luke 12:13

Jesus isn't falling for this distraction, no, not at all! To be an arbitrator was not his mission. As we have discussed previously, the Lord came to make dead men alive, not bad men good or good men better. This shows me that, in following my Lord, I don't want to get mired down by the lessor at the expense of the greater. People need Jesus ultimately over a better bank account. I want to focus and serve in areas that affect the eternal over the temporal.

What I'm not saying here, though, is that if you are a bank accountant or a car salesman, that Jesus cannot use you for things eternal. Opportunities will arise daily to make a difference for the Kingdom. The secret to a life well-lived is not your job but how you answer your daily calling of the Spirit and the nudges He places on your heart to which you obediently respond.

> And He said unto them, take heed, and beware of covetousness: For a man's life consists not in the abundance of the things which he possesses.
> Luke 12:15

This second warning involves not the day of popularity but the day of prosperity. In that Day, I need to heed His warning and look out against my tendency toward covetousness. I don't want to let my possessions possess me. This does not say possessions and prosperity are bad but it warns that they can be a great temptation. I must have control of them and not the other way around. I want to be liberated. The world says to buy, to accumulate. The Lord says to sell, to use my wealth for good, to give, especially things that hold me back and things that hold on to me too tightly.

Look at the result of holding on to riches and possessions too tightly;

> And a certain ruler asked him, saying, Good Master, what shall I do to inherit eternal life? And Jesus said unto him...you know the commandments, do not commit adultery, do not kill, do not steal, do not bear false witness, honor your father and mother. And he said, all these I have kept from my youth up.
> Luke 18:18-21

Notice Jesus' answer. He says to the seeker, "You know the commandments," but then lists five of the six commandments that deal with avoiding evil and does not mention the first four, which speak of man's relationship to God, nor does He mention the tenth commandment, that of coveting.

At this point, the ruler is feeling pretty good about his chances for eternal life...

But then the other shoe drops. The One called Faithful and True (Revelation 19:11) speaks truth.

> Now when Jesus heard these things, He said unto him, yet lack you one thing: Sell all that you have...
> Luke 18:22a

As we have discussed from the very beginning of this book, eternal life begins with repentance, with realizing that I am a sinner in need of God's grace. This was the ruler's sin. That of covetousness. He needed to realize that fact. That is why Jesus told him to sell everything. Unfortunately, this verse has been preached from pulpits across the ages as a word against prosperity. Nothing could be further from the truth! God will gift some of His followers with riches because He knows He can trust them to distribute their bounty to others to advance the Kingdom. But in this seeker's case, his possessions had control of him. For another, it could be something else, such as a job or a hobby, etc.

> And distribute to the poor, and you shall have treasure in heaven: And come, follow me.
> Luke 18:22b

"And come, follow me." That's it! Repentance of sin and confession of the Savior. This is eternal life! Jesus is saying eternal life puts God first. I want to do what it takes to make Jesus Lord. Do what it takes to go "all in." And not only did our Lord tell him how to have eternal life, but He told him how to have treasure, how to have riches, when he does inherit his eternal life. That is, give to the poor and you will have treasure in heaven.

Unfortunately, we know the rich young ruler's response. It is tragic indeed.

> And when he heard this, he was very sorrowful: For he was very rich. And when Jesus saw that he was very sorrowful, He said, how hardly shall they that have riches enter into the Kingdom of God! For it is easier for a camel to go through a needle's eye, than for a rich man to enter into the Kingdom of God.
> Luke 18:23-25

The man's possessions possessed him. Jesus wasn't trying to make him miserable, he wanted to set him free! In another gospel account, it says that Jesus had compassion on the man for his terrible predicament. The Lord went on to say that because of covetousness, a rich man will have difficulty entering the Kingdom of God. For indeed, it is difficult for a camel to enter into the side door, the eye of the needle, of the gates of Jerusalem. That camel must be unloaded and stoop very low to pass through. Exactly what a rich person also must do. I must unload the baggage (sin and stuff) holding me back and in humility reach out for my Savior. Then, I too will be able to pass through the needle's eye.

As an aside, this statement concerning riches highlights the truth of the first three Beatitudes: Blessed are the poor in spirit, happy are they that mourn, and blessed are the meek, for these three groups readily will inherit the Kingdom of Heaven, they shall be comforted, and they shall inherit the earth. All three of these things are what the rich young ruler wanted but was unable to obtain, secondary not to being rich, but because of his sin of covetousness.

Now, back to Jesus' second warning from Luke 12:

> And He spoke a parable unto them, saying, the ground of a certain rich man brought forth plentifully: And he thought within himself, saying, what shall I do, because I have no room where to bestow my fruits? And he said, this I will do: I will pull down my barns, and build greater; and there will I bestow all my fruits and my goods.
> Luke 12:16-18

Brothers and sisters, this is the world's way. This is greed in full bloom and display. I've got too much, what shall I do? I know, I'll expand, I'll grow, so I can accumulate more! It's always more more more. If you doubt me, look at the corporations of America. They have become behemoths in the business world, gobbling up smaller companies in their paths and ever expanding their barns. But follow the flow here in the words of Jesus. Ultimately these companies and their CEOs are only chasing after the wind.

> And I will say to my soul, soul, you have much goods laid up for many years; take thine ease, eat, drink, and be merry.
> Luke 12: 19

At some point, the coveter realizes he finally has enough, he can kick back and relax. He can enjoy. Little does he realize or even consider that what he has accumulated has absolutely no lasting value for him. When he dies, even if the company carries on, there is nothing in it for him. It's as if it didn't even exist. How sad, how heartbreaking. How important these words of Jesus are for those who have ears to hear!

> But God said unto him, you fool, this night your soul shall be required of thee: Then whose shall those things be which you have provided? So is he that lays up treasure for himself, and is not rich toward God.
> Luke 12:20-21

A life lived for the here and now is tragically missing the point of life. It is vanity and meaninglessness. It is pride and a waste. It is falling, oh, so short of what he could have been had he stored up eternal treasure in heaven rather than temporal treasure for his short time on the earth. This is why covetousness is so evil. It rips men and women off by taking their eyes of God and putting them on trinkets. Paul rightly tells us that covetousness is idolatry (Colossians 3:5). It is breaking the first and second commandments, those against worshipping false gods and worshipping God falsely.

> And He said unto His disciples, therefore I say unto you (*In light that you can't take anything with you*) take no thought for your life, what you shall eat, neither for the body, what you shall put on. The life is more than meat, and the body more than raiment. Consider the ravens, for they neither sow nor reap; which neither have storehouse or barn; and God feeds them: How much more are you better than the fowls? And which of you taking

> thought can add to his stature one cubit? If you then be not able to do that thing which is least, why take you thought (*worry*) for the rest? Consider the lilies how they grow: They toil not, they spin not; and yet I say unto you, that Solomon in all his glory was not arrayed like one of these. If then God so clothe the grass, which is today in the field, and tomorrow is cast into the oven; how much more will He clothe you, O ye of little faith? And seek not you what you shall eat, or what you shall drink, neither be you of doubtful mind. For all these things do the nations of the world seek after: And your Father knows you have need of these things. But rather seek you the Kingdom of God; and all these things shall be added unto you.
>
> Luke 12:22-31 (italics added)

That's the key. That's the whole enchilada. If I seek God and His kingdom, everything, every need, will fall into place. I don't need to covet. It's all about trust (Hebrews 13:5-6). And God is trustworthy. Take notice of how God operates. The birds, the flowers, things you have no control over. God works it out. Ultimately, I know this because He went to the Cross and died for my sins. Thus, I know He will freely give me everything I need. "He that spared not His own Son, but delivered Him up for us all, how shall He not with Him also freely give us all things?" (Romans 8:32)

In light that the Lord has it all covered, here is some good advice from Him:

> Fear not, little flock; for it is your Father's good pleasure to give you the kingdom. Sell all that you have, and give alms; provide yourselves bags which wax not old, a treasure in heaven that fails not, where no thief approaches, neither moth corrupts. For where your treasure is, there will your heart be also.
> Luke 12:32-34

It is ever so smart to use your money and possessions wisely, to pass them forward. As Jim Elliot has famously said, "He is no fool who gives what he cannot keep in order to gain what he cannot lose." So, the Teacher's first recommendation to keep my tendency toward covetousness at bay is to give my stuff away. Be generous, be magnanimous!

His second piece of advice is to be looking for His return:

> Let your loins be girded about, and your lights burning. (*We might say, keep your powder dry...be ready, be prepared.*) And you yourselves like unto men that wait for their lord, when He will return from the wedding; that when He comes and knocks, they may open unto Him immediately. Blessed are those servants, whom the Lord when He comes shall find watching: Truly I say unto you, that He shall gird himself, and make them sit down to meat, and will come forth and serve them. And if He shall come in the second watch (*midnight*), or come in the third watch (*3 am*), and find them so, blessed are those servants. And this know, if the goodman of the house had

> known what hour the thief would come, he would have watched, and not have suffered his house to be broken through. Be you therefore ready also: (*Pro tip*) For the Son of man will come at an hour when you think not.
> Luke 12:35-40 (italics added)

Being thoughtful and intentional that my Lord could come at any time, whether it be upon my death or at His Second Coming, will keep me away from the ever-so-strong temptation to covet. And my Lord teaches that it is certain that His return will be at a time when I think not. On a day which will be surprising to me. So, I want to always be ready.

Also, look what is in store for the servant looking for his master's return...the Lord will actually serve him! How outrageous is that. Jesus, the object of our affection, waiting upon us! No wonder Peter was scandalized when the Lord offered to wash his feet that night. He, like me, felt unworthy to be attended by his Lord. The greater waiting upon the lessor.

Conversely, look what can happen to me if I'm not looking to His return if I'm not living for heaven and driven by eternity:

> Then Peter said unto him, do you speak this parable unto us, or even to all? And the Lord said, who then is that faithful and wise steward, whom the lord shall make ruler over His household, to give them their portion of meat in due season? Blessed is that servant, whom the lord when He comes shall find so doing. Of a truth I say unto you, that He will make him ruler over all that He has. But if that servant say in his heart, my lord delays His coming; and

> shall begin to beat the menservants and maidens, and to eat and drink, and to be drunken...
> Luke 12:41-45

Two servants. The first is looking for his master's return and carrying on his business while waiting. To him, the Master will bestow honor and future responsibility in due season. That is, this parable is teaching that, as we look to the Lord's return, He will be pleased and we will receive rewards, praise, and wonderful roles to carry out in heaven.

But the second servant, the one who feels his master is not coming any time soon, falls prey to sin, harshness, and debauchery. Reading on in this parable, which I will let you do if you like, that servant's end is not good! You see, looking for the Lord's return keeps me from sin, while the converse is also true. Not looking for His coming makes me vulnerable to evil. It sets me up for failure. It makes me easy pickings for my flesh to whip me up, the world to trip me up, and for Satan to rip me up!

So, there you have it. The pitfalls of popularity and prosperity. That of hypocrisy and covetousness. Having the fear of man over the fear of the Lord in play and letting my possessions take possession of me. The antidote for these pitfalls: Confess the Lord to men every day, everywhere. And fear Him, not men. Elevate Him to His proper position, the love of my life, the source of my life, the reason for my life. Do this and you will say goodbye to hypocrisy. As for covetousness, look for opportunities every day to bless others by giving to them. I want to pass the stuff God has entrusted to me forward. And I want to always keep watch for His return. Indeed, the hour is late. Behold, the Lord is coming quickly!

Summary:

1. Hypocrisy is like leaven. It is insidious and subtle.
2. Mask wearing is fueled by the fear of men and the desire for popularity, prestige, power, priority, and/or preeminence.
3. The fear of the Lord will cause one to lose the fear of men and overcome hypocritical tendencies.
4. Confessing Jesus before men also throws water on the fire of hypocrisy.
5. The pitfall of prosperity is covetousness.
6. Covetousness is the desire to have and to hang on to more and more possessions. It is a physical manifestation of selfishness and is fueled by lust and the lack of trust in God's provision.
7. The Great Physician's two prescriptions for covetousness are to be generous and to be looking for His return.

For Further Study:

1. Jesus taught that the truth will always win out. Can you think of a time you witnessed hypocritical behavior being exposed? How did it look?
2. Is it easy to blaspheme against the Holy Ghost? Why or why not?
3. How does giving stuff away (money, time, talent, possessions) release a soul from coveting?
4. Is it bad to be wealthy? Why not?
5. Is it dangerous to be rich? Why?
6. Can it be an honor to be affluent? Why?

Money

Jesus had more to say about money and our attitudes surrounding it than just about anything else He taught about and warned against. One-sixth of the gospel narrative and twelve of thirty-eight parables allude to money and/or possessions in some way. The reason is... money really is a test. That is, the way men respond to money and their love of it determines their heart state. God is raising kids and He uses money and our attitude toward it to grow us up. His ultimate aim is that we learn to release our attraction to money and possessions; that we stop coveting earthly trinkets and baubles and look to the heavenly treasures and rewards that He has promised those who are faithful in their use of money.

Thus far in this book, we have learned from the Sermon on the Mount, the Constitution of the Kingdom, that we are to give alms in secret, not to be seen of men. We studied how hypocritical it is to show off our giving. Any reward we would receive was obtained when we gathered the praise of men. We extolled our Father for being a giver and applauded the fact that a charitable heart is wonderful. God being the ultimate giver, we noted that, when we are generous, we are imitating him! We affirmed that everything belongs to him. Remembering that fact is the proper attitude in big-heartedness. We called it the "sweet spot" of giving.

Later in the sermon, Jesus told us to lay up our treasure in heaven and said that the secret to doing that was to focus on the eternal and not the temporal. We reminded ourselves that human beings are the eternal things that make up our world. We want to pour into opportunities that build up people, over programs and organizations that focus on the worldly and not the eternal. In that same section, our Lord proclaimed that no man can serve two masters, we cannot serve God and Mammon. We realized that Mammon, indeed, is a spiritual force that tempts men to live for the trivial over the everlasting. Possessions over people, earthly kingdoms over heavenly homes.

Finally, in the last section, the Teacher warned us about the dangers of prosperity and the draw toward covetousness. We saw through parables that a life lived for possessions was tragically missing the point of life! We learned wonderfully from Him that the two responses against the temptation to covet were to give our stuff away (money, time, talent) and to be looking for His return.

Next, let's cover the Rabbi's words concerning the need to plan for "retirement."

> And He said unto His disciples, there was a certain rich man, which had a steward; and the same was accused unto him that he had wasted his goods. And he called him, and said unto him, how is it that I hear this of you? Give an account of your stewardship; for you may no longer be a steward. Then the steward said within himself, what shall I do? For my lord takes away from me the stewardship: I cannot dig; to beg I am ashamed. I am resolved what

> to do, that, when I am put out of the steward-ship, they may receive me into their houses.
> Luke 16:1-4

Follow the flow here. The rich man's accountant was caught with his hands in the cookie jar. He was about to be fired. He realized that life was soon going to get tough. He would need to learn a new skill, possibly one involving manual labor or he would have to humble himself and beg. Both were not good options for the man. So, he came up with the following plan:

> So, he called every one of his lord's debtors unto him, and said unto the first, how much do you owe my lord? And he said, a hundred measures of oil. And he said unto him, take your bill, and sit down quickly, and write fifty. Then he said to another, and how much do you owe? And he said, a hundred measures of wheat. And he said unto him, take your bill, and write fourscore. And the lord commended the unjust steward, because he had done wisely: For the children of this world are in their generation wiser than the children of light.
> Luke 16:5-8

In an effort to save his hide, the slippery accountant cleverly pulled in for his master some of the outstanding debt that he was owed. He obtained much of the rich man's accounts receivable for him. Money he apparently felt he would not ever get back. In that, the lord commended the accountant for his shrewdness. Now the point Jesus is making for us is piercing. Our Lord is noting that the children of the world are more aggressive in preparing for their futures than we, the children of the Kingdom, are in preparing for ours! They are saving up for their temporal and fleeting retirement while often we are not thinking about or acting toward our eternal and everlasting abode. Our Friend is gently warning that this ought not to be!

> And I say unto you, make to yourselves friends of the Mammon of unrighteousness; that, when you fail (*die*), they may receive you into everlasting habitations (*it will be there to greet you*).
> Luke 16:9 (italics added)

Make friends with money, Jesus is saying, by giving it away. Otherwise, it just leads to unrighteous things. But if you do, you will be blessed eternally. It's a good deal. I can't take it with me but this verse clearly says I can send it ahead!

Paul echoes this idea of using money for my eternal investment portfolio: "As it is written, he has dispersed abroad; he has given to the poor: His righteousness remains forever" (2 Corinthians 9:9). This chapter is full of wisdom concerning the use of money for good.

> For the administration of this service not only supplies the want of the saints, but is abundant also by many thanksgivings unto God: While by the experiment of this ministration they glorify God for your professed subjection unto the gospel of Christ, and for your liberal distribution unto them and unto all men: And

> by their prayer for you, which long after you
> for the exceeding grace of God in you.
> 2 Corinthians 9:12-14

This difficult "old English" section notes three wonderful benefits of passing money forward. People's needs are met, God is praised, and the recipients of your charity will pray for you. Once again, when you think about this critically, generosity is a "no-brainer!"

> He that is faithful in that which is least (*money*) is faithful also in much (*Kingdom matters*): And he that is unjust in the least is unjust also in much. If therefore you have not been faithful in unrighteous Mammon, who will commit to your trust the true riches.
> Luke 16:10-11 (italics added)

Giving releases ministry potential and opportunities that would not otherwise be available to you. Do you desire to be used by God? Remember, we said that money is a test. I have to be able to let it go. And when I do, I pass the test! And watch what happens. This is a law, just as strong as gravity. If I give, I receive. Period! God is looking for men and women He can trust with wealth because He knows they will use their blessing to bless others. He wants to bless you so you will bless others!

One last point from Jesus about generosity and then we will tie this topic up. That is, you should give without expecting to receive in return. If that is your attitude, your liberality will return to you in eternity.

> Then He said also to them that invited Him, when you make a dinner or a supper, call not your friends, nor your brothers, neither your kinsmen, nor your rich neighbors; lest they also bid you again, and a recompense be made you. But when you make a feast, call the poor, the maimed, the lame, the blind: And you shall be blessed; for they cannot recompense you: For you shall be recompensed at the resurrection of the just.
> Luke 14:12-14

So, we see that big-heartedness is glorious. We see that we can turn something that often causes men to stumble, i.e., money and the love of it, into something that will benefit others presently and you eternally. All that is needed is to become a conduit of grace, a vessel of open-handedness. As Levi Lusko has said, generosity puts a stake into the heart of idolatry (spirit of Mammon) and opens you up to prosperity.

In closing, God's financial plan is the opposite of the world's. When I bring in the "bread" to my home, the world says to first spend to live; then, if able, save some; and then, if any is left over, give. Contrastingly, the Designer's plan is the one that offers life. First give, then save, then use what is left to live.

> For wisdom is a defense, and money is a defense: But the excellency of knowledge is, that wisdom gives life to them that have it.
> Ecclesiastes 7:12

Money is a tool, that's all. And it can be a defense. But wisdom, especially in the use of money, brings life.

We said that God wants to bless you so you can bless others. When that happens, there will be two different attacks from the other team. The first is pre-giving selfishness, "I can't afford to do that now, I need it." The second is post-giving regret. "My, that was ostentatious. I can't believe I provided that much!" The relief for both of these temptations is to always remember that everything belongs to God. As we noted in an earlier chapter, all of our stuff really is just on loan from Him. We are caring for it, but it isn't really ours. When I do that, pre-giving selfishness and post-giving regret fade away.

Now for the application for our present day: In America, the Land of the Free and the Home of the Brave, we have a serious problem with our take on money (excuse the pun). We, as a nation, are not passing the test for the most part. Oh, there are pockets of generosity but, if calculated numerically, our gifting is in the single-digit percentage points of our total spending. I'm reminded of a warning given to Israel during a time when they were turning away from God's directives also. It sounds eerily like God could substitute our country's name in place of Sodom.

> Behold, this was the iniquity of thy sister Sodom, pride, fullness of bread, and abundance of idleness was in her and her daughters, neither did she strengthen the hand of the poor and needy. And they were haughty, and committed abomination before me: Therefore, I took them away as I saw good.
> Ezekiel 16:49-50

The sin for which we associate Sodom is not mentioned until the end. It was the end result, if you will. Before that, pride, fullness, and idleness set the stage for an unloving, uncaring hand toward the poor and needy. Let that not happen to us! Unlike Sodom, I want to belong to a country, to a city, to a church, that is magnanimous, that is loving, that is caring. It all starts with me; it all starts with you. Together, with the Lord's grace and help, we can make it happen!

Summary:

1. Money is a test and God is using our relationship to it as a means to mature us.
2. God is a giver and, as we are generous, we are imitating our Father.
3. Benefits of big-heartedness include meeting people's needs, God getting praise and glory, people becoming motivated to pray for you, and releasing ministry opportunities for you.

For Further Study:

1. What is the secret to storing up treasure in Heaven?
2. Is it always necessary to pay back someone who has been liberal to you in some way?
3. Why can fullness of bread and/or abundance of idleness sometimes be a bad thing?

Jesus' Words About Hell

This is the chapter I have been struggling over since I began to write this book! Unfortunately for me, Jesus has much to say about Hell and its reality. Thus, in a book about Jesus' parables and teachings, to omit His words discussing Hell would be to skip a major theme of His preaching and would water down the significance of His sacrifice to cover the sins of all mankind. I will say that it is unlikely that I understand the concept of eternal judgment correctly. For that matter, I suspect most preachers and teachers over the millennia have missed it to a great degree also. This I do know: God is love and love is kind and ever so longsuffering. Additionally, the Creator is compassionate and extremely merciful. But He is also just. His justice is His trait that we run full on against when we consider Hell, for the construct of justice implies payment for wrongdoing.

Since I don't really understand Hell and its ramifications that well, I will present two alternatives that I feel can be supported scripturally. Again, it is likely that neither is all that correct!

The first position on the nature of Hell, which has been mainline teaching for much of the last two millennia, is that Hell is the place where unrepentant souls spend eternity. It is a literal place created for Satan and his legions and is associated with torment, fire, and darkness. It is likely that Jesus spoke often about Hell as He did not, and does not, want anyone to be sent there. The Bible proclaims, "God, who desires all men to be saved and come to the knowledge of the truth" (1 Timothy 2:3-4). You see, Jesus saw Satan fall from heaven (Luke 10:18), He understands the reality of eternal judgment. Thus, in speaking often about Hell's reality, He is lovingly directing us away from it and toward Him. You might say that our Lord understood the stakes involved for mankind. Contrastingly today, Bible teachers, in my opinion, are reluctant to preach about Hell. It's embarrassing and quite frankly unbelievable that our loving God would send humans to Hell. In America's past though, this was not the case. The First Great Awakening, which started in New England in 1741 and was led by Jonathan Edwards and his famous message of "Sinners in the Hands of an Angry God," stirred thousands to repent and turn to the Lord as the reality of Hell became ever so genuine to the souls exposed to the evangelist's words. But today, sermons discussing Hell are few and far between. In reading the gospels, I sense Jesus would not agree with His church's approach of using kid gloves for the subject.

Let's hear some of the Teacher's warnings:

> Strive to enter in at the strait gate: For many, I say unto you, will seek to enter in, and shall not be able. When once the master of the house is risen up, and hath shut the door, and you begin to stand without, and to knock at the door, saying, Lord, Lord, open unto us; and He shall answer and say unto you, I know you not whence you are: Then shall you begin to say, we have eaten and drunk in your presence, and you have taught in our streets. But He shall say, I tell you, I know not whence you are; depart from me all you workers of iniquity. There shall be weeping and gnashing of teeth,

> when you shall see Abraham, and Isaac, and Jacob, and all the prophets, in the Kingdom of God, and you yourselves thrust out.
> Luke 13:24-28

Here we see that the offer of salvation is finite. It can only be received in this lifetime. Once the door of heaven is shut to a person, it cannot be opened. It is final and irrevocable! The reason it is taught that there is no second chance after unbelievers meet their Maker is that once an unrepentant soul sees God in all of His glory, that person would be forced to choose God and to love the Almighty against his will. The Creator does not want robots any more than a man would desire his wife to be forced to love him. Giving man free will was the risk our Maker took, full knowing some of His creatures would not choose Him. As was mentioned in the introduction of this book, God has sort of maintained a fine balance between keeping His presence evident, yet masked, so people who want to believe, may do so, while others who do not want to call Him Lord are also free to make that poor and unfortunate choice.

Perhaps the best-known words of Jesus concerning the nature of Hell are found in the story of the rich man and Lazarus. Let's look at this parable and see what the Lord has for us to know.

> Now there was a certain rich man which was clothed in purple and fine linen, and fared sumptuously every day.
> Luke 16:19

Here we meet an unnamed rich man who had a fine life, much like most of the people living today in the Western world. If you have a roof over your head and a car in the garage, you are richer than 90% of all who have ever lived. Being rich is not the problem in itself. But living in opulence can take one's eyes off of eternity by the distraction of sparkly things and bling as well as blinding one from the needs of others.

> And there was a certain beggar named Lazarus, which was laid at his gate, full of sores. And desiring to be fed from the crumbs which fell from the rich man's table: Moreover, the dogs came and licked his sores.
> Luke 16:20-21

We see a pathetic person who is destitute and in agony being in full view of the rich man, yet he did nothing to help the beggar's situation when it was in his power to do so. This is the wealthy man's sin; God wasn't calling him to change the world, only to change Lazarus' world! This he did not do. The rich man had the opportunity to help, yet he passed. We see in the next verse that this potential to help was perishable. It had an expiration date!

> And it came to pass, that the beggar died, and was carried by the angels to Abraham's bosom: The rich man also died, and was buried:
> Luke 16:22

That's it, any chance the rich man had to make a difference in life, even in Lazarus' life, was now over. Unlike tennis, no second serve! The rich man missed it! This is such a word to all of us rich men and women. I don't want a day to pass without responding to the Holy Spirit's nudges to intervene and help, to give to and to build up others. To make a difference in the world, to leave evidence of my footprint!

> And in hell he lifted up his eyes being in torment, and saw Abraham afar off, and Lazarus in his bosom. And he cried and said, father Abraham, have mercy on me, and send Lazarus, that he may dip the tip of his finger in water, and cool my tongue; for I am tormented in this flame. But Abraham said, son, remember that you in your lifetime received many good things, and likewise Lazarus evil things: But now he is comforted, and you are tormented. And besides all this, between us and you there is a great gulf fixed: So that they which would pass from here to you cannot; neither can they pass to us, that would come from there. Then he said, I pray you therefore, father, that you would send him to my father's house: For I have five brethren; that he may testify unto them, lest they also come to this place of torment. Abraham said unto him, they have Moses and the prophets; let them hear them. And he said, no father Abraham: But if one went unto them from the dead, they will repent. And he said unto him, if they hear not Moses and the prophets, neither will they be persuaded, though one rose from the dead.
> Luke 16:23-31

We learn that the rich man is in Hell, but we are not told the reason why. The parable implies that it was due to his absence of compassion for Lazarus, but we know from other scriptures concerning salvation that he also lacked faith in the Savior. That notwithstanding, we see in this story some characteristics of the rich man's situation. He could see, he was in torment secondary to flames, he was able to recall his mistakes in life and he was concerned for his loved ones still alive that they would not end up with his same fate.

Reading this story sort of makes you feel sorry for the rich man. I think that was one of the points that the Teacher was making. Life is short, don't make the mistake of the rich man as you live it! You don't want to have regrets! In looking at other pictures and listening to other words about Hell, one can come to the conclusion that this story really isn't about the nature of Hell at all! That is because God taught us that Hell was made for Satan and his henchmen. That is, unrepentant souls. Here we see the rich man is anything but unrepentant! We also note that the rich man sees into Heaven. This contradicts the teaching that Hell is the place of outer darkness (Matthew 25:30), a place devoid of light. No, I feel that this story is not really about the nature of Hell at all but about the importance of generosity and compassion. About love and charity, not about the exact nature of eternal judgment as has been taught by Jonathan Edwards and others over the centuries. Am I correct? Only time will tell. One thing for certain, I know that I, like our Father, do not want anyone to go there!

One more thing to note about this parable. Father Abraham said that, even if Lazarus would return from the dead, the rich man's brothers would not repent. That's it! Hell is separation from God for people who do not want Him. We know this is true because One did come back from the dead, His name is Jesus Christ, and yet many souls still do not repent and believe. That dear reader, not the nature of Hell itself, is the point of this story!

Continuing with Jesus' words, we need to consider His message given by Him in His revelation to the Apostle John.

> And the third angel followed them, saying with a loud voice, if any man worship the Beast and his image, and receive his mark in his forehead, or in his hand, the same shall drink of the wine of the wrath of God, which is poured out without mixture into the cup of His indignation; and he shall be tormented with fire and brimstone in the presence of the holy angels, and in the presence of the Lamb: And the smoke of their torment ascends up for ever and ever: And they have no rest day or night, who worship the Beast and his image, and whosoever receives the mark of his name.
> Revelation 14:9-11

> And the Devil that deceived them was cast into the lake of fire and brimstone, where the Beast and the false prophet are, and shall be tormented day and night for ever and ever.
> Revelation 20:10

This is serious stuff! Hell looks pretty permanent here! For ever and ever. That's unimaginable to me. More than anything else, this is the doctrine of Hell that trips me up. How can anything be so bad that the punishment goes on for eternity? Obviously, I don't understand. One thing these verses do teach me though, is they show me just how bad sin is.

Something else also reveals to me how bad my sin is...

Looking at the suffering our Savior endured to blot out my sins!

> The sorrows of death compassed me, and the floods of ungodly men made me afraid. The sorrows of hell compassed me about: The snares of death prevented me. In my distress I called upon the Lord, and cried unto my God: Psalm 18:4-6a

> My God, my God, why hast thou forsaken me? Why are you so far from helping me, and from the words of my roaring? O my God, I cry in the daytime, but you hear me not; and in the night season, and am not silent...Many bulls have compassed me: Strong bulls of Bashan have beset me round. They gaped upon me with their mouths, as a ravening and a roaring lion. I am poured out like water, and all my bones are out of joint: My heart is like wax; it is melted in the midst of my bowels. My strength is dried up like a potsherd; and my tongue cleaves to my jaws; and you have brought me into the dust of death. For dogs have compassed me: The assembly of the wicked have enclosed me: They pierced my hands and feet. I may tell all my bones: They look and stare upon me. Psalm 22:1-2, 12-17

Devils about him, joints dislocated, heartbroken, muscles in spasm, unimaginable thirst, spikes through His hands and feet while the mob stared at Him sucking for each breath! This is how the only sinless man who has, or ever will live, suffered Hell for you and me!

Just like I cannot understand the reality and implications of the nature of Hell, so too, I do not understand the veracity of the nature of the Savior's Passion. He went to Hell so I would not have to! Indeed, the grace of God is mocked if I blow off the horrible nature of sin and the existence of Hell.

> And I heard another out of the altar say, even so, Lord God Almighty, true and righteous are thy judgments.
> Revelation 16:7

Of course, the altar speaks of the Cross. We must view problems, or in this case, the authenticity of Hell, with the lens of Jesus' sacrifice. When we do that now, and when we become much more enlightened on that future day, we too will say righteous and true are all of your judgments O Lord!

Isaiah makes a comment and asks an important question which I need to consider when searching out God's judgments and ways.

> But now, O Lord, you are our father; we are the clay, and you our potter; and we are the work of thy hand.
> Isaiah 64:8

> For shall the work say of Him that made it, He made me not? Or shall the thing framed say of Him that framed it, He has no understanding?
> Isaiah 29:16

That verse has always cracked me up! It is the height of arrogance for any created being to put a morality trip on the Creator! A moment ago, we noted that Hell was made for unrepentant souls. That is, the definition of an unbeliever or an unsaved person is one who will not repent and call Jesus his Lord. This is one of the two arguments for the necessity of Hell being eternal. (I will discuss the second understanding momentarily.) We see in the Revelation examples of the unrepentant heart in the face of overwhelming motivation and evidence to do so:

> And the rest of the men which were not killed by these plagues yet repented not of the works of their hands, that they should not worship devils, and idols of gold, and silver, and brass, and stone, and of wood: Which neither can see, nor hear, nor walk.
> Revelation 9:20

> And there fell upon men a great hail out of heaven, every stone about the weight of a talent (150 lbs.): And men blasphemed God because of the plague of the hail; for the plague thereof was exceeding great.
> Revelation 16:21 (italics added)

These verses tell me that the story of the rich man and Lazarus is a parable and not the exact representation of Hell. In the Revelation, souls sent to the Lake of Fire do not repent. In Jesus' parable, the rich man obviously did!

Now for the second argument for the necessity of Hell being eternal:

> But whoso shall offend one of these little ones which believe in me, it were better for him that a millstone were hanged about his neck, and that he were drowned in the depth of the sea. Woe unto the world because of offenses! For it must needs that offenses come; but woe to that man by whom the offenses come!
> Matthew 18:6-7

You see, if I cause a "little one," one who is a literal child, or a child in the faith to stumble and lose their trust and belief in the Savior, well, I in effect have contributed to their downfall and to their future of an eternity in Hell. Thus, the punishment, in this case, is indeed, not greater than the crime. Eternity for eternity!

> Next, let's consider a second understanding of the nature of Hell which is less disturbing. But first, let me tell you about Ethan the priest. For Ethan was the psalmist who penned
> Psalm 89.

Ethan lived in a time in Israel's history when the nation had been conquered and no longer had a king. Ethan recalled the words recorded in Samuel promising that David would always have an heir upon the throne of Israel. Thus, he was disappointed with God because he understood the Davidic Covenant incorrectly. He did not realize that the Messiah, Jesus Christ, is the fulfillment of that Covenant. He did not understand that Jesus indeed has existed from eternity past and thus was sitting on the throne, but out of sight of his eyes. So too, there are things that I, that we, understand incorrectly that can disappoint us with God.

Hell, I feel, is one of those things that we will comprehend more clearly on that day when we see Him face to face.

> To whom shall you liken me, or who shall be my equal? Saith the Holy One...Hast thou not known? Hast thou not heard, that the everlasting God, the Lord, the Creator of the ends of the earth, fainteth not, neither is weary? There is no searching of His understanding.
> Isaiah 40: 25 and 28

> O the depth of the riches both of the wisdom and knowledge of God! How unsearchable are His judgments, and His ways past finding out! For who hath known the mind of the Lord? Or who has been His counselor?
> Romans 11:33-34

Indeed, there is no searching of His understanding. His ways are past finding out. No one can really know the mind of the Lord, for His thoughts are not our thoughts (Isaiah 55-8-9).

So, in that light, let us consider the second, mutually exclusive, understanding of Hell: The torture language is figurative!

Look at Jesus' tone when He talked about Hell. It certainly wasn't one of condemnation and judgment, but of compassion and mercy. For He came to seek and save the lost, not condemn them (John 3:17). Scholars say He was using a teaching method called "extreme statement" to emphasize what He was saying and to highlight the need to make our salvation sure. Jesus knows of the reality of Hell and thus He did not want to tone down the horror of being separated from the Father. In this understanding, Hell is estrangement from God. It is existence away from God (if that is even possible!) It is the consequence of one's choice, saying, "I am lord" instead of "Jesus is Lord." God is love, light, peace, hope, mercy, and truth. To be parted from that would be to exist in a world of evil, darkness, fear, and hopelessness. A place without grace or mercy! To me, that sounds like Hell!

But is Hell eternal torture or is the second death (Revelation 20:13-15) eternal death? Are these characteristics of the absence of God for a moment in time or for all of eternity? Do doomed souls cease to exist or do they go on forever? As I mentioned, I do not understand God's ways, neither do you. But one certainly may think that eternal torture doesn't fit with the nature of God. Again, the punishment doesn't seem to fit the crime. As bad as the Lord's Passion appeared, it doesn't seem to compare, in my puny mind, to the torment of eternal fire and eternal hopelessness! Christ's suffering for sin had an end. We cannot fathom how bad His separation from the Father was for him, but we comprehend that He was soon reunited with His Papa. For this reason, for now, I choose to understand the nature of Hell in this light. That is, separation from all that is good because of a man or a woman calling themselves "lord." It is eternal in the sense that there is no turning back. And it is ultimately annihilation in a lake of fire and brimstone after first seeing the Lord in all of His glory and bowing before that awesome reality (Philippians 2:10-11).

One last point which I think corroborates with this second view. In the Old Testament, the sacrifice for sin was the death of an animal. That is, the shedding of blood covered sin. Nowhere was the animal tortured. Its death was certainly bloody, and in certain instances painful, but it was always quick!

Either way, I feel the same way our Lord does, in that I do not want anyone to go to Hell. I do not desire souls to be separated from God for eternity. The reality of eternal judgment makes me want to share the good news of salvation. My prayer for myself, and for you, is for boldness and courage in making Jesus known to the lost of our world. I pray that we would ache in our hearts to see souls come to the saving knowledge of what our dear Lord has done for us all. That compassion for people in their state of ignorance or rebellion would drive us to share God's Word wherever and whenever we can.

Summary:

1. The summit of salvation blessings is Jesus' companionship. Hell is the absence of that!
2. Discounting the reality of sin and Hell waters down the significance of Jesus' sacrifice to cover the sins of mankind.
3. The concept of justice implies there will be payment, there will be punishment, there will be repercussions for and from sin.
4. It would appear from Jesus' teachings that salvation is no longer available to a person once they have died and can see Him in all of His glory.
5. Hell is a place of separation from God, made for devils. Unrepentant souls choose it!
6. The Savior suffered Hell for you and me!
7. It appears from the Revelation that the punishment for rejecting Christ's sacrifice may go on forever.
8. When questioning God's ways due to a lack of understanding the whole picture, end the sentence with a "+" (Cross), not a "?" (Question mark).

For Further Study:

1. Does Jesus stop loving souls who choose themselves over Him?
2. Why did our Lord speak often of Hell?

3. Why was giving man "free will" a risk to God?
4. What is the sin that seems to anger the Lord more than anything else? Hint: See Matthew 18:6-7.
5. Do you accept one of the views of Hell presented here over the other? Why?
6. Does the doctrine of eternal judgment (Hebrews 6:2) have an effect upon your witness for Christ?
7. How should you witness to a confused soul? To a rebellious one? Hint: See Jude 22-23.

Do This in Remembrance of Me

The Table of the Lord, the Sacrament of Communion, is one of the commonalities across Christendom. Believers will disagree on doctrinal issues, worship styles, and preaching methods, but they are unified across the denominations in their elevation of Jesus' request to celebrate and commemorate His death and resurrection by remembering Him at His table of bread and wine.

Let's look at the Savior's instructions to us:

> And when the hour was come, He sat down, and the twelve apostles with him. And He said unto them, with desire I have desired to eat this Passover with you before I suffer: For I say unto you, I will not any more eat thereof, until it be fulfilled in the Kingdom of God. And He took the cup, and gave thanks, and said, take this, and divide it among yourselves: For I say unto you, I will not drink of the fruit of the vine, until the Kingdom of God shall come. And He took bread, and gave thanks, and broke it, and gave unto them, saying, this is my body which is given for you: This do in remembrance of

> me. Likewise, also the cup after supper, saying, this cup is the new testament in my blood, which is shed for you.
> Luke 22:14-20

He took the bread and broke it, saying this is my body given for you. Of course, His body was broken for us. Certainly, the words of Isaiah were on Jesus' mind at that moment. In one of the most profound prophesies predicting His mission, we read:

> But He was wounded for our transgressions, He was bruised for our iniquities: The chastisement of our peace was upon Him; and with His stripes we are healed.
> Isaiah 53:5

Indeed, His body, the very body represented by the sacrament's divided bread was broken beyond recognition so we could be healed and made whole. "His visage was so marred more than any man, and His form more than the sons of men" (Isaiah 52:14).

In like manner, the Lord allegorically called the cup of wine the cup of the New Covenant, a blood covenant shed for the sins of the world. Of course, the disciples, and those of us who have followed, clearly see the connection to the words of Jeremiah concerning a future covenant with Him which was now being accomplished in Jesus' work.

> Behold, the days come, saith the Lord, that I will make a new covenant with the house of Israel, and with the house of Judah: Not according to the covenant that I made with their fathers in the day that I took them by the hand to bring

> them out of the land of Egypt; (*The covenant of the Law, which was a conditional covenant based upon their obedience.*) Which my covenant they brake, although I was a husband to them, saith the Lord. But this shall be the covenant that I shall make with the house of Israel: After those days, saith the Lord, I will put my law in their inwards parts, and write it in their hearts; and I will be their God, and they shall be my people. And they shall teach no more every man his neighbor, and every man his brother, saying, know the Lord: For they shall all know me, from the least of them unto the greatest of them, saith the Lord: For I will forgive their iniquity, and remember their sins no more.
> Jeremiah 31:31-34 (italics added)

That covenant with the house of Israel and Judah has, for the most part, not yet been realized as they continue to dismiss Jesus of Nazareth as a false messiah. On a day in the future, though, the Jews will realize their mistake, and as Zechariah predicts "they will look upon me whom they have pierced, and they shall mourn for him, as one mourns for his only son" (Zechariah 12:10). But we learn from the writer of Hebrews that the Church, made up of believing Jews and Gentiles, are living the new covenant of His blood now, ever since the day of Pentecost when the Spirit was given (Hebrews 8:1-13).

So, we have His broken body and His shed blood bringing us healing and forgiveness, Freeing us from the power of sin (his body) and the penalty of iniquity (his blood). Putting His law in our inward parts and causing the Father to remember our sins no more! But, along with these most profound truths, we have an instruction embedded. We are to do this often in remembrance of His great sacrifice and love. We are essentially to celebrate this whenever we eat. That is, every day! We are to live a lifestyle of communion. A life with the awareness of His presence as much as possible! When I think of the word "communion," to me it is synonymous with the concept of fellowship with our Lord. And the loveliness of this life is that, when I do this, peace of mind and vibrancy of heart are the result. I am whimsical as I live life beautifully in the light of His presence!

> And whatsoever you do, do it heartily as to the Lord, and not unto men: Knowing of the Lord shall receive the reward of the inheritance: For you serve the Lord Christ.
> Colossians 3:23

This verse is the communion lifestyle! As I live with the awareness of His thereness, all that I do, all that I accomplish, all that I think about, can be with Him in mind. No doubt, this way of life leads to victory and peace, no matter what the circumstances!

So, we see that this type of worship and intimacy with our Savior sprouts from His sacrifice made for us. For the Table of the Lord stems from His redemptive death for us. His body was broken, just as He broke the bread, showing that not only is this an outward celebration, but it is also an inward examination, something about which to be very sober and somber.

> For I received of the Lord that which also I delivered unto you, that the Lord Jesus the same night in which He was betrayed took bread: And when He had given thanks, He broke it,

> and said, take eat, this is my body, which is broken for you: This do in remembrance of me. After the same manner also He took the cup, when He had supped, saying, this cup is the new testament in my blood: This do you, as often as you drink it, in remembrance of me. For as often as you eat this bread and drink this cup, you do show the Lord's death until He come...But (*And*) let a man examine himself, and so let him eat that bread, and drink of that cup.
> 1 Corinthians 11:23-26 and 28 (italics added)

To examine myself means to give this meal worth. To be introspective. To be thinking about the many implications of this sacrifice to blot out my sins. And to be looking...Looking back to what He did, looking forward to His return, looking within myself in confession and looking around, aware of other people and His great love for them also! Truly the Lord's Table is both a party and a funeral reception. But even in His death, the wake can be a celebration, for after Good Friday came Easter Sunday!

The Bible pictures the Sacrament of Communion in many places. It is seen in the Exodus when manna fell from heaven, satisfying the children's hunger in the wilderness (Exodus 16). It is typified at the grandeur of Solomon's table (2 Chronicles 9) when the Queen of Sheba traveled from afar to see for herself whether the report she had heard of Solomon's majesty was indeed true. In the Acts of the Apostles, we can notice how it is associated with hope and protection as Paul offered it to the storm-tossed sailors on the night before their deliverance (Acts 27). Of course, Jesus equated bread with Himself, as told in the gospel of John, saying that He is the true bread from heaven, that He is the Bread of Life (John 6).

But the first mention of bread and wine is found in Genesis 14. As an aside, when a topic is first mentioned in the Bible often keys to its deeper meaning are embedded. Scholarly books discussing first mentions are available, discussing everything from the first mentions of integrity and love to government and faith, and so on.

In this section, the first mention of war is seen and we meet the mystical high priest Melchizedek. Five kings warred against four, including the kings of Sodom and Gomorrah. Abraham's nephew Lot was caught up in the conflict because he was a citizen of Sodom. That city with their king was on the losing side and Lot was taken captive one hundred miles to the north to the area of the tribe of Dan. This enraged Abraham, leading him to gather the three hundred and eighteen men of his household to free Lot. He led a guerilla nighttime attack and, with the Lord's help, was successful against a greater force. It was on his way back to his home on the plain of Mamre (meaning abundance) that he met Melchizedek, who brought forth bread and wine (first mention of these). We are told in the New Testament (Hebrews 7:1-3) that Melchizedek was the King of Jerusalem and that he had no beginning or end. In Hebrew, his name means King of Righteousness. So, track with me here. We have the King of Jerusalem, whose name means the King of Righteousness and he has no beginning or end. Who can this be? Why He is Jesus Christ, of course. This is an Old Testament appearance of Christ before He came as the babe of Bethlehem. Bible scholars call this a Christophany when we see Jesus appearing in the Old Testament. There are many other examples of this, which I will let you seek out on your own (three of many; Joshua 5:13-15, Judges 13:2-22, Genesis 18).

> And the king of Sodom went out to meet him after his return from the slaughter of Chedorlaomer, and kings who were with him, at the valley of Shaveh, which is the king's dale. And Melchizedek king of Salem (*Jerusalem*) brought forth bread and wine: And he was the priest of the most high God. And he (*Melchizedek*) blessed him, and said, Blessed be the most high God which has delivered your enemies into your hand. And he (*Abraham*) gave tithes of all (*He gave 10% of the spoil to Melchizedek*). And the king of Sodom said to Abram (*name of Abraham before God changed it*) give me the persons and keep the goods to yourself. And Abram said to the king of Sodom, I have lift up mine hand unto the Lord, the most high God, the possessor of heaven and earth, I will not take anything that is yours lest you should say, I have made Abram rich...After these things the word of the Lord came unto Abram in a vision, saying, fear not, Abram: I am thy shield and thy exceeding great reward. Genesis 14:17-23 and 15:1 (italics added)

What a story! And what a lesson for us. You see, along with Melchizedek being a type of Christ, we have the king of Sodom, who, of course, is a picture of Satan. The Enemy doesn't care about the goods, he wants the men, he wants their souls! Melchizedek, on the other hand, blesses Abram with bread and wine (*picturing the broken body and shed blood that Jesus explained to us*). Melchizedek then received tithes of Abram's spoils, which enabled Abram to defeat the temptation of the king of Sodom to keep all of the spoil but give away the souls of his men. Subsequently, the word of the Lord came to Abram, likely in response to some fear that may have been bubbling up in his heart at not keeping the spoils, saying that He, God, not the stuff, was Abram's exceeding great reward!

So it is for us. In remembering the Lord at His table, in celebrating communion, we are saying "Yes" to God and "No" to Satan! Blessing and protection are the results of the sacrament, just as they were to Abraham. Subsequently, communion directs us toward obedience and worship, which opens the door to revelation from God, just as it did for Abraham.

Lastly, before leaving this wonderful sacrament given to us, let us consider the miracle of the multiplication of the loaves and fish, for in this we will gain insight into the work of Jesus down through the centuries unto our present day.

> And when the day began to wear away, then came the twelve, and said unto Him, send the multitude away, that they may go into the towns and country round about, and lodge, and get victuals: For we are in a desert place. But He said unto them, give you them to eat. And they said, we have no more but five loaves and two fish; except we should go and buy meat for all this people. For there were about five thousand men. And He said to His disciples, make them sit down by fifties in a company. And they did so, and made them all sit down. Then He took the five loaves and the two fish, and looking up to heaven, He blessed them, and brake, and gave to the disciples to set before the multitude. And they did eat,

> and were all filled: And there was taken up of fragments that remained to them twelve baskets.
> Luke 9:12-17

There are so many types in this story! First, as a disciple of the King, I too can feed people when I have meager supplies. For example, at work I may run into a problem that is not in my specialty; no matter, with the Lord's help, I want to do what I can instead of passing on an opportunity to comfort. Same thing in ministry. I may be gifted in the areas of mercy and giving. That doesn't mean that, when asked to serve on a work detail or teach kids on Sunday, I should decline. Communion, the multiplication of the loaves shows me that with the Lord, food will miraculously be produced as I distribute it out.

We see also that the Lord does the miracle but the disciples partnered with him. They supplied the paltry provisions, they instructed the company to sit down in order to receive from Jesus, and they passed out the bread. Again, this confirms to me that I need to take seriously the opportunity to partner with the Lord, for this is His will. He could do everything himself, but He chooses to have us join along in His work. In this we see a blessing, do we not? Each of the disciples gleaned an entire basket of bread after all were fed. Of course, these fragments of bread allegorically reveal how the Word given to us by Jesus has been multiplied over the past two thousand years from the pulpits of preachers and teachers, from the desks of authors and speakers, from the easels of artists and painters.

So we see, in the Table of the Lord, that remembering His great sacrifice brings blessing and protection. Hope in God is linked to it, as well as the understanding that everything belongs to Him, making us want to give back to Him in the tithe and our offerings. It is associated with the healing of the body and the salvation of the soul. And, wonderfully, it directs us toward confession, obedience, and worship, all of which opens the door to intimacy with the Lord and revelation from the Lord.

In conclusion, if there is one verse that sums up our response to our Lord's Supper, it is this:

> Be still and know that I am God:
> Psalm 46:10a

Summary:

1. The Church of Christ has been living the New Covenant of His blood since the day of Pentecost, for He has written His Law in our inward parts.
2. The broken bread represents the body of Christ broken for us. It brings healing (Isaiah 53:5) and frees us from the power of sin (Romans 6:6).
3. The cup represents the shed blood of Christ bringing forgiveness and freeing us from the penalty of sin (Romans 5:9).
4. The communion lifestyle is to be aware of His presence often.
5. Communion says "Yes" to God and "No" to Satan. It is associated with blessing and protection, hope, and deliverance and directs us toward obedience and worship, which, in turn, opens the door to insight and revelation from God.

For Further Study:

1. Do you think the Lord's words about remembering His sacrifice at His table are a command or a promise? Or both?

2. What does examining yourself before partaking of the bread and the cup mean to you? If you have sinned today, does that disqualify you from partaking of His meal?

The Prophet

> The Lord thy God will raise up unto thee a Prophet from the midst of thee, of thy brethren, like unto me; unto Him shall you hearken. According to all that you desired of the Lord thy God in Horeb (*Mt Sinai where the Ten Commandments were spoken audibly by God*) in the day of the assembly, saying, let us not hear again the voice of the Lord our God, neither let us see this great fire any more, that we die not. And the Lord said unto me, they have well spoken that which they have spoken. I will raise them up a Prophet from among their brethren, like unto thee, and will put my words in His mouth; and He shall speak unto them all that I shall command him. And it shall come to pass, that whosoever will not hearken unto my words which He shall speak in my name, I will require it of him.
>
> Deuteronomy 18:15-19 (italics added)

Jesus Christ, as the Prophet Moses was foretelling, would come to the children of Israel at a future time. They were to be looking for this Prophet because they understood clearly that Moses' words were inspired by God. When Jesus walked among them, many indeed wondered if He was that Prophet (John 1:21 and 7:40). The reason a man speaking God's words was predicted to come was that the people were frightened at the prospect of God continuing to audibly speak to them as He did when He thundered the Ten Commandments from Mount Sinai (Exodus 20). Thus, God graciously offered up himself in a form that would not terrify His children. God became a man and dwelt among them (John 1:14).

And Moses said that the Prophet would be like him. How does that look? Are there similarities between Moses and Jesus that will reveal our Lord as the Prophet Moses spoke of? The answer, of course, is that there are many.

Both Moses and Jesus had earthly kings determined to kill them shortly after their births. In Moses' case, God comically delivered him by having Pharaoh's daughter find him in the very river in which he was destined to be drowned. As for Jesus, Herod became enraged after he learned from the Magi and the Jewish scribes that the prophesied King had been born in Bethlehem. In his fear of losing the crown, he had all of the baby boys of the region executed in a pathetic attempt to thwart God's plan. But his cruelty was too late as God had earlier warned Joseph to take Jesus and His mother and flee to Egypt.

Both Moses and Jesus were (will be) presented to the Jews twice. In both of their first comings, they were rejected and left from the presence of the Jews. Moses escaped to Midian and Jesus ascended to Heaven. Jesus told the Jews as He was being rejected by them, "You shall not see me henceforth, until you say, blessed is He that comes in the name of the Lord" (Matthew 23:39). Upon their second arrival, the Jews have revered Moses and will revere our Lord. Moses led the children out of Egypt; Jesus will rescue the children out of the clutches of Satan and the Antichrist.

The Bible reports that both were very meek (Numbers 12:3, Matthew 11:29). Both were envied (Numbers 12:1-2, Matthew 27:18). Moses' face glowed when he returned from the Mount. Jesus, upon the mount, was transfigured, shining like the sun! Moses rose in glory to the second in all of Egypt; Jesus as the Second Person of the Trinity is also bestowed with glory and honor. Moses ushered in the first covenant, that of the Law; Jesus opened the way for the New Covenant, the covenant of grace. Moses was a shepherd for his father-in-law Jethro. Jesus is the Good Shepherd for His Father, God Almighty. On numerous occasions, Moses interceded for the people. We understand that Jesus is at the right hand of God interceding for us (Hebrews 7:25). Moses parted the Red Sea; Jesus calmed the Galilean Sea. Moses smote the rock and out gushed water; Jesus was the Rock that was smitten and out gushed forth torrents of living water! Moses lifted up the Brazen Serpent in the wilderness and the people lived; Jesus told Nicodemus that He too would be lifted up as that serpent was, and the people would live. Moses fed the people manna from Heaven; Jesus, the true bread from Heaven, multiplied bread to His followers and ultimately gave His body as bread for our souls. This incomplete list of the similitudes between Moses and Jesus continues to be missed by the Jews. On a day not too far away, the veil will be lifted, though, and they will see and understand that Jesus is the Prophet of which Moses spoke (Romans 11:26).

The Bible speaks often of the office of prophet, which is called a gift. It is empowered by God's Spirit. Prophecy is either forthtelling or foretelling the Word of God. A prophet most often will speak God's Word to the people, that is, forthtell it. But, when we think of a Prophet with a capital "P," we are thinking about the ability to accurately predict future occurrences by the Spirit of

God. In the Old Testament, this was the way a true prophet could be discerned from one who was false.

> And if you say in your heart, how shall we know the word which the Lord hath spoken? When a prophet speaks in the name of the Lord, if the thing follow not, nor come to pass, that is the thing which the Lord has not spoken, but the prophet has spoken it presumptuously: You shall not be afraid of him.
> Deuteronomy 18:21-22

The penalty for being a false prophet was severe...death!

> But the prophet, which shall presume to speak a word in my name, which I have not commanded him to speak, or that shall speak in the name of other gods, even that prophet shall die.
> Deuteronomy 18:20

Thus, we understand that the Revealer of Secrets uses prophecy to unveil to mankind that He is the one true God. All other gods (devils) cannot foretell the future, they can only guess at it, leaving themselves with a track record that is far from 100%. In fact, God sort of brags about His prophetic ability to predict the future in Isaiah's inspired words.

> Produce your cause, saith the Lord; bring forth your strong reasons, saith the King of Jacob. Let them bring them forth, and show us what shall happen: Let them show the former

> things, what they be, that we may consider them; or declare us things for to come. Show the things that are to come hereafter, that we may know that ye are gods: Yea, do good, or do evil, that we may be dismayed, and behold it together. Behold, ye are of nothing, and your work of naught: An abomination is he that chooses you.
> Isaiah 41:21-24

> Behold, the former things are come to pass, and new things do I declare: *Before* they spring forth, I tell you of them.
> Isaiah 42:9

> Thus saith the Lord, the Holy One of Israel, and his Maker, *ask* me of things to come concerning my sons, and concerning the work of my hands *command* ye me. ... For thus saith the Lord that created the heavens...I have not spoken in secret.
> Isaiah 45:11, 18a, 19a (italics added)

It's as if God is daring us to prove Him in this arena of prophecy!

> Remember the former things of old: For I am God, and there is none else; I am God, and there is none like me. Declaring the end from the beginning, and from ancient times the things that are not yet done, saying, my counsel shall stand, and I will do all my pleasure.

> Isaiah 46:9-10
>
> I have even from the beginning declared it to thee, before it came to pass, I showed it thee: Lest thou shouldst say, Mine idol hath done them, and my graven image, and my molten image, hath commanded them. ...For mine own sake, even for mine own sake, will I do it: For how should my name be polluted? And I will not give my glory unto another.
> Isaiah 48:5, 11

There it is! God taunts other gods to foretell the future. He says that the fact that they cannot reveals to all that those gods are nothing! The Almighty declares that He will reveal things before they come to pass. The Holy One of Israel actually tells us to ask Him of things to come. He states that He has not spoken in secret and that He has declared the end from the beginning!

Why?

So that mankind would know that it's Him, and not another. Not an idol or the work of men's hands, and most important in our day of "scientific enlightenment," not mere coincidence or randomness! For He alone is to receive all glory and honor, blessing and power today and in eternity to come!

Now, in this book, we have been discussing at length Jesus' operation of the office of a prophet. That is, He constantly is speaking forth (forthtelling) the Word of God. In fact, we understand that He *is* the Word of God (John 1:14 and Revelation 19:13). But, here in this chapter, we want to consider Jesus the Prophet. Jesus, the One who foretells the future.

Early in the Savior's ministry, revival was breaking out wherever He traveled. People were being healed, devils were being cast out, and joy was filling the people's hearts. Of course, whenever a move of God occurs, there will be pushback from the powers of the darkness of this world. In this case, the god of this world mobilized the religious leaders to come against Jesus. While celebrating the Passover in Jerusalem, they commanded that He tell them by what authority He was doing these works and teaching these precepts. "If you have authority from God, show us a sign." To that, He gave a stirring personal prophecy which in His humanness must have been quite a painful revelation to Him. He said, "Destroy this temple, and in three days I will raise it up" (John 2:19). Standing upon the Temple Mount, Jesus metaphorically revealed that He would be physically destroyed by them and three days later be resurrected back to life. Apparently, this prophecy sailed over the Pharisees' heads because their response questioned the destruction of the actual Temple, not the temple of His body, as John explained to his readers.

Later, as pressure was building greater and greater from the religious legalists, they again asked Jesus for a sign validating His claims about speaking the words of God, words that came against the many commandments of men, such as the Sabbath laws, which they were propagating. Once again, the Lord prophesied exactingly about His death and resurrection, this time by using the sign of Jonah.

> An evil and adulterous generation seeks after a sign; and there shall no sign be given to it, but the sign of the prophet Jonah: For as Jonah was three days and three nights in the whale's belly; so shall the Son of man be three days and three nights in the heart of the earth.
> Matthew 12:39-40

Not coincidentally, Jonah told the men on the ship sailing for Tarshish that he needed to be thrown overboard, he needed to die, for the men to be saved (Jonah 1:12). So too, Jesus was adding that not only would He die and be raised back to life after three days, as was Jonah, but that His death would also save others, as did Jonah's. In Jesus' case, His death would not just save a few but would save all of mankind (John 3:16).

Not only did our Lord predict His demise and revival to those opposed to Him, but also to His followers.

> He said unto them, but whom say ye that I am? (*Still the most important question for all men and women, for all time!*). Peter answering said, the Christ of God. And He straightly charged them, and commanded them to tell no man that thing; saying, the Son of man must suffer many things, and be rejected of the elders and the chief priests and scribes, and be slain, and be raised the third day.
> Luke 9:20-21 (italics added)

This must have been particularly painful to Jesus because He well knew they were focused on prophecies of glory that were destined to be fulfilled at a much later time, in a day long after their lives were lived. Thus, He knew they would not get to see the promise of glory they were looking to and believing for...at least not in that day!

Jesus understood that the time He was living in was a day of unbelief by the Jews. He realized that, because they rejected Him, terrible things were in store for the children of Israel. He hoped to shake them out of their blindness by sharing what the scriptures said of Him as well as predicting who they would follow in the future and what would soon happen to them.

> Search the scriptures; for in them you think you have eternal life: And they are they which testify of me.
> John 5:39

Like John 3:16, this is one of the key verses in all of God's Word that unlocks so much else. In this case, Jesus is revealing to His detractors that the Old Testament is about Him. It's more than just Jewish history and poetry, more than laws and precepts, because it speaks of our wonderful Savior on nearly every page. People, pictures, prophecy, and poems, picture, typify, proclaim, and sing of him. From Adam to Esther, from the Tree of Life to the Passover sacrifice, from Micah 2 to Isaiah 53, from Psalm 22 to the Song of Solomon, Jesus is illustrated in vivid pictures and types in a way that even little children can comprehend. All that was and is needed is for the child of God to look for Him. This is the way we today need to read the Old Testament, that is, considering where and how He is pictured on every page! This is what "turned on" the early church after their "Road to Emmaus" experience. They finally realized that the Old Testament is all about Jesus!

> And you will not come to me that you might have life. I receive not honor from men. But I know you, that you have not the love of God in you. I am come in my Father's name, and you receive me not: If another shall come in his own name, him you shall receive.
> John 5:40-43

Bible scholars teach that, during the time of Jacob's Trouble (Jerimiah 30:4-7), the Jews will initially follow after the charismatic world leader that John in the Revelation of Jesus Christ calls the Beast. We also know this figure that the Jews will call "lord," as the Antichrist. Jesus predicted to the Jews who were rejecting Him that their nation would be duped into following a false messiah, one who does not seek God's honor, but his own.

> How can you believe, which receive honor one of another, and seek not the honor that comes from God only? Do not think that I will accuse you to the Father: There is one that accuses you, even Moses, in whom you trust. For had you believed Moses, you would have believed me: For he wrote of me.
> John 5:44-46

Game, set, match! "You're going to seek a false messiah and you didn't listen to Moses. For I am that Prophet, like him, of which he spoke."

Later, when the Redeemer made His triumphal entry into Jerusalem on His fateful last week, He prophesied serious repercussions that would happen to Jerusalem and the Jews because they did not recognize the time of God's visitation unto them.

> And when He had come near the city, and wept over it, saying, if you had known, even thou, at least in this thy day, the things which belong unto your peace! But now they are hid from your eyes.
> Luke 19: 41-42

Jesus cried these words of grief over Jerusalem on Palm Sunday. He was saddened because this day was prophesied to the Jews in their scriptures (Psalm 118:19-26 and Daniel 9:25) and He realized they did not understand its meaning. He saw what they did not, that it was hidden from their eyes!

> For the days shall come upon thee, that thine enemies shall cast a trench about thee, and compass thee round, and keep you on every side, and shall lay you with the ground, and your children within you; and they shall not leave in you one stone upon another; because you knew not the time of your visitation.
> Luke 19:43-44

The One the Bible calls Emmanuel, God with us, was among them, and they knew it not! Consequently, the repercussion of their unbelief, their denial, and their blindness was that Jerusalem would be destroyed. The city of the great King would be leveled. Indeed, that did happen less than forty years later, as General Titus and his Roman legions compassed Jerusalem and after a long siege broke through and leveled the city. Jesus predicted this disaster was the direct consequence of their rejection of His saving grace.

Not only did the Prophet speak of the destruction of Jerusalem but He also exactingly foretold of the demise of the place where God's glory resided. He told His followers that the Temple would also come to ruin.

> And Jesus went out, and departed from the temple: And His disciples came to Him for to show Him the buildings of the temple.

Matthew 24:1

In context, this remark comes after Jesus had a very difficult encounter with the Jewish leaders. It was most uncomfortable for the disciples to be part of because their Master laid all of the past sins of the Jews squarely upon that very generation. As they were leaving the Temple Mount, His disciples were trying to spin some positivity onto the encounter. "Look how beautiful our religion is, Jesus, there must be some good that you see. Look at these beautiful buildings that glorify God." To this, Jesus gave the stirring prophecy of the Temple's total destruction.

> And Jesus said unto them, see you not all these things? Truly I say unto you, there shall not be left here one stone upon another, that shall not be thrown down.
> Matthew 24:2

Titus had commanded his men to spare the Temple when they broke through the walls and entered the city. But we know that was not meant to be, for Jesus had prophesied to the contrary. History records that a lone soldier tossed a torch into the Temple that started a conflagration so hot that the gold overlay of the Temple melted between the huge stones. To get the gold, the soldiers tossed the Temple. Literally, no stone was left unturned. No stone was left upon another, just as Jesus had said would occur.

The Prophet spoke one last word against the Jews as they were in the process of murdering Him. As He was carrying His cross on the Via Delarosa, "the Sorrowful Way," He prophesied very bad news to the daughters of Jerusalem because of the deeds of their fathers on that day.

> And there followed Him a great company of people, and of women, which also bewailed and lamented him. But Jesus turning unto them said, daughters of Jerusalem, weep not for me, but weep for yourselves, and for your children.
> Luke 23: 27-28

This is so sad to me. The women of Jerusalem, innocent bystanders if you will, are going to be part of the carnage, part of the curse that was going to come down on the Jews because of the sins of the fathers. And the children, too! Yes, sin stinks. Often, we think we can pay the price of rebellion and stubbornness when we decide to willfully miss the mark. But what I, what we, fail to factor into the equation is the collateral damage to others. Damage to our families, our kids, and even our grandkids! Generational curses are put into motion.

> For, behold, the days are coming, in which they shall say, blessed are the barren, and the wombs that never bore, and the breasts that never gave suck.
> Luke 23:29

This is terrible! For a woman of Jerusalem two thousand years ago, bearing and raising children was her one desire. Women did not have multiple irons in the fire as they do in our day. So, for Jesus to say that the future was going to be so bad because of the deeds of that day, that it would be a curse to bear and to nurse children, the situation would have to be nothing short of a disaster!

Read on, for that is indeed what happened!

> Then they shall begin to say unto the mountains, fall on us; and to the hills, cover us. For if they do these things in a green tree, what shall be done in the dry?
> Luke 23:30-31

The King was in their midst and they slew Him. What could they expect to happen afterward?

As we noted, less than one generation later, Jerusalem was leveled. Some of the Jews fled to Masada, where, after a three-year siege, they committed mass suicide over being taken by the Romans. Subsequently, emperors inspired by the god of this world were very heavy on the Jews. Millions were killed, persecuted, and scattered during the rule of the Romans. Later, the Ottoman Turks, under the religion of Islam, kept their thumb over the few Jews that were left in what was now called Palestine. Most of the Jews migrated in the first millennium to Russia and Eastern Europe. There they were also persecuted and killed. The Jews of Europe in these latter days have been particularly singled out, as our recent history so very well documents.

For nearly two thousand years, the Jews have suffered as an ethnic group. The reason? It may be hard to hear, but Jesus clearly states it was because they rejected Him. As we stated earlier, the most important question that all must answer is, "Who do you say that I am?" Just like the Jews, if you, if I, reject His gracious offer of forgiveness and salvation, if I step over His dead body, if you will, I am speeding headlong against the immovable object. Against the irresistible force. Nothing of lasting good will ever come to the person, people group, political viewpoint, or governmental providence that pits itself against Jesus of Nazareth. This was true for the Jewish nation two thousand years ago and it is true for our nation today. If America, which calls itself a God-fearing nation, continues to flout God's laws and precepts, we too can expect Him to withdraw His blessing from us. Not because He is mean and vindictive but because He is just. He has clearly stated that whatsoever a man sows, he can expect to reap. If we as a nation sow unbelief, strife, and falsehoods, what can we expect to come of that? History shows us very clearly. Nations and people groups who have rejected God's message of peace don't last long. In the case of the Jews, a miracle has occurred in the face of their unbelief secondary to promises God made to the Patriarchs, Abraham, Isaac, and Jacob. He promised them that He would not allow them to be destroyed completely. He would chastise them if they sinned, as He has done, but would also revive them in the latter days, as He is doing. Those with eyes to see will note that this is indeed happening right before us, for we have witnessed the return of the Jews to Israel and the formation of the Jewish state.

For us in America, what can we do to mitigate the crop we have planted from springing forth to our destruction? God is so gracious, as His Word plainly tells us how to return to Him.

> If my people, which are called by my name (*That's us Christians!*), shall humble themselves, and pray, and seek my face, and turn from their wicked ways; then I will hear from heaven, and forgive their sin, and will heal their land.
> 2 Chronicles 7:14 (italics added)

Four things we believers, His people, need to do to save our land. Humble ourselves, pray for the nation, lean in to Him, and repent of our sins. Sins of sowing discord among the brethren, sins of neglect of the poor and needy, sins of pride and partisanship.

The Welsh revival of 1904 was centered upon this verse. Evangelist Evan Roberts taught four responses to this verse, responses you and I should also make. Confess sin and make restitution. Forsake sin. Respond to the Spirit promptly. Profess Jesus Christ publicly.

His Word also tells us how to stay in the place of grace where His blessings pour forth.

> But you, beloved, building up yourselves on your most holy faith, praying in the Holy Ghost, keep yourselves in the love of God, looking forward for the mercy of our Lord Jesus Christ unto eternal life.
> Jude 20-21

The key verse in this entire little book is to keep ourselves in the love of God. That is, to stay in the place where God's blessings are not hindered to flow down upon us. As we have discussed, sin and unbelief are the inhibitors. The medicine is threefold. Build ourselves up in our faith; that is, stay in God's Word. Pray in the Spirit, meaning let the Spirit lead my prayers. And look for the mercy of our Lord Jesus Christ, that is, look for His return, live for heaven.

Okay, so the Jews of Jesus' day were living in the greatest generation in the history of the world and they didn't get it. They missed the First Coming of the Messiah. They had many signs that they didn't see, didn't comprehend, didn't look for. Let's not let that happen to us. We too have signs of the soon coming of the Lord. Of His Second Coming. We will talk about many of these ciphers in our next three chapters, entitled "The Last Days." I don't want to be surprised, I don't want you taken aback on that day, not too far away, when we hear the Shout, the Voice, and the Trump of God calling us to meet our Lord in the air (1 Thessalonians 4:16). I want us to be ready!

Summary:

1. Moses prophesied that one like him would arrive. The people were instructed to look for and to listen to Him.
2. A prophet is one who forthtells and/or foretells the Word of God.
3. Jesus used the Old Testament pictures of the Temple and Jonah to reveal that He would die and be resurrected three days later.
4. Jesus taught that the Old Testament speaks of Him in people, pictures, prophecies, and poems.
5. Jesus prophesied that Jerusalem and the Temple would be razed because of the Jews' collective unbelief in and rejection of Him.
6. Jesus also taught there would be a generational curse upon the Jews because they dismissed Him.

For Further Study:

1. The scribes knew the King would be born in Bethlehem from Micah's prophecy. But how did the Magi know that a great King in Israel had been born?
2. Consider the biblical definition of a prophet. Do you know any personally?
3. Fulfilled prophecy is one way we know that the Bible is inspired. Can you think of other proofs?
4. How is Jesus like Moses? Can you think of other Old Testament characters who picture Christ?
5. Do you find prophecy interesting or perplexing?
6. How can you tell if a prophecy is from God or another source?

7. The Almighty declares that He will reveal things before they come to pass. Can you think of any prophecies which He has declared that have yet to come to pass?
8. What is the most important question of all time?
9. Have you ever had a sin lead to collateral damage you were not counting upon?
10. Do you think recent events in our world are the result of our collective moving away from God or just a coincidence?
11. What does the Bible say we can and should do to mitigate any judgment upon our land secondary to our collective rebellion and unbelief?

The Last Days: The Parable of the Fig Tree

It has been nearly two thousand years since our Lord ascended into heaven. Ten days later, the Holy Spirit descended upon the earth. In the interim, we have had the Comforter with us, for that third person of the Trinity first came upon the disciples on the day of Pentecost. But importantly, immediately after Jesus soared away, the disciples were informed by heavenly messengers that He would physically return to our planet once again.

> And when He had spoken these things (*that the Holy Spirit would come upon them.*), while they beheld, He was taken up; and a cloud received Him out of their sight. And while they looked steadfastly toward heaven as He went up, behold, two men stood by them in white apparel: Which also said, you men of Galilee, why stand you gazing up into heaven? This same Jesus, which is taken up from you into heaven, shall so come (*back*) in like manner as you have seen Him go into heaven.
> Acts 1:9-11 (italics added)

This is the "hope" that we believers in Jesus Christ hold, that our wonderful Risen Lord will return in power and great glory to rule and reign upon our earth.

Jesus had much to say about this future day while He was present with us during His First Advent. In a book about parables and teachings of the Great Physician, we must include His words on this very important topic. For, as John has taught, it is the hope of the Lord's return that purifies us while we wait for Him (1 John 3:2-3).

We learned in our last chapter that Jesus powerfully prophesied that the Temple would be destroyed secondary to the collective unbelief in, and rejection of, our Lord by the Jews. The disciples wrongly concluded that this prophecy was talking about the End Times, that it was talking about the onset of the Kingdom Age for which they were so hopefully looking. Hence, they asked the following question:

> And as He sat upon the mount of Olives, the disciples came unto Him privately, saying, tell us, when shall these things be? And what shall be the *sign* of thy coming, and the end of the world? And Jesus answered and said unto them...
> Matthew 24:3-4a (italics added)

Pay attention! The Prophet is about to foretell the future to His men. He is ready to answer the question we all want to know. When will things be made right? When is thy Kingdom to come and thy will to be done? Spoiler alert...the sign is in the parable of the Fig Tree. Jesus will speak to that in a moment. But first, there will be birth pangs!

> Take heed that no man deceive you. For many shall come in my name, saying, I am Christ; and shall deceive many.
> Matthew 24:4-5

The implication is that believers and seekers will be deceived by false messiahs. Indeed, this has happened. Billions follow the errant teachings of Mohammed, Buddha, and Hinduism. Not only religious leaders, but secular false Christs have led men astray. Men such as Hitler, Jim Jones, Charles Manson, and many many others have collectively duped us by their pseudo-righteousness! Jesus says, don't fall for it. In a moment He will tell His men how to discern the real from the imitation. Another spoiler alert... His return will be like lightning! No doubt, no wonder. It will be obvious!

> And when you shall hear of wars and rumors of wars: See that you be not troubled: For all these things must come to pass, but the end is not yet. For nation shall rise against nation, and kingdom against kingdom: And there shall be famines, and pestilences, and earthquakes, in various places. All these are the beginning of sorrows.
> Matthew 24:6-8

Luke adds that in addition to this list of birth pangs, there will also be signs in the sun, Moon, and stars and that the seas and the waves will roar (Luke 21:25).

This is huge! These three little verses have described very accurately the last two thousand years. Jesus said that the time leading up to His return would be like the beginning of sorrows.

Of course, sorrows are another term for what we know as labor pains or birth pangs. And just like birth pangs, they will start out infrequently and far apart but, as the day of the delivery approaches, that is, as the day of our Lord's return nears, they will become more and more frequent and intense. This is indeed what has happened over the past two millennia in each of these categories of distress which our Lord called out.

First, wars have gone from local and regional conflicts to worldwide conflagrations. In the future, as the day approaches, I can't help but think that the nuclear option will be in play as part of this prophecy of increasing labor pains.

Famines have always been part of the curse upon mankind ever since God told Adam that the earth would no longer bring forth fruit in abundance. But as time has marched forward, we see Jesus' words about hunger reach epic proportions. One-third of the souls living on our planet go to bed without proper nutrition. Hundreds die every day from starvation. Indeed, famine has taken on a labor-like rhythm.

I write this chapter in 2020 amid the painful pang of the Corona virus. This is but another of the many pestilences, many pandemics if you will, which our world has endured. Again, there have always been diseases that have ravaged mankind. Leprosy, the bubonic plague, smallpox, cholera, TB, typhoid, malaria, and Spanish flu as notable sporadic sorrows of the past two thousand years. But, in the last generation or so, the pangs are getting closer. Polio, HIV, Herpes, HPV, Ebola, West Nile virus, H1N1, Swine and Avian flu, Zika, and now Covid 19. If the Lord tarries we can expect further global pandemics to wreak havoc just as the Prophet foretold. One of the plagues during the world's time of true labor, the time we understand to be described in the Book of Revelation, is that men who take the Mark of the Beast will suffer grievous boils as a result of that poor choice (Revelation

16:2). To my reading, that likely is some sort of infectious or toxic reaction to the implanted mark itself.

Next, we come to the shaking of the earth. Quakes have always been part of life for mankind. In the Bible, earthquakes seem to be supernaturally timed to bookmark dramatic events that the Almighty wanted to emphasize. We remember the earth quaking as He prepared to audibly speak the Ten Commandments to the children of Israel (Exodus 19:18). Later, when Jonathan and his armorbearer stepped out in faith against the Philistine garrison, the earth trembled as they defeated the numerically greater enemy. Of course, the most significant set of earthquakes of all time occurred in Jerusalem the hour that our Lord died upon the Cross for the sins of all mankind and then again three days later as an aftershock rolled away the stone! But as awesome as these earthquakes were, they did not occur very often in biblical times. Not so for our day today. Scientists tell us that over the past one hundred years we have seen a logarithmic increase in activity of the earth's crust. Not only minor tremblers as a result of increased fracking, but also many large and devastating upsets have been endured. San Francisco, Los Angeles, Mexico City, Istanbul, Japan, Alaska, Indonesia, and other large population centers have been hit with this pang of which Jesus spoke. In the future, it would not surprise me that the San Andreas or Cascadia faults will clash leading to death and destruction unlike we have ever seen. Again, from the Revelation, it would appear that a great earthquake, the culmination of this prophecy, will occur which will move every mountain and island out of its place (Revelation 6:12-14).

Lastly, Luke added in His account of Jesus' words, that there will be labor-like signs in the moon and the stars and the sea will roar. The Bible tells us, "The heavens declare the glory of the Lord and the firmament shows His handiwork" (Psalm 19:1).

Indeed, God has placed His very word in the stars for all to see. The Magi understood this to be true as they traveled to worship the King based upon the signs in the sky they had observed which announced His arrival. Joshua spoke to the sun and God caused the day to be extended so he could defeat his enemies (Joshua 10:12-14). But once again, something new is happening in the sky. Blood moons, super conjunctions, comets, and meteor showers appear almost nightly in the sky. Of course, these signs, too, will increase as the day draws near. As for the oceans raging, 2020 was a banner year for hurricanes in the Atlantic basin. There were so many tempests that the entire alphabet was required in naming them; but that was still not enough, so the Greek alphabet was also employed. In addition to storms, we have witnessed the labor pains of tsunamis in the Indian and Pacific Oceans leading to death and destruction on a scale never before experienced. It is noted that the tsunami which occurred from the Indonesian earthquake of 2004 was the largest natural disaster in the history of our world.

Indeed, our planet is experiencing false labor, just as Jesus said it would. Paul summed up this concept well when he said: "For we know that the whole creation groans and travails in pain together until now" (Romans 8:22).

> Then they shall deliver you up to be afflicted,
> and shall kill you: And you shall be hated of all
> nations for my name's sake.
> Matthew 24:9

Persecutions await the evangelist speaking of the Lord. When I witness the Lord to people, I don't want to make the mistake of telling them everything will be wonderful in their lives. Clearly, Jesus taught that the world and its system will be at odds with His Kingdom and His followers. No, one must always factor in eternity when deciding for the Lord. The future choice is clear. Misery or majesty! Present comfort with future destruction, or present discomfort with future glory! But, even in our discomfort, He is with us, giving us peace in the midst of the storm: "These things I have spoken unto you, that in me you might have peace. In the world you shall have tribulation: But be of good cheer; I have overcome the world" (John 16:33).

> And then shall many be offended, and shall betray one another, and shall hate one another.
> Matthew 24:10

This is important. John Bevere in his book, *The Bait of Satan*, has rightly preached that "offenses" are being used greatly by our Enemy to bring us down. Jesus said that offenses would be on the increase as time marched forward. What is an offense? Simply put, an offense is anything that we are counting on that does not come to pass. It is an unexpected action or event. Your spouse giving you a hard time for something seemingly trivial, your car breaking down on the way to work, your back going out lifting a suitcase, the flight to Hawaii being rescheduled at the last moment...and on and on. When the unexpected occurs, and I am not ready for it, I will be offended. And when people are the cause of an offense, then betrayal and hatred are the result. And betrayal doesn't have to be a Benedict Arnold or a Judas Iscariot. Simply put, betrayal is choosing yourself over another. And hatred doesn't have to be active disdain toward a person. To be loveless toward another is a form of hatred in God's economy.

Now for the good part. The way to keep Jesus' prophecy from coming true for you... Expect the unexpected! Don't count on life being perfect, smooth, and/or regulated. Don't let distractions bother you. Rather, look to them as opportunities for personal growth as well as occasions to help others. Lastly, don't expect people to always be there for you, do the correct thing, or act in a way that you desire. If you remember this and put it into use, you will not be an "end-times" causality to offenses, to the bait of Satan.

> And many false prophets shall rise, and deceive many.
> Matthew 24:11

Aware as we are that we live in a day of fake news, many are still taken captive and deceived by false prophets. Earlier we learned that there will be false Christs, those who say they are the "anointed ones." False prophets are a bit more subtle, but still very dangerous. A false prophet speaks with authority, as if what he or she is saying is true, only it's not! Our world has many false prophets on the scene today. The entertainment industry especially is a breeding ground for such false prophetic activity.

> And because iniquity shall abound, the love of many shall wax cold. But he that shall endure unto the end, the same shall be saved.
> Matthew 24:12-13

In a moment, we will learn that Jesus will liken the last days to the days of Noah. In Genesis 6, speaking of Noah's day, the Bible states in Verse 5, "The wickedness of man was great upon the earth, and that every imagination of the thoughts of his heart was only evil continually." Unfortunately, this verse could easily describe large pockets of our world today. Thus, we see also another clue to the loveless state of the last days. Besides "offenses," the abundant sin running rampant will cause many to lose their love for God and fellow mankind.

Along with this warning about the End Times, Jesus gives an important directive. Endure! "Never give up." You can say that three times as Winston Churchill famously did, if you like. Claim God's promises, know He is in control, even when things look bad, and you will be saved. In this case, the word for saved is "ozzo." This word implies not only eternal life but salvation in all aspects of this life. Saved from unforgiveness, from lust, from anger, from envy, from worry, etc.

Okay, thus far Jesus has spoken of how the days of the end will look as time marches toward its culmination. A series of non-specific occurrences and behaviors, if you will. Next, we come to a specific event that, when it occurs, will signal that the birth is soon to occur, an event so familiar to the Jews that it needed no further exposition from Jesus. And, importantly, it is an event that our Lord links to the time of Great Tribulation.

> When you shall therefore see the abomination of desolation, spoken by Daniel the prophet, stand in the holy place (whoso reads, let him understand): Then let them which be in Judea flee to the mountains: Let him which is on the housetop not come down to take anything out of his house: Neither let him which is in the field return back to take his clothes. And woe unto them that are with child, and to them that give suck in those days! But pray you that your flight be not in winter, neither on the Sabbath day: For then shall be Great Tribulation, such as was not since the beginning of the world to this time, no, nor ever shall be.

Matthew 24:15-21

When this was spoken, the abomination of desolation had occurred relatively recently in the history of the Jews. They were aware of what the Lord was saying. The Greek ruler, Antiochus Epiphanes, to the horror of the Jews of his day, desecrated the Temple by slaughtering pigs in the Holy of Holies. Jesus is saying that something like that will again occur, signaling the onset of the Great Tribulation. A day so bad for the Jews that, if they do not immediately flee from Judea, they will not escape. Zechariah adds insight to Jesus' words, stating that when this prophesied event occurs, only one-third of the Jews will make it to safety (Zechariah 13:8-9).

So, we see that with the abomination of desolation occurring, Jesus has moved His teaching of the End Times from the days leading up to His return, the pre-tribulation era of the last two thousand years, to the very time of the end. A short seven-year time frame known as the Tribulation by the New Testament writers but understood to the Jews as the day of Jacob's Trouble (Jeremiah 30:4-7).

Continuing with this future day:

> And except these days should be shortened, there should no flesh be saved: But for the elect's sake these days shall be shortened.
> Matthew 24:22

The Tribulation will be a time of great discomfort. The Revelation teaches that a charismatic world leader will figuratively ride in on a white horse, pronouncing peace at a time when the world is ripe for a one-world government. We understand this one to be the Antichrist. Riding in with him, though, will be the other three horsemen of the Apocalypse, War, Famine, and Death. Continuing with John's vision of this time, there will be plagues and judgments that will make problems the world has experienced thus far seem trivial in comparison. But God will use this time of hardship, this time of Jacob's Trouble, to bring His elect, both Jews and Gentiles to a place of saving grace. The Bible states that a multitude, too numerous to count, will stand before the throne, having come out of the Tribulation and clothed in white (Revelation 7:1-14).

> Then if any man shall say unto you, Lo, here is Christ, or there; believe it not. For there shall arise false Christs, and false prophets, and shall show great signs and wonders: Insomuch that, if it were possible, they shall deceive the very elect. Behold, I have told you before (*it happens*).
> Matthew 24:23-25 (italics added)

False Christ and false prophet appearances will crescendo from our present day to the time of Jacob's Trouble with the arrival of the Antichrist and the False Prophet. These two, along with Satan, will form an unholy trinity that will have the power to astound the fooled of the world with apparent signs and wonders. Again, from Zechariah, we learn that the idle shepherd (Zechariah's identification of the Antichrist) will have an apparent mortal wound from which he will recover. This will amaze the world, which will interpret this wonder as an "evident" resurrection (Zechariah 11:17). John reveals that the False Prophet will have the power to call down fire from the sky to deceive men and women. This sign will cause them to worship the first Beast whose deadly wound was healed (Revelation 13:12-13). Jesus is lovingly telling us not to fall for these tricks. Once again, He is foretelling the future as only God is able. You may also remember, from an earlier chapter, that Jesus told us not to be too impressed by miracles, by signs and wonders, for Satan himself can appear as an angel of light. No, the teacher told us to judge for identification by looking at the fruit produced by the wonder-worker. In the case of the Beast and the False Prophet, the fruit will be most foul!

> Wherefore if they shall say unto you, Behold, He is in the desert; go not forth: Behold, He is in the secret chambers; believe it not. For as the lightning comes out of the east, and shines even unto the west; so shall also the coming of the Son of man be...Immediately after the tribulation of those days shall the sun be darkened, and the moon shall not give her light, and the stars shall fall from heaven, and the powers of the heavens shall be shaken: And then shall appear the sign of the Son of man in heaven: And then shall all of the tribes of the earth mourn, and they shall see the Son of man coming in the clouds of heaven with power and great glory.
> Matthew 24:26-27, 29-30

As was pointed out at the beginning of this chapter, Jesus' return will be obvious to all. No private audiences will be made available. When the Lord returns, all will see. On the night our Lord was betrayed, He told the high priest, Caiaphas, that He indeed was the Messiah and that He would one day see Him (the Son of man) sitting on the right hand of power and coming in the clouds of heaven (Matthew 26:64). Zechariah prophesied that when the Lord returns the entire world will mourn, asking, "Where did you get those wounds?" To that Jesus will reply, "I received them in the house of my friends" (Zechariah 13:6).

Next, after speaking of the days of false labor followed by the days of true labor, the Prophet will answer His disciple's initial question. He is now going to tell of the sign which will identify the season of His return and of the end of the age. It is a sign that we will note in our day today has already come to pass!

> Now learn a parable of the fig tree; when his branch is yet tender, and puts forth leaves, you know that summer is nigh: So likewise you, when you shall see these things, know that it is near, even at the doors.
> Matthew 24:32-33

His return is even at the door! For this parable is speaking of the nation of Israel. In the Bible, whenever a fig tree, vine, or olive tree is mentioned, an application to the children of Israel is always present. In this case, looking at the fig tree, we understand that Israel has endured a period of winter, so to speak, over the past nineteen hundred years. In 70 AD, the people were dispersed and the Promised Land was left to lie fallow, becoming irrelevant to the world. Israel was that frozen tree that during the winter appears to have died. But then a miracle occurred! Israel was born in one day.

> Hear the word of the Lord, you that tremble at His Word...A voice of noise from the city, a voice from the temple, a voice of the Lord that renders recompense to His enemies. Before

> she travailed, she brought forth; Before her pains came, she was delivered...Who has heard such a thing? Who has seen such things? Shall the earth be made to bring forth in one day? Or a nation be born at once? For as soon as Zion travailed, she brought forth...
> Isaiah 66:5-8

These four questions of the Almighty were indeed answered on May 14, 1948! On that Day, Israel was reborn. The valley of dry bones took shape (Ezekiel 37). By the pen of the United Nations, Israel once again became a sovereign nation. After the long winter, the fig tree has budded and brought forth leaves. No, the summer fruit is not yet on the tree because the nation does not recognize Jesus as their King but, indeed, the sign that Jesus' disciples were seeking has occurred. The fig tree has put forth leaves. Israel has been reborn. The sign the disciples requested marking the nearness of the Lord's return has occurred. This should give all believers pause. We are living in the last days! In the days immediately before the Second Coming of Jesus Christ. We don't know the day or the hour (Matthew 24:36), but we can know the season. Spring has come. Look up, dear believer, your redemption and the redemption of the world draw nigh!

Summary:

1. Immediately after Jesus ascended up into Heaven, we believers were told by God's angels that He would return.
2. The sign Jesus' disciples were seeking concerning His Coming and the End of the world is found in the Parable of the Fig Tree.

3. Jesus said much would happen before His return. Wars, birth pangs, and persecutions.
4. False messiahs and false prophets will arise. The first will say, "Follow me," the latter, "Listen to me." Beware of both! You can know a tree by its fruit.
5. The Abomination of Desolation (a world leader desecrating the Temple), spoken by Daniel the prophet, will signal the onset of the Great Tribulation.

For Further Study:

1. What happens in the hearts of men and women who are thinking about and longing for the return of the Lord? See 1 John 3:2-3
2. Why are famines, pestilences, earthquakes, and oceans raging compared to birth pangs?
3. What is an offense? How are offenses a sign of the End Times? See Matthew 24:10, 12-13. How do you protect against being offended?
4. What should you immediately think of when a fig tree is mentioned in the Bible? What happened on May 14, 1948? In June of 1967?

The Last Days: The Times of the Gentiles

In our last chapter, we learned of the Parable of the Fig Tree and how it is the sign that would signal the nearness of the end of this age. We rejoiced in realizing that on May 14, 1948, this sign occurred. We also noted that our Lord said much would happen in the time between His first and second comings to our planet. Wars, birth pangs, persecutions, false messiahs, and false prophets would be in play.

But there is more to consider. The Prophet foretold three other signs that make our day today the time of the end of the age. Signs that will also motivate us to look with great anticipation for the Coming of our Risen Savior!

> But as the days of Noah were, so shall also the coming of the Son of man be. For as in the days that were before the Flood they were eating and drinking, marrying and giving in marriage, until the day that Noah entered into the ark. And knew not until the Flood came, and took them away; so shall also the coming of the Son of man be.
> Matthew 24:37-39

Do you believe the Flood actually occurred? Jesus did!

Some things in the Bible may be so miraculous and unusual that they are hard to believe. When this is the case, we often can look at our Lord's take on the difficult subjects. He spoke of Jonah and the whale, of the fate of Sodom and Gomorrah, of Adam and Eve, and here it would seem to appear that He believed that a worldwide flood did indeed occur. If these beliefs were good enough for him, so it will be for me!

Back to the sign of Noah. As we discussed earlier, wickedness was a continual pastime in Noah's day, not unlike our day today. Also, in Noah's story, we are told that it was in a time when men were multiplying upon the earth (Genesis 6:1). This also likens our day to Noah's. Indeed, over the past century, the population of the world has skyrocketed, never before seen, and this can be said of no other time. It would appear to me that the 21st Century will be the fulfillment of Jesus' comparison to Noah.

Note also that, in Noah's day, the people were taken by surprise. This also is in play in our day. Unbelievers, for the most part, have heard the gospel message as well as the teaching of the return of Christ, yet they mock it. Let that not happen to us. Paul gives good advice when talking about this same subject:

> But of the times and the seasons, brethren, you have no need that I write unto you. For yourselves know perfectly that the day of the Lord so comes as a thief in the night. For when they shall say, peace and safety; then sudden destruction comes upon them, as travail upon a woman with child; and they shall not escape. But you, brethren, are not in darkness, that the day should overtake you as a thief. You are all children of the light, and the children of the

> day: We are not of the night, nor of the darkness. Therefore, let us not sleep, as do others; but let us watch and be sober.
> 1 Thessalonians 5:1-6

Our world is heading toward the birth, yet the masses are asleep, unaware of the impending labor. But we can and should be awake, mindful of the times and the seasons. We should live life understanding that our "Hope" could come back on any day.

In Luke's gospel account, Jesus also likens the time around His return, i.e., the days we are living in now, to the days of Lot. Let's listen:

> Likewise, also as it was in the days of Lot; they did eat, they drank, they bought, they sold, they planted, they builded: But the same day that Lot went out of Sodom it rained fire and brimstone from heaven, and destroyed them all. Even thus shall it be in the day when the Son of man is revealed.
> Luke 17:28-30

It was business as usual in the day of Lot. They were busy, full, and growing. Just as in our day. Of course, when we think of Sodom, celebrated sexual aberration first comes to mind. Again, in our time today, the alternative lifestyle is elevated greatly. The act of sodomy is no longer taboo, only calling it sodomy is. It's now sanitized, re-labeled, and propagated as acceptable, if not desired. At no time prior has this been the case. In the past, sodomy was hidden and not out in the open as it is in our day and as it was in the days of Lot.

Ezekiel gives us additional insight into the days of Lot, which is helpful in our comparison to our times now.

> Behold, this was the iniquity of thy sister Sodom, pride, fullness of bread, and abundance of idleness was in her and in her daughters, neither did she strengthen the hand of the poor and needy. And they were haughty, and committed abomination before me: Therefore, I took them away as I saw good.
> Ezekiel 16:49-50

Pride, abundance, trivial pursuits, and lack of compassion, in addition to the abomination in God's eyes that we associate with Sodom, were the hallmark of the days of Lot. Indeed, this is what we also see in much of the world today. Business as usual, rights of the individual over the group, abundance of material possessions, food, and free time with a noticeable blind spot toward the poor and needy of our world.

So, we see that, just as in the days of Noah, the days of Lot resemble our day like no time before!

Notice also, in both accounts Jesus uses to illustrate His near return, that immediately after the subjects were rescued (Noah and Lot), judgment fell. That is, the Flood began when Noah and his family entered the ark and the fire and brimstone fell immediately after Lot, his wife and daughters, left the city. In like manner, we will see the departure of God's people in our day today immediately before the judgment of the tribulation proceeding forth. That is, Jesus will next tell of the rescue of His own before allowing tribulation, before letting the final judgment begin. Paul has echoed this paradigm in preaching that believers are saved from the wrath to come (1 Thessalonians 1:10, Romans 5:9).

So, pay attention! For the Prophet is now about to give the last event of the pre-tribulation era (our day today) and the signal to the start of Jacob's Trouble with His following words to the disciples. These are words to which we may want to attend, for they are speaking of the next event on the prophetic clock!

> Then shall two be in the field; the one shall be taken, and the other left. Two women shall be grinding at the mill; the one shall be taken, and the other left.
> Matthew 24:40-41

The word "taken" is used three times in association with the Lord calling His people unto himself (Matthew 1:20, Matthew 17:1, and John 14:3). This verse is speaking of the Rapture of the church, the departure of believers before the day of wrath, just as occurred with Noah and Lot. Paul described these words of Jesus with his own amplified preaching.

> But I would not have you ignorant, brethren, concerning them which are asleep (*those who have died believing in Christ*), that you sorrow not, even as others which have no hope (*who don't understand that death is not the end*). For if we believe that Jesus died and rose again, even so them also which sleep (*have died*) in Jesus will God bring with Him. For this we say unto you by the word of the Lord, that we which are alive and remain unto the coming of the Lord, shall not prevent (*proceed*) them which are asleep (*have died*). For the Lord himself shall descend from heaven with

> a shout, with the voice of the archangel, and with the trump of God: And the dead in Christ shall rise first. Then we which are alive and remain shall be caught up (*Raptuso in Latin*) together with them in the clouds, to meet the Lord in the air: And so, shall we ever be with the Lord.
> 1 Thessalonians 4:13-17 (italics added for clarity)

> Behold, I show you a mystery (*something which had not been previously revealed*): We shall not all sleep (*die*), but we shall all be changed. In a moment, in the twinkling of an eye, at the last trump: For the trumpet shall sound, and the dead shall be raised incorruptible, and we shall be changed. For this corruptible must put on incorruption, and this mortal must put on immortality.
> 1 Corinthians 15:51-53 (italics added for clarity)

Simultaneously with our ascent to meet the Lord, we shall be changed from mortal men and women to immortal beings ready to live on into eternity with our Lord. Oh, happy day that will be!

Most importantly, don't sleepwalk through life. The clock is approaching midnight!

> Watch therefore: For you know not what hour your Lord does come. But know this, that if the goodman of the house had known what watch (*what time of night*) the thief would come, he would have watched, and would not have suf-

> fered his house to be broken up. Therefore, be you also ready: For in such an hour as you think not the Son of man comes.
> Matthew 24:42-44 (italics added for clarity)

The word from our Lord is that we are to be watching, we are to be awake. We don't want to be taken by surprise!

And while we are watching and waiting, we are to be working. Going about the King's business as we patiently watch for him.

> Who then is a faithful and wise servant, whom the Lord had made ruler over His household, to give them meat in due season? Blessed is that servant, whom the Lord when He comes shall find so doing. Truly I say unto you, that He shall make him ruler over all His goods.
> Matthew 24:45-47

Do you want to be great in the Kingdom of God? Then finish strong. Run through the tape! I want to be watching and working as I wait, for I don't know the day or the hour but it is clear what season in which we are living. The day of the Lord is at hand!

Now, in finishing Jesus' answer to His disciples concerning the sign of His return, the Master includes some important additional details that mark the time leading up to the end in Luke's account of this same question.

> And when you shall see Jerusalem compassed with armies, then know that the desolation thereof is nigh. Then let them which are in Judea flee to the mountains; and let them

> which are in the midst of it depart out; and let not them that are in the countries enter thereinto. For these be the days of vengeance, that all things which are written may be fulfilled. But woe to them that are with child, and to them that give suck, in those days! For there shall be great distress in the land, and wrath upon this people. And they shall fall by the edge of the sword, and shall be led away captive into all nations:
> Luke 21:20-24a

The Jews were told in Matthew's rendering that, when they see the abomination of desolation, they need to escape. But we must note that, though these instructions are the same, to run, to get away, the setting is vastly different. Luke is talking about something that has already occurred to us, the fall of Jerusalem in 70 AD, while Jesus in Matthew's gospel is speaking of escaping from the city when they see the abomination of desolation, an event which is still in the future to us. But in Jesus' next words, He gives another prophecy that would be, and has been, fulfilled before the day of His return.

> And Jerusalem shall be trodden down of the Gentiles, until the Times of the Gentiles be fulfilled.
> Luke 21:24b

In June of 1967, this prophecy was fulfilled! In 586 BC, the Jews lost Jerusalem to the Babylonians and never regained control of the city until that fateful day when General Moshe Dayan and the Israeli freedom fighters took control of the Old City. On that day, the Times of the Gentiles were fulfilled. We are living in a day when all of the prophecies the Lord gave to His disciples telling of His return have been fulfilled. We are in overtime! We are past the due date! Again, I'm pleading with you...Look up, His coming is nigh!

Summary:

1. The "Rapture" of the Church will occur before the onset of the Tribulation, just as Noah and Lot were "taken" out of harm's way before judgment fell in their stories.
2. Paul tells us in 1 Thessalonians 5 that we believers do not need to be caught off guard as concerning the return of the Lord.
3. The Rapture of the Church is the next event on the prophetic clock in our day today!
4. The Lord desires that His followers be watching and working as we wait for His return. (See Matthew 24:42-47.)
5. The Times of the Gentiles were fulfilled on June 7, 1967.

For Further Study:

1. What happened in June of 1967?
2. Do you believe that the Flood of Noah actually occurred? Did Jesus believe it happened? What about Sodom and Gomorrah? Jonah and the whale?
3. What are the four signs from Genesis 6 that liken our days to the days of Noah?
4. What are the five signs from Ezekiel's prophecy that liken our day to the days of Lot?
5. What does "finishing strong" look like to you?
6. What are the four fulfilled prophecies of Jesus that lead us to conclude we are in the Last Days?

The Last Days: The Third Day

We understand that Jesus has given us four signs from the gospels that reveal we are in the very last days. First, the fig tree has budded; second, the Times of the Gentiles have been fulfilled; third and fourth, we are living in days like Noah's and days resembling Lot's.

In addition, the Bible has four other prophecies, spoken to us by other spirit-filled men, that also tell us we are in the last days. We have already articulated Isaiah's inspired words telling us that Zion would be born in one day, that day occurring on March 14, 1948. If Jesus' and Isaiah's words were not enough, let's listen to Ezekiel, Hosea, and David.

> The hand of the Lord was upon me, and carried me out in the spirit of the Lord, and set me down in the midst of the valley which was full of bones...and, lo, they were very dry. And He said to me, Son of man, can these bones live? (*Come back to life?*). And I answered, O Lord, only you know. Again He said to me, prophesy upon these bones, and say unto them, O you dry bones, hear the word of the Lord. Thus saith the Lord God unto these bones: Behold I

> will cause breath (*the Spirit*) to enter into you, and you shall live: And I will lay muscle upon you, and will bring up flesh upon you, and cover you with skin, and put breath (*the Spirit*) in you, and you shall live; and you shall know that I am the Lord. So, I prophesied as I was commanded: And as I prophesied, there was a noise, and behold a shaking, and the bones came together, bone to his bone. And when I beheld, lo, the muscle and the flesh came upon them, and the skin covered them above: But there was no breath in them.
> Ezekiel 37:1-8 (italics added for clarity)

This prophecy is exactly where we are living today! Ezekiel, we will see in a couple of verses, was speaking of the nation of Israel. He was told by God to go out to a valley full of dead men's bones and was asked by God if he believed that the Restorer of All Things could bring these bones back to life. The prophet rightly deferred, saying only the Almighty would know such a thing. To that, God told Ezekiel to prophesy to the bones and they would come together in form and receive breath and live. Ezekiel did that and the bones came together, bone in bone, with muscle, flesh, and skin appearing. But as we read, Ezekiel noted that there was still no life in the re-formed body.

On March 14, 1948, the first part of this prophecy was fulfilled. There was a great noise and shaking (the Holocaust) which resulted in the bones coming together and taking the nature of a body. But, as the prophecy proclaims, the body had a form but there was still no breath. Now we understand that Bible interprets itself. When breath is used, God is speaking of His Spirit. The Spirit of God is not yet upon Israel as I write these words in

2021. Israel is a secular nation that does not recognize Jesus as its King.

But that is about to change.

> Then He said to me, prophecy unto the wind, prophecy, Son of man, and say to the wind, thus saith the Lord God; come from the four winds, O breath, and breathe upon these slain, that they may live. So I prophesied as He commanded me, and breath came into them, and they lived, and stood up upon their feet, an exceeding great army. Then He said unto me, Son of man, these bones are the whole house of Israel.
> Ezekiel 37:9-11

Ezekiel prophesied a second time, which has yet to occur, and Israel will come back to life spiritually. In reading on into the next chapter of Ezekiel's revelation, it would appear that the time of this revival will occur after God rescues the nation from a northern invader (Russia and her allies), causing the Jews to believe in the one true God and ultimately to call upon Jesus as Savior. Folks, we are living in the space between Verses 8 and 9. Israel has had a form since 1948 but the Spirit has not yet come upon her, giving her spiritual life. This will happen soon and is yet another proof that we are living in the last days. Indeed, this prophecy runs parallel with Jesus' Parable of the Fig Tree. The bones have come together just as the fig tree has budded but there is no breath in the bones today just as the fig tree in our day is yet to produce summer fruit. But summer is coming, the bones will receive life and the fig tree will bring forth fruit, in a day, not very far away!

Next, our sixth proof that we are living in the last days comes from the voice of Jesus as spoken by Hosea.

> I will go and return to my place, until they acknowledge their offense, and seek my face:
> In their affliction they will seek me early.
> Hosea 5:15

Jesus is speaking, saying to the Jews that He will reluctantly withdraw Himself from them until they realize their need for Him. This is prophecy, certainly, but it also applies to our personal lives. If we go our selfish way, God sometimes will back off and allow us to wallow in our stupidity until we come to our senses. Now, the prophecy here states that in their "affliction" they will seek Him early. That is, early in the tribulation time frame, early in the time of Jacob's Trouble (Jeremiah 30:1-7), they will call out to Jesus and He will answer. I remind you of the words Jesus boldly proclaimed to the Jews during the week of His murder. "You will not see me again until you say, blessed is He who comes in the name of the Lord" (Luke 13:35).

> Come and let us return unto the Lord: For He hath torn, and He will heal us; He hath smitten, and He will bind us up.
> Hosea 6:1

This very next verse is the prophetic response of the Jews to the Lord's departure when they finally come to their senses and see their need for Him. "Let's return to him. We have been torn and smitten for the past two thousand years. Now is the time for us to be healed, for our wounds to be bound up."

When will this be?

> After two days will He revive us: In the third day He will raise us up, and we shall live in His sight.
> Hosea 6:2

Once again, the Bible interprets itself. A day in God's economy is equal to one thousand years and one thousand years is equivalent to one day (Psalm 90:4, 2 Peter 3:8).

Two days ago, Jesus left and returned to His place. Then, nineteen hundred years later, Israel came back to their land in 1948. But we understand that they are not yet revived. They are still secular and not followers of Jesus, but their revival will happen soon. After two days (two thousand years), they will seek His face. Interestingly to me, a year in Jewish reckoning is three hundred and sixty days, not three hundred and sixty-five. Thus, doing the math, if we take two thousand years and subtract five days from each of those years, we lose ten thousand days or approximately twenty-seven years. Dear reader, Jesus died and ascended to Heaven around 30 AD. If we move forward nineteen hundred and seventy-three years instead of two thousand years, we come to 2003 AD. Thus, to me, we are no longer in the second day of this prophecy. We are after the second day and the Jewish revival can come at any time! In addition, we see that He will raise them up on the third day. We are on the third day! The third day is the time of the return of Christ and includes the thousand-year time frame that the Book of Revelation calls the Millennium. Now, if the thousand-year reign of Jesus begins on the third day, it would seem that Jesus will make His appearance early on that third day. Again, look up...we are early in the third day!

Our last proof of the veracity that today we are living in the last generation comes from the words of David, the sweet psalmist of Israel.

Psalm 102 is a prophetic song that sings of the difficulties of the last two thousand years of Jewish history as well as telling us of their revival and of when the return of the Lord will be. Let's listen:

> Hear my prayer, O Lord, and let my cry come unto thee...
>
> For my days are consumed like smoke, and my bones are burned as a hearth. (*The Holocaust*) My heart is smitten, and withered like grass; so that I forgot to eat my bread. By reason of the voice of my groaning my bones cleave to my skin. I am like a pelican in the wilderness: I am like an owl of the desert. I watch, and am as a sparrow alone upon the house top. (*These three birds do not live in the wilderness, the desert or the house top; things are out of sort.*). My enemies reproach me all the day; and they that are mad against me are sworn against me. (*anti-Semitism*). For I have eaten ashes like bread, and mingled my drink with weeping, because of thine indignation and thy wrath: (*As we have seen due to their rejection of Messiah.*). For thou has lifted me up, and cast me down...
>
> But thou, O Lord, shall endure forever; and thy remembrance unto all generations. Thou shall arise and have mercy upon Zion (*Israel*): For the time to favor her, yea, the set time, is come...
>
> When the Lord shall build up Zion, He shall appear in His glory.

Psalm 102:1-16 (excerpts, italics added for clarity)

When the Lord shall build up Zion, He shall appear in His glory! It could not be clearer. The children of Israel were without a homeland until 1948. They were dispersed, persecuted, burned, and discriminated against, as the prophecy speaks. But not so today. Zion is a nuclear nation that is a force to be reckoned with. It is built up and, as we have seen, its increase has been due entirely to the Lord's providence and will. Surely, with Zion built up, Jesus will soon return in His glory!

Okay, I know what you may be thinking. In every generation since Christ's first advent, men and women have felt they were living in final days. What makes you so sure that we are so special?

Obviously, I have already answered why I feel we are so blessed. The words of Jesus and the others make it clear to me that now is the time. But, if I am wrong and the Lord delays His return, that's okay, too! Walking with Christ's return in mind is the way to live. My heart is purified (1 John 3:1-3) and I am happy, blessed, and empowered with the knowledge that everything the Lord has said is coming to pass. It's a good deal! And besides, if I die before His return, well then, I'll meet Him at that time. Either way, it won't be long. The same can be said for you!

Summary:

1. The world today is right in the middle of the Ezekiel 37 "dry bones" prophecy!
2. According to Hosea, Jesus will return early in the third day after the Jews seek His face. We are early on the third day of this prophecy in our world today.

3. David has sung that the Lord will appear in His glory after Zion suffers a period of severe persecution followed by being built up (militarily, economically). Our day today would seem to fulfill this prophecy.

For Further Study:

1. Spiritualizing the Dry Bones Prophecy, are there people in your life who are dry and seemingly without life whom God wants you to speak to? Do you think they too can live?
2. Can you think of any other biblical proofs that speak to the soon return of the Lord which were not mentioned? Hint: See Zephaniah 3:9, Zechariah 12:1-3 and 9, Daniel 12:4.
3. In God's economy, a day is as a thousand years and a thousand years as one day. According to the Word of God, how many days ago did Adam walk the earth?
4. In the Creation account, what did God do on the seventh day? Do you see a pattern here for us to consider in our day today?

Faith

The Father is looking for faith in His children. He desires believers over just followers. If that were not true, then, as we have discussed previously, He would simply reveal Himself to mankind in all of His glory. As we have noted, though, if He did such a thing, faith in and toward Him would not be required or even available. Thus, the Lord keeps Himself veiled to some degree so that those who wish to believe in Him and call Him "Lord" may do so, while those who do not want Him in their lives are also free to make that tragic choice. Indeed, God has given us, in contrast to the rest of the universe, free will. Everything else bows to His Word and His will. Allowing us a degree of independence was the risk He took to have a two-way love relationship with mankind.

The Bible emphasizes faith throughout its pages, both in the Old Testament and the New. In fact, without faith, it is impossible to please God at all (Hebrews 11:6).

So, just what is faith?

> Now faith is the substance of things hoped for,
> the evidence of things not seen.
> Hebrews 11:1

Faith accepts as truth things that are not yet seen. Faith says circumstances will come to pass as God has promised. Thus, the strength of my faith comes from the object of my faith. If I have faith in God, well, that is founded upon the Rock. If I have faith in man, obviously that can let me down. One of the Bible's most famous proverbs speaks to this truth. "Trust in the Lord with all of your heart and lean not upon thine own understanding. In everything acknowledge him and He will direct thy paths" (Proverbs 3:4-5). Additionally, faith in God is rational, not wishful, based on our past experiences with Him. That is, He has done what He said He would, He came to earth the first time, died for our sins, and defeated death. Thus, we can believe that He will do what He says is still to come to pass. That is, to save our souls and come back to earth a second time.

Everyone uses faith all of the time. The chair I'm sitting on, the car I'm driving—I'm exercising faith that they will not fail every time I sit on that seat or operate my automobile. These are fallible examples, thus it should be easy to have faith in God and His Word, two things that are infallible.

Also, when God's Word states that faith is the substance, or reality, of things hoped for, it is not saying, "Oh, I hope what God says will come to pass." Not at all; hope is the absolute expectation that what the Creator says about me will become my experience at a future time. No doubt at all! For when God makes a promise, faith believes it, hope anticipates it, and patience waits for it.

Jesus had much to say about faith in His words to us. And, since the faith of His children pleases God, as mentioned above, we should not be surprised that our Lord delighted when He saw it demonstrated in people whom He encountered.

> And when Jesus entered into Capernaum, there came unto Him a centurion, beseeching Him, and saying, Lord, my servant lieth at

> home sick of the palsy, grievously tormented.
> And Jesus said...
> Matt 8:5-7a

Here we have a high-ranking soldier of the occupying army appealing to a poor Jewish rabbi for help. And it is not help for himself but for his servant. Someone who likely is Jewish but has become attached to the foreign power structure. One might think that Jesus will have nothing to do with this "enemy of the nation" and his traitorous servant. But that is not what happens. Let's listen:

> I will come heal him. The centurion answered and said, Lord, I am not worthy that you should come under my roof: But speak the word only, and my servant shall be healed. For I am a man under authority, having soldiers under me: And I say to this man, go, and he goes; and to another, come, and he comes; and to my servant, do this, and he does it. When Jesus heard this, He marveled...
> Matthew 8:7b-10

You see, the centurion humbled himself greatly. He called Jesus "Lord." He realized he was not dealing with just a poor Jewish Bible teacher but with the Lord! He demonstrated saving faith in his declaration of Jesus' power and authority. Of course, he was able to think abstractly in realizing that the same power he wielded in the physical world in getting his will done was available to Jesus in the spiritual one. Making this connection was what caused our Lord to marvel! For faith sees the unseen world as though it is the true reality. Faith sees what the eyes cannot and is what the Messiah is looking for from all of us.

Let's watch our Lord draw out saving and healing faith in another, one whom we might initially overlook as not being someone the Lord would reach out to:

> Then Jesus went thence, and departed into the coasts of Tyre and Sidon (*modern-day Lebanon and apart from Israel*). And, behold, a woman of Canaan came out of the same coasts, and cried unto Him, saying, have mercy on me O Lord, thou Son of David; my daughter is grievously vexed with a Devil. But He answered her not a word. And His disciples came and besought Him, saying, send her away; for she cries after us.
> Matthew 15:21-23 (italics added)

This is starting to look a little harsh! A poor woman cries to the Lord and all He does is ignore her. But remember, we must always look at the tone of the gospel words. We know that Jesus isn't cruel, so we must go beyond the written word, beyond the "text message," if you will, and see what the Lover of our Souls is up to. In this case, this foreign woman had heard about Jesus, had heard that they called Him the Son of David, but she had no personal experience with Him. Jesus wanted this to change, thus, to get her to go where He wanted her to be, He initially snubbed her.

> But He answered and said, I am not sent but unto the lost sheep of the house of Israel.

> Then came she and worshipped Him, saying,
> Lord, help me.
> Matthew 15:24-25

Jesus responded to her plea for help as well as His disciples' request for relief by giving his "mission statement." He was sent to seek and save the lost, starting with Israel. Not looking good for the woman and her daughter at this point. But the thing that occurred next in the exchange is what our Lord was looking to bring out. She worshipped Him. No longer was she using a prayer formula that she had learned from others. No, she was pleading and crying from her heart. Now she recognized Jesus for who He was. She called him, "Lord." Not only the son of Israel's greatest king but the very King himself.

One more thing for Jesus to bring out, mainly for His disciples (all of us down through the ages) to consider, before healing the woman's daughter.

> But He answered and said, it is not meant to take the children's (*Israel's*) bread, and cast it to the dogs (*puppies, not homeless scavengers; the Gentiles*). And she said, truth, Lord: Yet the dogs (*puppies*) eat the crumbs which fall from their master's table. Then Jesus answered and said unto her, O woman, great is your faith: Be it unto thee even as you will. And her daughter was made whole from that very hour.
> Matthew 15:26-28 (italics added for clarity)

Indeed, Jesus was sent to the lost sheep of the house of Israel but He is showing to us that He was not bound to that calling nor was that going to ultimately be the extent of His mission.

Healing the Canaanite woman's daughter pictures for us in a way that cannot be forgotten that the Gentiles (many of us reading these words) were to be called into the household of faith. We puppies, we Gentiles, get to partake, not only in the crumbs, but now we are enjoying the entire meal! And it is all through faith. No works. Just pressing in and worshipping the Savior. For by grace through faith we are saved, and not of works lest any man boast (Ephesians 2:8-9). It is this kind of faith that caused our King to exclaim, "O, woman, great is your faith." A faith that connects the dots, that once again sees into the invisible world, that realizes crumbs from Jesus will be enough; it is that faith that brings joy to our Lord.

Other times in the gospels, the Teacher develops faith in His listeners by using examples where we might have faith in people who would be unworthy of such respect, yet we offer it anyway. To follow are two parables that contrast fickle men to a gracious Father, to make a point about faith. The first comes immediately after the disciples were taught the Lord's Prayer:

> And He said unto them, which of you shall have a friend, and go unto him at midnight, and say unto him, friend, lend me three loaves: For a friend of mine in his journey is come to me, and I have nothing to set before him? And he from within shall answer and say, trouble me not: The door is now shut, and my children are with me in bed; I cannot rise and give thee. I say unto you, though he will not rise and give him, because he is his friend, yet because of his importunity he will rise and give him as many as he needs.
> Luke 11:5-8

This is a contrast parable in that we have a sleepy and grumpy friend who will meet our request, not out of a magnanimous heart, but to get us out of his hair. The Teacher wants us to see that the Father is not sleepy, grumpy, and just a neighbor. He is alert, kind and our papa! We can expect much much more in that setting. Jesus cements this with His next words:

> And I say unto you, ask, and it shall be given you; seek, and you shall find; knock, and it shall be opened unto you. For every one that asks receives; and he that seeks finds, and to him that knocks it shall be opened. If a son shall ask bread of any of you that is a father, will he give him a stone? Or if he ask a fish, will he for a fish give him a serpent? Or if he shall ask an egg, will he offer him a scorpion? If you then, being evil, know how to give good gifts unto your children: How much more shall your Heavenly Father give the Holy Spirit to them that ask Him?
> Luke 11:9-13

How ridiculous would it be for a human father to give evil gifts upon the request of a son? Likewise, it is far more preposterous that our Heavenly Father will not give us good gifts when we ask. Faith says God is good. It cries that His gifts are good (Psalm 84:11-12).

Next, the second contrast parable:

> And He spoke a parable unto them to this end, that men ought always to pray, and not faint. Saying, there was in a city a judge, which

> feared not God, neither regarded man: And there was a widow in that city; and she came unto him, saying, avenge me of mine adversary. And he would not for a while: But afterward he said within himself, though I fear not God, nor regard man; yet because this widow troubles me, I will avenge her, lest by her continual coming she weary me.
> Luke 18:1-5

Here we have an unjust judge in a court of law who encounters a widow, a stranger to him, and one who is alone. He has no motivation to help her, but notice that, because of her frequent requests, he complies as he grew weary of her entreaties.

The point is, this is not our Father! He is our Dad, not an unjust judge. We are His bride, not a poor widow. We are not alone, we have an Advocate. We are His child, not a stranger, and we don't have to go to a court of law, we can come before the throne of grace! When I look at my requests to the Father in this light, I am sort of embarrassed by my lack of faith!

Jesus confirms my suspicion with His next words:

> And the Lord said, hear what the unjust judge said. And shall not God avenge His own elect, which cry day and night unto him, though He bear long with them? I tell you that He will avenge them speedily.
> Luke: 18:6-8a

We have nothing to fear. Our God is faithful, He does not grow weary, and He is kind.

Yet our Lord ends this contrasting parable with words of warning to His praying followers.

> Nevertheless, when the Son of man comes (*back*), shall He find faith on the earth?
> Luke 18:8b (italics added)

Will the Lord find faith in His children when He returns? As we discussed in our last section dealing with the End Times, will we continue to endure when the birth pangs get closer and more intense? Will we have praying faith? The way to stay strong is to keep our eyes on the Giver, not the gifts. Praying faith is not to get the goods but to enjoy the One who is good. It is not to claim the promises, but to embrace the Person. You see, Satan delights in our fear as God does in our faith. I want to speak words of faith even when I don't see it. I want to walk by faith and not by sight (2 Corinthians 5:7). And I don't want to be afraid of sudden fear. No, fear is not the opposite of faith, it is but an occasion for faith!

Jesus tells us ultimately that we need even to take no thought for our very lives! The Father has everything under control. Just trust, just believe, just have faith.

> And He said to His disciples, therefore I say unto you, take no thought for your life, what you shall eat; neither for your body, what you shall put on. The life is more than meat, and the body is more than raiment. Consider the ravens: For they neither sow nor reap; which neither have storehouse or barns; and God feeds them: How much more are you better than fowls? ...Consider the lilies how they grow, they toil not, they spin not; and yet I say

> to you, that Solomon in all of his glory was not arrayed like one of these...And seek not what you shall eat, or what you shall drink, neither be of a doubtful mind. For all these things do the nations of the world seek after: And your Father knows that you have need of these things.
> Luke 12:22-24, 27, 29-30

Don't worry about things. When I do that, I am just revealing my lack of faith in the God who has everything under control! It is so easy to forget that God "has got this" in our day-to-day lives. Temporary amnesia concerning God's sovereignty is my dilemma so often. Probably yours, too, I suspect.

But unbelief, lack of faith in God, is the thing to fear. Hebrews 4:1 tells us that an entire generation of children could not enter into the Promised Land only because of their collective unbelief in the promises of the Lord. Remember how we started this chapter. It is faith that pleases God. So, it only goes to reason that lack of faith will get the opposite effect.

So, how do we snap out of an unbelief cycle when one gets going?

> Be anxious for nothing; but in everything by prayer and supplication with thanksgiving let your requests be made known unto God.
> Philippians 4:6

Unbelief is toxic if it persists, so when I note it, I want to take that worry to the Father in prayer with thanksgiving. Talking to God and being thankful is the winning combination. In fact, when I, when you, thank God after you receive from Him, that's gratitude. But if you thank Him before you receive the blessing, well, that's faith! And that kind of faith is a key to receiving from the Giver. Let me show you:

> Therefore, I say unto you, whatsoever things you desire, when you pray, believe that you will receive them, and you shall have them.
> Mark 11:24

This promise is outrageous! I'm not saying I totally understand all of the ramifications of this, but Mark 11:24 is certainly something I want to recall when I believe I am praying in the will of God. What a promise!

Back to the children of Israel and how their unbelief kept them from entering into the Land: When we read the story in Numbers, it sounds a lot like cowardice. The ten spies told the people that there were giants in the land. Thus, they freaked out and rebelled against Moses and the Lord. But, really, cowardice is simply the combination of unbelief and selfishness.

Don't forget this equation the next time you find yourself losing heart. The cure for cowardice is to trust God and to foster a sense of duty!

So unbelief is related intimately to fear. And what I tell myself about myself, my self-talk, is directly linked to fear and faith. Fear establishes the limits of my life, the fences of which I will not or cannot cross. Faith breaks those walls! Self-talk is so important. It must be positive and not negative. Be a Tigger and not an Eeyore. Speak words of life to yourself, not of death!

Also, what I fear reveals what I value the most yet trust God the least to have things turn out the way I would like. Will that girl I was infatuated with as a teenager love me back? Will the book I'm writing become a bestseller? Things like this we may desire, yet fear is not the Lord's will. When this occurs, and it often will in our fallen state, I must remember the promise of Romans 8:28, "And we know that all things work together for good to them that love God, to them who are the called according to His purpose." God has a handle on the future that is far above my comprehension and understanding. This promise is critical in beating back the fear of dashed expectations. With God in control, the future may not turn out like I imagine, no it will be better!

So I want to make friends with my problems, trusting God to weave them into a pattern of good. As I have heard my Pastor Levi Lusko teach, the problem is not the problem; it's my perception of the problem that is the problem!

One last thought about fear and faith...The desire to live life risk-free is a form of unbelief! Often, getting close to the Lord and stepping out on a limb in faith go hand-in-hand. Fear keeps that from happening. I must remind myself that "perfect love casts out fear" (1 John 4:18). God is love and He is perfectly lovely. With Him, I want to "go for it." I want to "go all in" as much as possible. That is where the intimacy with Him resides. Again, fear and unbelief keep that from happening.

Next, let's consider how obedience is tied to our faith in God. James, the Lord's half-brother, gives the connection in his famous faith without works teaching. His faith without a response preaching. His faith without obedience epistle.

> What does it profit, my brethren, though a man say he has faith, and has not works? Can faith save him? If a brother or sister be naked, and destitute of daily food, and one of you say unto them, depart in peace, be warmed and filled; notwithstanding you give them not those things which are needful to the body,

> what does it profit? Even so, faith, if it has not works, is dead, being alone. (*In true faith we see action, compassion, and evidence.*) Yes, a man may say, you have faith, and I have works: Show me your faith without your works, and I will show you my faith by my works. You believe that there is one God; you do well: The devils also believe, and tremble. But will you know, O vain man, that faith without works is dead? Was not Abraham our father justified (*proved*) by works, when he offered Isaac his son upon the altar? See you how faith wrought with his works, and by works was faith made perfect? And the scripture was fulfilled which said, Abraham believed God, and it was imputed unto him for righteousness: And he was called the Friend of God. You see then how that by works a man is justified (*proved*), and not by faith only. Likewise, was not Rahab the harlot justified (*proved*) by works, when she had received the messengers, and had sent them out another way? For as the body without the spirit is dead, so faith without works is dead also.
> James 2:14-26 (italics added for clarity)

Two stories from the OT demonstrate the relationship of faith and works, between faith and response, between faith and obedience.

Abraham believed God's promise to him that he would father a child in his old age and we are told he was reckoned as righteous at that point (Genesis 15:1-6). Paul would say he was justified at that point, i.e., made free. Yet Abraham's faith was demonstrated later when he was called to sacrifice the very son God had blessed him with (Genesis 22:1-12). James defines justification slightly differently, saying Abraham was proved free at that later point.

Which one is correct, made free or proved free? I believe both are!

It was his obedience that made him the Father of Faith and one whose great faith has been noted throughout the ages. And it was his obedience that led to many additional blessings from the Father (Genesis 22:15-18). The same thing for us, as we have discussed earlier in talking about the awards banquet in heaven; we too will receive rewards based upon our works, based upon our obedience. No, we are saved by faith in Jesus Christ alone (Ephesians 2:8-9) but our works do follow us, they reveal the changed heart within us. And, as we have seen, will not be forgotten by our Lord!

Rahab confessed that the God of Israel was the true God (Joshua 2:1-11) but her faith was shown in her hiding the spies, much to her great risk. This is what landed her in "the hall of faith" found in Hebrews 11.

You see, the actual measure of my spiritual condition lies in my obedience, not my anointing! I may be a "ten-talent" believer but, if I am repeatedly going my own way, doing my own thing, over following in my Lord's leading, well, that will profit me nothing! Ultimately, little of eternal value will result from my faith-without-works lifestyle. My talents will be squandered due to my lack of obedience.

In contrast, great faith is obedience despite the consequences. It is activated by living in the fear, the respect, the awe of the Lord. When a man or a woman is walking in the fear of the Lord, he or she obeys instantly, even when it is painful, when it doesn't make sense. The fear of the Lord is to tremble at His Word, to willingly obey God even when compromise or disobedience seems to be the better course. It is when I choose His presence over my comfort. When I fear the Lord, I embrace His heart and want His will over my own. Again, the fear of the Lord is not being afraid of him, it is having that "first love" feeling for Him perpetually. It is to be terrified at the thought of being away from Him. And it is modeled by Jesus. When I look at His life, every one of these attributes of the fear of the Lord Jesus displayed in His relationship to His Father.

Ultimately a faith that works is related to love. Out of faith come works of love, loving God, and loving people. And, I remind you that love is a verb, it is a decision, not a feeling. John and Paul teach the same idea as James, only calling the evidence of saving faith love, instead of the possibly confusing term of works.

> But whoso has this world's good, and sees his brother have need, and shuts up his heart of compassion from him, how dwells the love of God in him? My little children, let us not love in word, neither in tongue, but in deed and in truth.
> 1 John 3:17-18

> For in Jesus Christ neither circumcision avails anything, nor uncircumcision; but faith which works by love.
> Galatians 5:6

Lastly, let us make the distinction between saving faith and our ongoing faith as we live out our lives...

Ha, there is no distinction! "As you have therefore received Christ Jesus the Lord, so walk you in Him" (Colossians 2:6). We received Christ by hearing the Word, believing, and then confessing it, that is, acting upon it. Likewise, in my day-to-day life, I hear a word from God, e.g., write a letter to a friend, I believe it is from God, then I act upon it, I write the letter. My walk is simple really. Scripture, prayer, act, then repeat! Scripture, prayer, act, repeat! As I do this, the most important doctrine in all of Paul's epistles is fulfilled.

> For by grace are you saved through faith; and that not of yourselves: It is the gift of God: Not of works, lest any man should boast. For we are His workmanship, created in Christ Jesus unto good works, which God has before ordained that we should walk in them.
> Ephesians 2:8-10

We are saved by faith. It is a gift. If I worked for my salvation, it would no longer be a gift. Thus, there is no room for boasting. No pride, no feeling that it is something I deserve. But the connected truth is that the response to the said gift is a life of good works, a life of active love that God has already set in motion for me to grab hold on to. How cool is that!

In conclusion, to live a life of faith pleases God, causing Him to marvel. It sees into the invisible world and overcomes fear and cowardice. It leads to an "all in" attitude which brings intimacy with him. Said intimacy makes it easy to live in obedience to His leadings as we never want to be apart from him.

Summary:

1. Faith pleases God, accepts as true things that are not yet seen, and is rationally based upon our past experiences with him.
2. The strength of my faith comes from the object of my faith. Faith in God is on solid ground while faith in man can let me down.
3. When God makes a promise, faith believes it, hope anticipates it, and patience waits for it.
4. Fear is not the opposite of faith but an occasion for faith.
5. Fear can establish limits in my life. Faith can break those limits.
6. Thanking God after you receive a blessing is gratitude. Thanking God before you receive a blessing is faith. According to Mark 11:24, this type of faith opens the floodgates of your prayer life.
7. Cowardice is the combination of unbelief and selfishness coming together. Trusting God and fostering a sense of duty is the antidote.
8. We are saved by faith, yet our works do follow us and are the response, are the evidence of our faith.
9. Great faith is obedient to God's leading and is the true measure of my spiritual condition, not my anointing, which are only the gifts He has given me by His grace.
10. There is no difference between saving faith and life living faith. Both hear the Word, believe it, and then act upon that Word.

For Further Study:

1. What would your life look like if you really believed Luke 11:9, in which Jesus said to ask, seek, and knock and you will receive, find, and have opened?

2. Which is correct? To pray with specificity or to pray, "Thy will be done?" Can they both be true?
3. How does remembering God is in control and He is good (Romans 8:28), overcome one's fear of dashed expectations?
4. In your walk with the Lord, what do you lose when praying for a risk-free life?
5. Regarding faith and works, are these statements true or false? "It doesn't matter what I do" and "It only matters what I do."
6. How do the fear, the respect, the awe of the Lord activate faith?
7. James calls the evidence of my faith "works." What do Paul and John in their epistles call that same evidence?

Forgiveness and Reconciliation

Jesus had much to say about the importance and beauty of forgiveness. We will see in a moment that He parabolically teaches that we have been infinitely forgiven by the Father and therefore we are expected to forgive one another. He also made the connection that, as we forgive, we lose bitterness and set the stage for both healing and reconciliation.

You may recall that we discussed forgiveness in Chapter 4 of this book when we considered the Lord's Prayer. We learned that to forgive means to release a debt. In contrast, Jesus taught that, if we cannot forgive men their trespasses, our trespasses will also not be forgiven by the Father and will continue to bother us as we live our lives. The importance of burying the hatchet was emphasized. But we made the distinction that forgiveness was not the path to salvation, clearly, that being our faith in Christ, but the ability to forgive does place us on the road to freedom in this life! We also commented that forgiveness is so beautiful because it does not demand any action by the debtor, only the one doing the forgiving. There is no requirement for the trespasser to apologize for forgiveness to occur. But, of course, if the wrongdoer does ask for pardon, then the stage is set for reconciliation. Lastly, we saw that forgiveness is not the same as forgetting. We noted that forgetting might even be considered foolish if, after releasing a person who has wronged us without that person seeking restitution, we go ahead and forget the injustice. That just sets the stage for the same abuse to again occur. No, forgiveness is not the same as forgetting. Only God can do that! (Psalm 103:12)

In this chapter, I would like to discuss two parables that Jesus shared. The first one illustrates the importance of forgiveness. We will note, as with faith and works from our last chapter, that there is tension between salvation and the ability to forgive our neighbor. That is, Jesus will clarify for us that forgiveness is actually a proof, another evidence of the changed heart of the saved soul. Again, forgiveness is not the requirement for salvation, but the confirmation. The second parable will give much insight into the pathway to reconciliation with our neighbor as well as explain the different ways the Lord works to reconcile men and women unto himself.

Forgiveness and the Unforgiving Servant:

> Then came Peter to him, and said, Lord, how often shall my brother sin against me, and I forgive him? Until seven times?
> Matthew 18:21

The Law stated that a man was to forgive his brother three times before disassociating with him. This question of Peter's came on the coattails of the discussion Jesus had with His disciples on who would be the greatest in the Kingdom of Heaven. Peter, after learning it is the one who becomes as a child, must have thought he was being pretty magnanimous by suggesting he could forgive his brother seven times.

Of course, God is so completely different from us. Look at Jesus' response: "I say not unto thee, until seven times: But, until seventy times seven" (Matthew 18:22). In the realm of forgiveness, four hundred and ninety times would be an uncountable, an unattainable number. That's the idea. We are to forgive our neighbor and then keep forgiving. This is so counter to the world's way. God would have it be mercy over judgment. The world we live in is just the opposite. Judgment over mercy is the default setting. This worldview often spills over to us Christians. We are pretty good at recognizing that we have been forgiven; the problem is that we forget that others are too! As has been said, my job is to love and leave the judging to God. Often, I get this mixed up and do the judging and leave the loving to God! In fact, to the extent that I am judgmental and legalistic is the degree that I am loveless. Better to be magnanimous and whimsical. This is such a better way to live than one who is self-wired to be critical and harsh. Solomon locks in this truth with these beautiful words found in Proverbs 19:11, "The discretion of a man defers his anger; and it is his glory to pass over a transgression."

Jesus emphasizes this truth with the following awesome and equally convicting parable about forgiveness in the Kingdom.

> Therefore, is the kingdom of heaven likened unto a certain king, which would take account of his servants.
> Matthew 18:23

We've talked about this before. Obviously, God is the "certain king." We are the servants. And, as we have seen previously, at the end of the age, the Lord will take account of His servants. We noted that Paul called this the "Bema Seat," also known as the awards banquet. It is the time when the things we did in faith, hope, and love will be acknowledged and will carry forward with us into the Kingdom Age (1 Corinthians 13:13).

> And when he had begun to reckon, one was brought unto him, which owed him ten thousand talents.
> Matthew 18:24

A talent is fifty pounds of gold. Thus, ten thousand talents is half a million pounds of gold! Clearly an incalculable amount and one that no one can pay off. This is all of us. We are the ones brought to Him owing an unpayable amount.

> But forasmuch as he had not to pay, his lord commanded him to be sold, and his wife, and children, and all that he had, and payment to be made.
> Matthew 18:25

This is a type or a picture of Hell, of separation from God, as we have discussed earlier. Not a good spot for men and women at this point in the parable. But things are about to get much better...

> The servant therefore fell down, and worshipped him, saying, Lord...
> Matthew 18:26a

The servant worshipped the king. He called him "Lord." He was saved. He was born from death to life. This point in the parable typifies the new birth! And look what happens...his debt will be completely forgiven as he prays to the king.

> ...have patience with me, and I will pay thee all. (*Not true, but God ignores that little blind*

> *spot, moving on.*) Then the lord of that servant was moved with compassion, and loosed him, and forgave him the debt.
> Matthew 18:26b-27 (italics added)

The most common emotional response seen in the Gospels by Jesus toward others is his profound compassion! This is me; this is you. We have received forgiveness and empathy from our Lord. We no longer owe an impossible debt that can never be repaid. This parable shows the utter folly of a works-based road to Heaven. Being a good person, having good works, can never cover the multitude and debt of sin we have incurred.

If the parable ended here, we could all celebrate and revel in the kindness we have received. But it doesn't; there is a huge warning that all children of God must incorporate into their lives. If we don't, we risk losing everything!

> But the same servant went out, and found one of his fellow servants, which owed him a hundred pence: (*Two days wages; not insignificant, but certainly not a half million pounds of gold.*) And he laid hands on him, and took him by the throat, saying, pay me that you owe. And his fellow servant fell down at his feet, and besought him, saying, have patience with me, and I will repay you all.
> Matthew 18:28-29 (italics added)

This sounds very familiar. Like us, the servants who owed the king an incalculable amount, the second servant, who owed two days' wages, asked for mercy. You can make the argument that this request wasn't even necessary for him to receive forgiveness from the man whom the king had already forgiven, but to his credit, he does indeed beg for patience, knowing that this amount, two days wages, can indeed be paid off in time.

On a tangential note, this portion of the parable shows that nothing we need to forgive others of even comes close to what we've been forgiven of by the Father. Let that sink in for a moment...rape, racism, murder, etc. Are you saying these sins are less serious than what the Lord has delivered me from you may be thinking? Well, yes! God is holy and we are not. In His economy, those sins, as bad as they are to us, are only two days' wages compared to the mountain of debt we have acquired. Every time a man looks at a woman with lust it compares to rape, each time I show partiality it equates to racism, and as often as I am angry without a cause it is equivalent to murder.

Okay, moving on, look at what the unforgiving servant does next. It is not good, and we must learn from his selfish and forgetful mistake.

> And he would not: But went and cast him into prison, till he should pay the debt. So, when his fellow servants saw what was done, they were very sorry, and came and told their lord all that was done.
> Matthew 18:30-31

Not only did the unforgiving servant forget that he had been pardoned greatly, but apparently, he seemed to think that his lord would not learn about his inability to imitate his master in the area of forgiveness and compassion. Of course, this is not the case with our God. He sees all, He doesn't grow faint or weary (Isaiah 40:25-28).

> Then his lord, after that he had called him, said unto him, O thou wicked servant, I forgave thee all that debt, because you asked me: Should not you also have had compassion on your fellow servant, even as I had pity on you? And his lord was angry, and delivered him to the tormentors, till he should pay all that was due him. So likewise, shall my Heavenly Father do also unto you, if you from your heart forgive not your brother.
> Matthew 18:32-35

Lack of forgiveness is tormenting in itself. I need to forgive for myself, more than for the other person in debt to me. Unforgiving people are small, petty, bound, angry, and bitter. These are the characteristics that merciless people end up demonstrating! As Lewis Smedes has famously said, "To forgive is to set a prisoner free and then to discover that the prisoner is you."

On another note, we see that the unforgiving servant was delivered to the tormentors. This is the warning I spoke of earlier! Jesus' statement of being delivered to the tormentors is His way of describing Hell, of telling about separation from the Father. How can this be? For, at the beginning of the parable, which clearly speaks of the Kingdom of Heaven, the servant was forgiven his debt. We would say that he was saved. There are two points of view to explain this. The first explanation is that the servant was not really saved.

As we discussed earlier, the ability to forgive is one of the evidences of our salvation. The inability to forgive may indicate a person who has head knowledge of Jesus but no heart relationship with the Lord. That person misses Heaven by eighteen inches, the distance from the head to the heart! How sad!

The second way of looking at this apparent change of heart by the Father is that the servant was saved but then walked away from his salvation. This one is above my pay grade because I would like to believe that, once a person is saved, he cannot lose his salvation. But that may not be the same as walking away from it! Peter seems to preach in his second epistle that the state of apostasy is worse than the state of ignorance. He appears to say that one can walk away from their salvation and that state is worse than not ever believing at all.

> For if after they have escaped the pollutions of the world through the knowledge of the Lord and Savior Jesus Christ, they are again entangled therein, and overcome, the latter end is worse with them than the beginning. For it had been better for them not to have known the way of righteousness, than, after they had known it, to turn from the holy commandment delivered unto them.
> 2 Peter 2:20-21

This is sobering! But, as we have discussed many times in this book, God is love. We must always read the Bible with that tone in mind. He is not heavy-handed and mean. But love allows for choice. In our case of free will, we may have the choice to walk away from Him. It is His love that cries out in sadness if and when one should do that! But it is His love that allows one to make such a tragic mistake. For, without free will, a love relationship with Him is impossible.

Okay, now back to this important parable for those of us who do not desire to live a life like the unforgiving servant. We see that the response to God's grace is to give grace to others.

And there is a tension to grace. It is as if we have a debt of grace that we owe to others because of what Christ has done for us. The definition of grace is undeserved, unearned favor. Thus, to respond in grace to another can be to love a person when they are undeserving and not expecting it from me. It can be to give acts of service—James would call it works—to people who cannot return the blessing. And, most certainly, it is to forgive others, to release them, even when they are undeserving, just as our Lord did for us (Romans 5:8). Our response to this kind of grace is to continually promote mercy over judgment!

There is also an expiration date on the grace we have received from the Father. That is, it is over when we die. Therefore, we must prioritize our lives accordingly. Choose light over the allure of darkness. There is a gravitational pull in this life from the Devil, the world, and our flesh to trivialize our lives. Don't do it! Keep running and, as in a race, pick up the pace as you see the finish line drawing near!

Bitterness vs Health:

A moment ago, we shared that to forgive is to set a prisoner free, only to find out that the prisoner is me. This is because unforgiveness travels with bitterness. There is hardly anything more toxic to the soul than a bitter heart (Galatians 5:15). That person becomes defined by their dysfunction while the forgiving soul is defined by their deliverance! One of the first Bible verses my former pastor taught his kids was Ephesians 4:32. It is a good one to memorize. "And be ye kind one to another, tenderhearted, forgiving one another, even as God for Christ's sake has forgiven you." This verse is the answer to Verse 31 where Paul preaches to put away all bitterness. Forgiveness is always the way to leave bitterness behind.

In Exodus 15, there is a wonderful Old Testament picture of this principle. The children of Israel had departed Egypt and were in the desert. It was dry and dusty. They were tired and thirsty. Then, all of a sudden, they came to an apparent oasis with a pool full of water for the people and their livestock. Unfortunately, though, the water was bitter, so the people complained against God and Moses for bringing them to such a place. But God was teaching them about bitterness, unbeknownst to them at that time. He told Moses to cast a tree into the pool and the waters would become sweet. In Old Testament typology, the tree is a type of the Cross of Christ, a picture of His sacrifice for us. When we consider the Cross, when we become Cross-eyed, so to speak, bitterness departs. This is the lesson: Never forget what Jesus has done for us. It is health to our souls. Indeed, continuing in Exodus 15, because of this deliverance, God revealed to Moses and Israel, for the first time, another name of His. A name that describes His nature. "Jehovah Raphe," the God who heals. For indeed, remembering what the Lord has done for me brings sweetness to my soul, removes bitterness, and promotes health to my body.

The Good Shepherd, the Lost Coin, and the Prodigal Son:

Along with the way of forgiveness, this chapter is also about reconciliation. Jesus will now teach us from three of His most famous parables that show how God reconciles men and women to Himself as well as giving us a template on how we should reconcile with others. We will see that the three stories are one teaching about forgiveness and reconciliation. I would go so far as to say Luke 15 is the greatest chapter in the Bible illustrating the beauty of these two principles. Let's look at the Good Shepherd, the Lost Coin, and the Prodigal Son.

> Then drew near unto Him all the publicans and sinners for to hear Him. And the Pharisees and the scribes murmured, saying, this man receives sinners, and eats with them.
> Luke 15:1-2

Setting the stage for His great teaching, the Pharisees and the scribes were the legalists of Jesus' day. They were the loveless and judgmental, holier-than-thou leaders who had no interest in reconciling and receiving those not as versed in God's Word. Obviously, their religiosity conflicted head-on with Jesus' mission of seeking and saving the lost. But due to their hypocrisy, Jesus can now unleash this great teaching upon them as a rebuke and on the humble as a directive.

> And He spoke this parable unto them, saying, what man of you, having a hundred sheep, if he loses one of them, does not leave the ninety and nine in the wilderness, and go after that which was lost, until he finds it? And when he has found it, he lays it upon his shoulder, rejoicing. And when he comes home, he calls together his friends and neighbors, saying unto them, rejoice with me; for I have found my sheep which was lost. I say unto you, that likewise joy shall be in heaven over one sinner that repents, more than over ninety and nine just persons, which need no repentance.
> Luke 15:3-7

There is sarcasm in Jesus' words toward the murmurers. He equates them with the ninety-nine who need no repentance.

Of course, this is not true in any man's case but they were not in a frame of mind to accept that basic biblical doctrine (Psalm 14:1-3).

We see that the kingdom mentality has the Good Shepherd going after the lost lamb. This first of the three parables speaks of a blundering believer who foolishly walks into sin. In this case, Jesus, the Second Person of the Trinity, is pictured seeking out the wandering soul. Paul teaches us the same approach for the blundering believer. "If a man be overtaken in a fault, you which are spiritual, restore such a one in the spirit of meekness" (Galatians 6:1). We see Jesus walking with this one who has been separated from the flock. We are to do the same. Go get the sinner who has been foolish and walk with him, reconciling him back into the fellowship of believers. Bring that lamb back to the flock.

> Either what woman having ten pieces of silver (*Her dowry; very valuable to her!*) if she lose one piece, does not light a candle, and sweep the house, and seek diligently until she find it? And when she has found it, she calls her friends and her neighbors together, saying, rejoice with me; for I have found the piece which I had lost. Likewise, I say unto you, there is joy in the presence of the angels of God over one sinner that repents.
> Luke 15:8-10 (italics added)

In this second part of this threefold parable, we have not a foolishly lost lamb being spoken of but a carelessly lost coin. Instead of the blundering believer we see the beguiled brethren! This one is tricked, so to speak, by being inattentive. Also, in this portion of the parable, we see the Holy Spirit pictured by the woman who diligently searches out her house to regain the lost portion of her dowry. For us in reconciling the beguiled brethren, we want to share truth, to talk with him, correct him with right teaching from the Word to bring him back into the fellowship.

So, in the cases of the foolish lamb and the careless woman losing her coin, we who are spiritual are to make the first move to have reconciliation occur. We will see that this is not the case in the Parable of the Prodigal Son. We must hold back, pray for that one, but most critically for reconciliation to occur, we must wait!

> And He said, a certain man had two sons: And the younger of them said to his father, Father, give me the portion of goods that falls to me. And he divided unto them his living. And not many days after the younger son gathered all together, and took his journey into a far country, and there wasted his substance with riotous living. And when he had spent all, there arose a mighty famine in that land; and he began to be in want. and he went and joined himself to a citizen of that country; and he sent him into his fields to feed swine. and he would have filled his belly with the husks that the swine did eat: But no man gave unto him. And when he came to himself, he said, how many hired servants of my father's have bread enough and to spare, and I perish with hunger! I will arise and go to my father, and will say unto him, Father, I have sinned against heaven and before you, and am no more worthy to be called your son: Make me as one of your hired servants. and he arose, and came to his

> father. But when he was yet a great way off, his father saw him, and had compassion, and ran, and fell on his neck, and kissed him. And the son said unto him, Father, I have sinned against heaven, and in your sight, and am no more worthy to be called your son. But the father said to his servants, bring forth the best robe, and put it on him, and put a ring on his hand, and shoes on his feet. And bring hither the fatted calf, and kill it; and let us eat, and be merry: For this my son was dead, and is alive again; he was lost, and is found.
> Luke 15:11-24

In this, one of the most famous of all of Jesus' parables, we see a defiant brother whose sin is that of rebelliousness. In this case, the Father is pictured, completing the Trinity of Son, Holy Spirit, and Father, but here we see that he does not go after his son but patiently and longingly waits for him to return. This advice is crucial for the Church, for parents of adult children, for families, to understand. We must let a rebellious member of our church or a defiant adult child go when they are sucked into the sin of rebelliousness. Pray for that person, that child, for sure, but don't go after them. That will wreck whatever work God will perform in their heart as they realize their sin and stupidity. If your heartstrings lead you to rescue the runaway before God's work is done, the sin problem will remain and you will keep having to do the rescuing (Proverbs 19:19).

A vignette in First and Second Corinthians illustrates this approach well. In Paul's first Epistle to Corinth, there was a man of the congregation living in sin with his mother-in-law. The Corinthians were proud of their liberality and tolerance in allowing this behavior to go on unmentioned in their midst. Paul, in no uncertain terms, told the church to disassociate with the man in the hopes that he would come to his senses concerning this blatant sin. Indeed, that apparently occurred, for in his second epistle Paul told the believers to accept the man back into their fellowship as he had repented and should be exonerated. This is how we must deal with the sin of rebelliousness. It is very hard to do but, oh, so important.

Jude sums up this difference between the foolish and careless versus the rebellious and hardened in his words about evangelism to the lost. "And to some have compassion, making a difference: And others save with fear, pulling them out of the fire" (Jude 22-23). That is, share grace with the broken. "Jesus loves you and died for your sins. Know that the goodness of God leads to repentance," etc. But to the hardened, share the Law. "All (You) have sinned, the wages of sin is death, the plane is going down and you don't have a parachute!" If I don't plow the soil of the defiant brother's heart with tough love, then he will remain like the first category of soil in Jesus' Parable of the Sower and the Seed. That soil, you may remember, was the pathway that was compacted down by foot traffic and could not receive the seed.

Notice, also, that all three of these parables have a happy ending. There is great rejoicing! These stories reveal that we can trust the Father, Son, and Holy Spirit to rescue our loved ones. He will go about it differently, depending upon the circumstances, but He will not lose His sheep, His dowry, or His sons (John 17:12). Truly, reconciliation is wonderful and God is faithful.

David sings of pardon and peace with God with these beautiful lyrics:

> Blessed is he whose transgression is forgiven, whose sin is covered. Blessed is the man unto whom the Lord imputes not iniquity.
> Psalm 32:1-2

This song, which was Paul's springboard for his teaching of salvation by faith over works, found in Romans Chapter 4, sings of course, of what the Lord has done for us and pictures what we must do in our interactions with others. Indeed, the ability to forgive is a major doctrine of the Bible and one at which all believers must become very adept.

In conclusion, we have talked much of the fear of the Lord (the respect and the awe of the Lord) in this book. And again, this mindset is in play in the area of forgiveness and reconciliation, for the fear of the Lord, combined with the decision to love God and others, is the one-two punch for a successful life. But there is a difference to understand between selfless love, described in 1 Corinthians 13, and the fear of the Lord. That is, love is a verb, it is a decision, not a feeling, while the fear of the Lord is an actual mindset, it is a paradigm. Thus, the fear of the Lord is not as vulnerable to attacks from Hell as our fickle feelings can be. The fear of the Lord causes men to depart from evil (Proverbs 16:6) and thereby enables us to live holier than when we are just walking in the decision to love God and people.

Why is this important? We talked about the possibility of walking away from our salvation earlier. As far as I can tell, there are two ways believers can accomplish this terrible outcome for their lives. First, persistent unrepented sin (1 Corinthians 6:9-10) and, second, persistent bitterness and unforgiveness. But there are three ways to protect against this possibility. They include living in the fear of the Lord, realizing the price He paid to deliver us and looking for His return. Living in these three things will keep you in the center of His heart.

Lastly, there is a circle involving the fear of the Lord and forgiveness which leads to beautiful intimacy with our God. Let me show you: The fear of the Lord leads to repentance (Proverbs 16:6), which leads to the ability to forgive (as we learned what the Lord did for us, we want to forgive others as the parable of the unforgiving servant teaches). He who is forgiven much loves much (Luke 7:47). And this love we have for God leads to much intimacy with him. All of which results from our worldview of living in the fear of the Lord.

So, in coming full circle, the God who is Love has forgiven and reconciled the entire world. But reconciliation is a two-way street. Love does not force itself. Forgiveness implies reconciliation, but both parties must act for it to occur. Salvation works the same way! It is not the nature of love to force a relationship; but its nature is to open the way.

Summary:

1. Forgiveness is most beautiful. It drives away bitterness and sets the stage for both healing and possible reconciliation.
2. The ability to forgive others is another evidence, like a life filled with good works, of the changed heart of the saved soul.
3. The Parable of the Unforgiving Servant shows that a "works-based" theology is utterly ridiculous in obtaining salvation.
4. That same parable teaches that any sin we may forgive another of is two days' wages compared to the mountain of debt we have incurred and been forgiven of by God.

5. The Parable of the Unforgiving Servant implies that the response to God's grace is to give grace to others.
6. Bitterness is toxic to the soul and hurts the bitter person, not the one who is the cause of those feelings.
7. The Parables of the Good Shepherd, the Lost Coin, and the Prodigal Son reveal three different ways a believer can backslide...foolishness, carelessness, and rebelliousness.
8. The Parables of the Good Shepherd and the Lost Coin show us to imitate God and go after the blundering believer and the beguiled brethren. Walk with them and share truth in love and meekness.
9. God is love. It is not in His nature to force a relationship with men and women. But it is in His nature to open the way!

For Further Study:

1. How is forgiveness different from reconciliation?
2. According to Proverbs 19:11, what does God consider glorious?
3. What is the most common emotional response of Jesus toward others who come to Him in humility?
4. Do you feel that every person who has wronged you is worthy of forgiveness? Would / should God forgive Adolph Hitler if he had asked for it in true repentance? How does that make you feel?
5. Can a person know much about the Lord and the Bible and not be saved? Can a saved person lose his salvation? Can she walk away from it?
6. What is grace? How can you extend it to others?

7. What often happens in the heart of a person that you treat with love who is undeserving and unexpecting it from you?
8. What does the story in Exodus 15 teach about bitterness?
9. According to the Parable of the Prodigal Son, what is the best way to reconcile with a rebellious adult? Does the Bible suggest using that method for a young child? Hint: See Proverbs 19:18, 22:6&15, 23:13-14, and 29:15.
10. According to Jude, what is the best way to share the truth with the broken? To the hardened?
11. How is living in the fear of the Lord different than the desire to walk in love toward God and others?

Servanthood

We are saved and destined for heaven by grace alone through faith alone. But, as we have talked much about in this book, there is tension, there is a tie, there is a yin and yang between faith and works, between faith and the ability to forgive, between faith and the desire to live holy. Such is the case with service and servanthood. Jesus had much to say about the heart of a servant and, of course, He demonstrated that to the Nth degree with His death on the Cross to blot out the sins of mankind.

So, let's dive into Jesus' words concerning servanthood. Along with the Parables of the Sower and the Seed and The Prodigal Son, the Parable of the Good Samaritan is one of the most famous of all of Jesus' teachings. I dare say that most people of Western civilization have heard of the term if not the story itself. The Good Samaritan has leaped out of the bounds of Christianity and is part of the world's consciousness. In this chapter, let's see what it means. Everyone can relate to it. We all want to make a difference. We all see ourselves as the Good Samaritan! Spoiler alert; that is not what Jesus was talking about! Hopefully, by the time we come to the end of the parable, we will see that nothing could be further from the truth. We are not the Good Samaritan! This parable is not about what we should do; oh, that may be a secondary meaning, but it is really about what He did!

Yes, we are in this story, but we are not the heroes. Jesus is the Good Samaritan. We are, at first, the victim taken out by robbers and near death when Jesus rescues us, later we are the innkeepers whom Jesus partners with to help other near-death prey recover while He is away.

The Good Samaritan

> And, behold, a certain lawyer stood up, and tempted him, saying, Master, what shall I do to inherit eternal life? He said unto him, what is written in the law? How do you read it?
> Luke 10:25-26

Jesus perceived what the lawyer was up to, thus He answered the question with a question to see where the lawyer was setting his trap.

> And he (*the lawyer*) answering said, thou shall love the Lord thy God with all thy heart, and with all thy soul, and with all thy strength, and with all thy mind; and thy neighbor as thyself.
> Luke 10:27 (italics added)

Not bad! The pharisaical lawyer quoted from the Torah (Deuteronomy 6:5 and Leviticus 19:18) in what Jesus taught at another time as the two greatest commandments of the Law, love God and love your neighbor. Thus far, Jesus still didn't know entirely where the religious leader was going with his question. That was about to change:

> And He (*Jesus*) said to him, you have answered right: This do, and you shall live. But he (*the lawyer*), wanting to justify himself, said unto Jesus, and who is my neighbor?
> Luke 10:28-29 (italics added)

There it is! The lawyer wanted to prove that it was possible for him to obey the entire Law. In effect, he was saying he had no sin and thus didn't need the message of repentance that both Jesus and John the Baptist were preaching as needful and necessary. But he had a little problem. When Jesus said, "Good, now go do that, love God and everyone else," the lawyer realized he had a dilemma. That is, he didn't love everyone else. Only certain people who were like himself. Like many in our day today, he was a racist! So, he sought to justify himself by asking his second question, "Who is my neighbor?" He couldn't meet the Law's demands so he tried to change the definition.

This time, Jesus doesn't answer the question with a question. No, this time He spoke the great parable we know as the Good Samaritan. It's comical really. Jesus uses a Samaritan, someone hated by the Jews, yet obviously full of goodness as seen in the story, to show the lawyer and everyone else who has ever justified themselves, that we are not as good as we think we are.

> And Jesus answering said, a certain man went down from Jerusalem to Jericho, and fell among thieves, which stripped him of his raiment, and wounded him, and departed, leaving him half-dead. And by chance there came down a certain priest that way: And when he saw him, he passed on the other side. And likewise, a Levite, when he was at the place,

> came and looked upon him, and passed by on the other side.
> Luke 10:30-32

The road from Jerusalem to Jericho was also called the "valley of the shadow of death." It is a fifteen-mile downhill walk through a narrow dry-creek gorge in the bleak Judean desert. Robbers and thieves would notoriously lie in wait and plunder unsuspecting travelers. Thus, people would travel this road in groups, and only in a dire emergency would a person dare travel the road unaccompanied. You see, in this parable, we all are the man who fell among the thieves. Before Christ came into our lives, we too were traveling the dangerous roads of this planet on our own. And Satan and his hordes were lying in wait for us. At a certain point, we were all taken out by sin and stupidity. We were half dead, lying on the side of the road without hope, without help. The priest and the Levite are the philosophies and religions of the world, based upon good works and good ideals which ultimately will not save in the day of disaster. On another level, the priest and the Levite feared for their own lives. Surely, they felt a trap was being laid by the thieves which would entangle them next. You've been there, I've been there. Scams and fake news everywhere. What are we to believe? So we disengage. But not so with the hated Samaritan. And not so with our Lord.

> But a certain Samaritan, as he journeyed, came where he was: And when he saw him, he had compassion on him. And went to him, and bound up his wounds, pouring in oil and wine...
> Luke 1033-34a

We saw in the last chapter that Jesus' most common response toward the lost is compassion. Once again, we see that on display. The Savior had empathy for us. He bound up our wounds using oil and wine. In Bible typology, these two liquids nearly always typify the work of the Spirit and of the Cross. We would say that here is where the half-dead man, where we in the story, were saved. Where we went from death to life.

But when I was saved, when you were delivered, we were not the finished product that we will someday be. The parable addresses that next, along with veiling a prophecy about the age we live in for good measure.

> And set him on his own beast, and brought him to an inn, and took care of him. And on the morrow when he departed, he took out two pence (*one day's wage*), and gave them to the host, and said unto him, take care of him; and whatsoever you spend over this, when I come again, I will repay thee.
> Luke 10:34b-35 (italics added)

The inn, of course, is the body of fellow believers. It is the church of Jesus Christ. It should always be the place where the wounded and the bewildered can find refuge. It should be a place where the young in the Lord can be nurtured, grow, and mature. Where they can be kept safe from further successful assaults from thieves and robbers.

Now for the prophecy: The Samaritan departed after giving the innkeeper two pence. In this, we see Jesus departing and giving gifts (the Holy Spirit) to the church while we wait for His return. I see the two pence as two thousand years. You may think that's a stretch, but our Lord could have said three pence, but He didn't. Nonetheless, the Samaritan gave the innkeeper the charge to care for the victim and said he would return. When that day was to occur, he beautifully said that he would repay the innkeeper for whatever he spent over and above what he was initially given. As we have stated several times, this is what we too will experience on that day our Lord returns. The Good Samaritan will repay us for the good works, for the gold, silver, and precious stones (1 Corinthians 3:9-15) we have accumulated in our service to Him.

> Which now of these three, think you was neighbor unto him that fell among the thieves? And he (*the lawyer*) said, he that showed mercy on him. Then said Jesus unto him, go, and do thou likewise.
> Luke 10:36-37 (italics added)

The lawyer couldn't even bring himself to say the name "Samaritan" to Jesus. He could only choke out, "The one who showed mercy." But he was convinced, no doubt. Did he repent? We aren't told. I would like to think that he left and pondered these beautiful words of our Lord, doing an about-face. That's what we did. Not only were we the half-dead victim in this story, but we've all been the racist lawyer at times, too. Jesus' words have penetrated us and I like to think it did that for that lawyer, too!

Now for the application to our lives: Coming full circle, we are saved by grace through faith alone. We don't do good works to get life but doing good works should be a way of life! And we can't save the world, but we don't have to...Jesus already has done that!

But we want to pay attention to the parts that make up life. You see, my agenda for any given day is planning. Yours I suspect, too. But this is not God's outline for my day. He uses distractions and opportunities that crop up to direct us, to nudge us, to what He would have us do. Look at Jesus in the gospels. He would pray and then go with the flow of the day as it occurred. Many times, He would be going in one direction and a need would come up that changed His course, in His case, seamlessly. This is also how it should be for us. I want to let my schedule be determined by the daily distractions and opportunities that come up. Let me repeat that: Distractions and opportunities are God's agenda for me. I'm not saying I can't have a schedule, can't have a plan, but I must be willing to adjust on the fly as things intervene. When I do this, I become an agent of grace, hands and feet of Jesus, able to respond to the needs around me and glorify the Lord in the process.

So how does this happen? By giving distractions our focus. We want to live intentionally in the present instead of just trying to get through the next line item on our schedules. Indeed, a to-do list can be a good servant, but it is a bad master!

But there are three common human responses to unplanned distractions and opportunities of which we must be aware. First, we often have "No" as our default setting. We need to be cognizant of that negative tendency and change our setting to "Yes." Secondly, we often look horizontally. "How will this affect me?" Not the best in God's economy. This is another default setting we need to change. I want to be vertical in my decision making. That is, "Is God in this?" That's the question that I want to go to as a first thought. Lastly, we often decide too quickly when a distraction or opportunity presents itself. The remedy is to count to five, to wait a moment before responding.

Now, all of this good advice is predicated upon not being too busy. When that is the case, our ability to love God and our neighbor is severely stifled by the pressure of the schedule. So, part of the strategy for success is to not book yourself too tightly. That only leads to the other side getting an advantage over you. Stack the odds in your favor by leaving room in your day, every day.

In concluding our discussion of the Good Samaritan, we see three levels to this parable. First, Jesus is the Good Samaritan. He is the one hated by the establishment but who ultimately saves us helpless victims of the Devil when others cannot. He departs for a time but not until He first gives gifts to us to use in helping other victims of the god of this world. And He promises to return in the future with further payment in His hands for the good we have done while He is away. Second, we want to be like the Good Samaritan as much as possible. But third, we are shown that we are not really the Good Samaritan most of the time. Like the hypocritical lawyer, we often justify ourselves and prefer people who are like us over those who are different.

Jesus' Example of Servanthood

> Now before the feast of Passover, when Jesus knew that His hour was come that He should depart out of this world unto the Father, having loved His own which were in the world, He loved them unto the end...He rose from supper, and laid aside His garments; and took a towel, and girded himself. After that He poured water into a bason, and began to wash the disciples' feet, and to wipe them with the towel wherewith He was girded.

John 13:1, 4-5

Jesus stepped away from the feast, laid aside His garments, took the raiment of a Servant, and did the unthinkable, that is, He washed the feet of His men. The greater stooping before the lesser in extreme humility! This section pictures what Christ did in going to the Cross for the salvation of mankind. He left the perpetual feast He shared in Heaven with the Father and the Spirit and laid aside His garment of deity, becoming a human being. If that were not enough, He came not as a rich or famous leader but as an obscure and common man who was willing to serve, paying the ultimate price to rescue others.

> Let this mind be in you, which was also in Christ Jesus: Who, being in the form of God, thought it not robbery to be equal with God: But made himself of no reputation, and took upon Him the form of a servant, and was made in the likeness of men: And being found in the fashion as a man, He humbled himself, and became obedient unto death, even the death of the cross.
> Philippians 2:5-8

Jesus did not have to do any of this! He chose to become a man, to become a servant, to humble himself, and to be obedient. Reflect on these truths...this is so not what we are like naturally. The good news is, with His help through the Spirit it is what we can become!

> After He had washed their feet, and had taken His garments, and was set down again, He said

> unto them, know you what I have done to you? You call me Master and Lord: And you say well; for so I am (*I Am, the name for God*). If I then, your Lord and Master, have washed your feet; you also ought to wash one another's feet. For I have given you an example, that you should do as I have done to you.
> John 13:12-15 (italics added)

This is a huge key in spiritual life. What we observe Jesus do in the Gospels is what we want to emulate. He is the vine and we are the branches (John 15:5), He is our source and strength, He is our inspiration. When we see Jesus loving the poor and down-trodden, giving worth to women and strangers, we want to be inspired to do the same. Of course, we won't do it as well as He does, that's not the point, but we can turn ourselves in the same direction He is going. I don't want to swim against the current of His love and beauty!

> Truly, truly, I say unto you, the servant is not greater than His lord; neither he that is sent greater than He that sent him. If you know these things, happy are you if you do them.
> John 13:16-17

"Happy are you if you DO these things." That one little word "do" is enormous. There is a risk for Christians that, in agreeing with the Word (knowing the Word), we think we are doing it. But doing is an action verb. It takes effort, not just agreement! I can agree with everything Jesus examples and teaches, but if I do none of it, well, that is of no profit!

So, we see that Jesus, the G.O.A.T. (greatest of all time) became the servant. Let's look at some other words of the Teacher to see how greatness and servanthood tie together:

> And He came to Capernaum: And being in the house He asked them, what was it that you disputed among yourselves on the way? But they held their peace: For on the way they had disputed among themselves who should be the greatest. And He sat down, and called the twelve, and said unto them, if any man desire to be first, the same shall be last of all, and servant of all.
> Mark 9:33-35

So many paradoxes in Christian life: Give and you will receive, die and you will live, and here, become last and you will be first. Be we know intuitively that this is true. No one wants to spend much time with a braggart. You know, that one who is ever building himself up at the expense of others. We are attracted to whimsical and humble people, as is the Lord. The Bible teaches "Humble yourself and you will be exalted" (1 Peter 5:6) and "Pride goeth before destruction and a haughty spirit before a fall" (Proverbs 16:18). We understand, when we think about it, that to be great we must stoop down.

Wonderfully, after Jesus spoke this great truth, He expounded upon it with five examples of greatness, five ways to live in the largeness of our Lord's spirit and example.

> And He took a child, and set him in the midst of them: And when He had taken him in His arms,

> He said unto them, whosoever shall receive one of such children in my name, receives me:
> Mark 9:36-37

First, treat all men equally, whether they can help me or not! Not only will I be great if I do that, but look at the promise attached...Jesus interprets this beautiful behavior as doing it unto him!

> And John answered him, saying, Master, we saw one casting out devils in your name, and he follows not us: And we forbade him, because he follows not us. But Jesus said, forbid him not: For there is no man which shall do a miracle in my name, that can lightly speak evil of me. For he that is not against us is on our part. For whosoever shall give you a cup of water to drink in my name, because you belong to Christ, truly I say unto you, he shall not lose his reward.
> Mark 9:38-41

Second, be as magnanimous as possible! Be inclusive, not legalistic and judgmental. In fact, the extent that I am critical and disapproving will be the extent that I am loveless!

> And whosoever shall offend one of these little ones that believe in me, it is better for him that a millstone were hanged about his neck, and he were cast into the sea.
> Mark 9:42

Thirdly, be sensitive to weaker people in the faith. I don't always need to be right. More important, I need to love. Look at Jesus: Talk about the greater tolerating the miscues of the lessor! The disciples, we disciples, are continually putting our feet in our mouths. What does He do? He just keeps loving us. He continues building us up, not tearing us down. This is my task when dealing with the weaker one, the little one in the faith. I want to edify, not cause to stumble.

> And if your hand offend you, cut it off: It is better for you to enter into life maimed, than having two hands to go into hell...And if your foot offend you, cut it off: It is better to you to enter halt into life, than having two feet and be cast into hell...And if your eye offend you, pluck it out: It is better for you to enter into the Kingdom of God with one eye, than having two eyes to be cast into hellfire:
> Mark 9:43, 45, 47

What is this about! Sounds pretty harsh! Cut off your hand and foot and pluck out your eye if they cause you to offend or you will risk hellfire? Yes, exactly! In other words, be radical against my own sin. Deal strongly with the things in my life that separate me from God. Remember, Hell is separation from God. Not where I want to be. Jesus is once again using an extreme statement to get our attention. He is not saying that if our hands, feet, or eyes cause us to sin we will lose our salvation; this goes against so much else in the Word which we have discussed often, concerning the road to life by grace through faith. No, this is an emphatic way of saying to us that we are to be sensitive to others and harsh with ourselves! Often, we naturally gravitate in the other direction. That is, we are tough on others and go easy with ourselves. Jesus is saying just the opposite. To be great, I need to deal with my sin radically.

As I consider this fourth premise of greatness, my prayer is that of the psalmist: "Order my steps in thy word: And let not any iniquity have dominion over me" (Psalm 119:133).

> Have salt in yourselves, and have peace one with another.
> Mark 9:50

Salt is that essential ingredient that preserves and enlivens our food. In the east, as we have discussed previously, it was used as currency in many places. Also, it was part of contractual agreements and peace treaties between people groups. To have salt in ourselves means to live in peace with one another. Jesus, as the Prince of Peace, is saying that greatness lives peaceably one with another.

So, as we observed in Jesus, greatness stoops down. That kind of greatness treats all men equally, is magnanimous and sensitive to people who are weaker. It deals with our own sin radically and it lives at peace with all men.

The Servant's Heart

A moment ago, we heard Jesus proclaim that, if any man desires to be first, He shall be last of all and servant of all. Our fleshly nature hates this, yet, when we think about it for more than a moment, we realize it is, oh, so true. Ultimately, when we run against the wind of truth, we nearly always come to regret it later.

Jesus' Parable of the Wedding Feast brings this point home well. While dining at the home of one of the chief Pharisees Jesus spoke these beautiful words;

> And He put forth a parable to those which were invited, when He noticed how they chose out the chief seats; saying unto them, when you are invited of any man to a wedding, sit not down in the highest seat; lest a more honorable man than you be invited of him. And he that invited you and he come and say to you, give this man your seat; and you begin with shame to take the lowest seat. But when you are invited, go and sit down in the lowest seat; that when he that invited you comes, he may say unto you, friend, go up higher: Then shall you have praise in the presence of them that sit at meat with you. For whosoever exalts himself shall be abased; and he that humbles himself shall be exalted.
> Luke 14:7-11

This is a great key to life. Don't think about myself, don't think about my position, don't think about how others view me. You see, it is not about me. And life is not about how others see me, either. Really, the only important thing is how my Lord perceives me. And because of what He has already done, I can be comforted knowing that I am robed in His righteousness, lacking nothing in His eyes!

So the servant's heart is a humble one. A good working definition of humility I've heard is that a humble person loves people over self, is aware of God nearly all of the time, and trusts God over self for decision making. We see from the Parable of the Wedding Feast that this approach leads to praise from the "Man" while the "me first" attitude brings embarrassment.

What are some other attributes of the servant's heart? For one, you are willing to help others in need. There are nine words that the servant uses frequently. "What do you need and how can I help?" A warning, though... use these words only if you mean it.

Another characteristic of servanthood is that it contains the same ingredients as unconditional love. That is, they both are patient, kind, gentle, unselfish, not thinking evil, not easily provoked, etc. Servanthood is as love on another level because they both involve a choice. "I choose today to lay down my life." Along with that, neither love nor servanthood responds to coercion or manipulation. It's not "have to," but "get to." A quick way to lose any self-respect I have is to let others take advantage of me in that way. Again, partnering with the Spirit gives me direction on when and how to serve.

On that line, though, sometimes God will occasionally test my heart by asking me to serve in ways I am not well suited for. You see, my primary ministry of service will always be according to the gifts and abilities He has given me, but my secondary area is whatever is needed at the moment! The servant recognizes this and is willing to step out in faith as this occurs. An example of something that is always needed is sharing the good news of Jesus Christ to the lost. But some are not well suited to evangelism. No matter, we still need to engage people with content in humility and service. Love without the gospel and the gospel without love—both fall short!

Lastly, in considering the servant's heart, if you are wondering, "Am I being a servant?" The best way to know is this. "How do I respond when people treat me like one?" It's most important not to seek recognition from others when I serve. If I do, that praise will be the sum of it. Rather, the words of Paul hit the mark when he said, "And whatsoever you do, do it heartily, as unto the Lord, and not unto men: Knowing that of the Lord you shall receive the reward of the inheritance: For you serve the Lord Christ" (Colossians 3:23-24).

Discipleship and Servanthood

So we see that servanthood can often be hard. It is optional, involving a choice, and it is exactly what our Lord did in relation with us, motivating us to move in that direction in our daily lives toward others.

And there is a cost. When I say the nine words of service... "What do you need and how can I help?", I need to be ready to respond. I need to do a cost analysis, if you will. Can I pay the price?

Jesus explains this relationship very poignantly with these challenging words:

> And there went great multitudes with him, and He said unto them...
> Luke 14:25

These multitudes had seen His miracles and heard His gracious words and were hungry for more. Jesus understood they were interested and curious but not altogether invested yet. They were believers but not disciples! Therefore, He spoke these words:

> If any man come after me, and hate not his father and his mother, and wife, and children,

> and brethren, and sisters, yea, and his own life also, he cannot be my disciple.
> Luke 14:26

Once again, the Teacher is using the rhetorical device of the extreme statement. He is teaching the New Testament version of the First Commandment, which is, "I am the Lord thy God and you shall no other gods before me" (Exodus 20:2-3). Jesus, rightly equating Himself with the Father, is really stating the obvious. We are to realize who He is and love Him over the seven people groups that tend to often be elevated to the place of idols in our minds and lives.

> And whosoever does not bear his cross, and come after me, cannot be my disciple.
> Luke 14:27

During the time of Roman rule, to bear one's cross was a common idiom that is not understood well in our day. A Roman soldier could come up to any non-Roman and order them to carry a load, up to one mile. (Now we can understand our Lord's statement, found in Matthew 5:41, that when a man bids you go one mile, go two for good measure!) To bear one's cross was the idiom describing this practice. Jesus is saying to bear your cross and follow Him is to embrace His agenda, not your own. It's not talking about flogging or crucifying oneself at all. But it is speaking about counting the cost. He is describing how to go from being just a believer to a disciple.

> For which of you, intending to build a tower, sits not down first, and counts the cost, whether he has sufficient to finish it? Lest haply, after

> he laid the foundation, and is not able to finish it, all that behold it begin to mock him, saying, this man began to build, and was not able to finish.
> Luke 14:28-30

Not counting the cost in life, not taking care of the details can be humiliating. And counting the cost has two facets to it. Number one, "Can I finish what I start? Do I have the resources to do this?" It looks at the cost of doing something. Is the reward of the accomplishment worth the energy expended to get there? In the case of following Jesus, the answer is a resounding "Yes!" Short-term discomfort on one hand vs long-term glory on the other. Sort of a no-brainer! The second component to counting the cost is counting the opportunity cost of not doing something. Am I more concerned with making mistakes or missing opportunities? The opportunity costs of not doing things God calls me to do can be enormous! I miss out on blessings that He would have bestowed upon me! I wonder if, when we are in heaven, we will shed more than a few tears when we learn of the many opportunities we were offered, yet passed upon!

So, it is very important to look at both sides of this equation when deciding to be His disciple or not. That is, with the Spirit's help, do I have what it takes to go for it and what am I going to miss out on if I decide to go through the motions instead of going "all in"?

> Or what king, going to make war against another king, sits not down first, and consults whether he be able with ten thousand to meet him that comes against him with twenty thousand? Or else, while the other is yet a great

> way off, sends an ambassador, and desires conditions of peace. So likewise, whosoever he be of you that forsakes not all that he has, he cannot be my disciple.
> Luke 14:31-33

Discipleship is limited to those who are willing to pay the price. Francis Chan has famously said, "What the world needs is Christians who don't tolerate the complacency of their own lives. It needs sanctified disciples over justified saints." And many of the Bible's promises apply only to disciples living spirit-filled lives. Touchstones like Philippians 4:6-7 or Malachi 3:10-11 seem to necessitate a certain level of commitment to obtain the juice. Thankfully, others still can be obtained by those of us less invested. Promises such as those found in Romans 8:1 and 8:31-39. As an exercise, sometime look at your favorite Bible promises and meditate upon whether they apply to all saints or only to disciples. If conditions are present to obtain the promise, well then, you have your answer!

Later in His ministry, near the time of His death, Jesus was asked if some Greeks who had come up to the feast of Passover could speak to Him and hear from him. They, like us in the West, were curious about Jesus. And, like us in America, they came from a country with a fatalistic philosophy (humanism) and foolish mythology (gods that cannot save). They were seeking more than what the world was offering. They knew there must be something greater. As Solomon has penned, "He has set eternity in our hearts" (Ecclesiastes 3:11).

Let's listen to the Master's response:

> And Jesus answered them, saying, the hour is come, that the Son of man should be glorified.

> Truly, truly, I say unto you, except a kernel of wheat fall to the ground and die, it remains alone: But if it dies (*is buried, is planted in the ground*), it brings forth much fruit.
> John 12:23-24 (italics added for clarity)

Jesus spoke to these Greeks in a way they could understand; that is, science, not scripture. Everything they were looking for, everything in life is about what He was soon going to accomplish. About His death and resurrection. The reason for everything is found at the Cross. The love that held Him up and the power that raised Him up is all I need and was all they needed. To understand Jesus, we must look at His death and resurrection. Before His death, He was alone in power and majesty. He was that kernel of grain in one place, in one time only. But after being planted in the ground, so to speak, He brought forth tremendous fruit. He raised an army of followers, little Christs, Christians spread out throughout the world and over time testifying to His words and His finished work.

> He that loves his life shall lose it; and he that hates his life in this world shall keep it unto life eternal.
> John 12:25

I know I don't need to tell you by now that this is an extreme statement. A secret to life is to die. Die to self, die to my agenda, that is, stop thinking about myself all the time and live for him. Yet another way of our Lord telling us to go "all in."

> If any man serve me, let him follow me; and where I am, there shall also my servant be: If any man serve me, him will my Father honor.
> John 12:26

As we have said, following my Lord can be hard. Toughing it out instead of quitting.

Persecutions and misunderstandings, etc. But guess what: The servant travels wherever Jesus goes. You are never alone. And, along with that, the servant shall be honored by the Father. It's a good deal!

So, we see that servanthood was first modeled by Jesus, the only true Good Samaritan. Wonderfully, after He rescued us from the thieves (Satan and his minions), we get to partner with Him in serving others on the way to eternity. He further demonstrated servanthood in washing the disciple's feet, picturing for us His incarnation as a man and subsequent sacrifice for the sins of the world. He told us, happy are we if we do the same; that is, sacrificially die to self to bring life to others! We understand that the love He demonstrated holds the same attributes as servanthood, being patient, kind, generous, selfless, calm, etc.

He also taught us that true greatness is becoming like a child versus being a self-promoter. Being teachable, dependent, trusting, and humble. It's not desiring distinction or authority and it's not thinking evil of others. Child-like living is being curious and creative. We saw that the great one treats everyone the same, is magnanimous and sensitive to those weaker in the faith. He deals with his own sin radically while going easy on flaws he sees in others and he lives at peace with all men as much as is possible.

We learned that humility is at the heart of the servant's heart! (Pun intended.) We smiled when we considered that the way to know if you are living with a servant's mindset is how you respond when people treat you like a subordinate! Lastly, we considered that discipleship is intimately related to servanthood. That there is a cost involved in going from being a justified believer to a sanctified disciple. But our analysis revealed that the cost of going all in and the opportunity cost of not doing that isn't even close. As a disciple, not only is our debt paid, but we get to live outwardly in the righteousness of God. This makes us very dangerous to Satan and the world. You have Christ in you dear disciples...so go for it, nothing can stop you!

Summary:

1. Jesus is the Good Samaritan. At best, we are the innkeepers who partner with the Lord to help other near-death victims of the Devil recover while He is away.
2. We see from the Parable of the Good Samaritan that all men and women are our neighbors, regardless of whether they are like us or not.
3. We don't do good works to get life, but doing good works should be a way of life! The good news is that there is no pressure. We don't have to save the world. Jesus has already done that!
4. We humans often fail when presented with unplanned distractions because we say "No" too quickly and without thinking.
5. Jesus' example of servanthood, God becoming a man, shows us that no type of service is beneath us!
6. Jesus answered the disciples' dispute about who would be greatest by saying that he that would be first should be servant of all.
7. To be great, according to Jesus, I should be radical in coming against my own sin yet sensitive about the flaws, weaknesses, and sin I see in others.

8. A proud person loves self over others, does not think often of God, nor is in need of His help in decision making. According to the Parable of the Wedding Feast, this worldview leads to embarrassment.
9. Servanthood and unconditional love share the same attributes.
10. Counting the cost of following Jesus can move a believer to a disciple and will result in later blessings, rewards, and glory!
11. According to John 12:26, the servant travels with Jesus and shall be honored by the Father.

For Further Study:

1. When is it a good opportunity to answer a question with a question, as Jesus did?
2. Does fear for your safety and well-being sometimes keep you from imitating the Good Samaritan? You want to do good. How can you come against that?
3. What New Testament promise is pictured by the Good Samaritan giving two pence to the innkeeper to use in the care of the wounded victim while He was away? Hint: See Ephesians 4:7-12.
4. Distractions and opportunities are part of God's daily agenda for you. What changes do you need to make to allow this to occur?
5. Which is better, busyness or slothfulness? I know, that was easy! But can one be too busy?
6. What has Jesus from the Word told you to do which you have to this point left undone? Was there an expiration date to this request? If not, go do it!
7. What heart state do legalism and judgmentalism lead to?

8. Have you ever used the nine words of a servant? How did it turn out?
9. How are you gifted by the Lord? Hint: See Romans 12:6-8. What is your primary ministry of service? Have you ever served in ways in which you are not gifted in well? How did that go?
10. Is the idiom "no good deed goes unpunished" biblical? How do you respond when people treat you as a servant, as a lessor?
11. What is the flaw in this popular preaching phrase: "Witness, witness, witness and, when necessary, use words?"

Israel

Truly God is good to Israel (those governed by God), to those of an upright heart (Psalm 73:1). But as with many things we have discussed in this book, there is a tension between God's goodness and what might be perceived by us as His severity. Jesus had many words of correction and reproof that He gave to the Jews, which, on the surface, may seem harsh and unloving to our little minds. As we have deliberated previously, sometimes the loving thing to do is to be stern and forthright to jolt sinners out of their stupor and error. Such was often the case in the Teacher's dealing with His fellow countrymen. They needed an intervention; they had hardened their hearts and moved away from the one thing that could save them. They lost their faith, forgot the promises given to them, and felt their traditions and works were good enough to satisfy God. Jesus' words to them challenged their preconceptions clearly and directly.

The temptation for us today is to dismiss these directives given to Israel as no longer relevant to our situation. Hopefully, you will feel differently after we consider some of the Lord's words, making applications to them for our lives today.

"Blessed is he, whosoever shall not be offended in me" (Luke 7:23). These words of Jesus were true in His day as well as for us today. You see, God's promises always come true. What God says, IS (Isaiah 46:9-10)! But His thoughts are not our thoughts and His ways are not our ways (Isaiah 55:8-9), His understanding is unsearchable (Isaiah 40:28); we cannot really comprehend His mind and His methods. Thus, we often get confused, we get things wrong. Such was the case with First-Century Israel. They were looking for the Messiah, but they anticipated incorrectly how He would appear. Their scriptures told of a conquering king (Isaiah 2:2-4, 9:6-7 and 11:1-10) and also of a suffering servant (Isaiah 52:13-15 and 53:1-12; Genesis 3:15 and 22:1-14). The latter was dismissed. Their scriptures also clearly spoke of a new covenant (Jeremiah 31:31-34 and Ezekiel 18:31-32) that would replace the first covenant of the Law. This, too, they refused to see. Ultimately, most of Israel was offended by our Lord, suffering a fate that history documents as not being good.

As I look at the Bible as one big storybook, I see that the hinge point between experiencing the goodness of God versus His severity (Romans 11:22) is based upon faith. "Without faith, it is impossible to please God" (Hebrews 11:6). Everyone whose story is positive demonstrates faith that obeys, faith that waits upon the Lord. Conversely, those whose stories have bad endings lack faith and rebel against the Lord. The unsearchable part to me is that some of the rebellious ones are given a second chance while others are not. Satan, Cain, Esau, Saul, Korah, Achan, Ananias, and Sapphira, the world before the Flood...these top the list of the rebellious unforgiven, while Jacob's sons, Aaron, David, Jonah, Paul, and all of us who call Jesus Lord, are walking in His goodness and grace. We have been forgiven! Why is this so? I have no idea! But it sobers me and motivates me to stay in the place of the love of God (Jude 21).

And, before I get too judgmental about the ways of God, I must always remember that the very same Being who is a consuming fire (Hebrews 12:29) was also nailed to a wooden beam for me. He humbled himself and became a man, lived a perfect life, and then died for me, yes, but also died for the sins of the whole world. When I end a sentence about God with a question mark, I need to pivot and end that same sentence with a cross! (+ instead of ?). I need to be Cross-eyed!

With this introduction, let us consider some of the difficult encounters Jesus had with the Jewish leaders (representing the nation of Israel), looking at the prophetic implications as well as applications for us.

The Parable of the Workers in the Vineyard

In Bible typology a vineyard always has an embedded meaning to Israel. Let's see what this parable is saying, both to them and us.

> For the kingdom of heaven is like unto a man that is a householder, which went out early in the morning to hire laborers into his vineyard. And when he had agreed with the laborers for a penny a day (*one full day's wages*), he sent them into the vineyard. And he went out about the third hour, and saw others standing idle in the marketplace, and said unto them; go you also into the vineyard, and whatsoever is right I will give you. And they went their way. Again, he went out about the sixth and ninth hour, and did likewise. And about the eleventh hour he went out, and found others standing idle, and said unto them, why stand you here all day idle? They said unto him, because no man has hired us. He said to them, go you also into the vineyard; and whatsoever is right, that you shall receive. So, when evening was come, the

> lord of the vineyard said unto his steward, call the laborers, and give them their hire, beginning from the last unto the first. And when they came that were hired about the eleventh hour, they received every man a penny. But when the first came, they supposed that they should have received more; and they likewise received a penny. And when they had received it, they murmured against the goodman of the house. Saying, these last have worked but one hour, and you have made them equal with us, which have borne the burden of the heat of the day. But he answered one of them, and said, friend, I do you no wrong: Did you not agree with me for a penny? Take what yours is, and go your way: I will give unto the last, even as unto you. Is it not lawful for me to do what I will with mine own? Is your eye evil, because I am good? So, the last shall be first, and the first last: For many be called, but few chosen.
> Matthew 20:1-16 (italics added)

You may remember, when we discussed this parable earlier, that this story doesn't feel very fair. The workers who labored for the entire twelve-hour workday received exactly the same as the ones who worked less and, in some cases, quite a bit less. Disappointing for the first laborers, but that was the arrangement they had negotiated. That was the point of this story. This parable speaks of God's grace. Grace by definition is not equal. On the contrary, it is capricious and totally up to the pleasure of the one bestowing the unmerited and undeserved favor. It cannot be earned.

You see, the first group of workers was in an entirely different category. They had a contract. The others did not. Thus, the late-comers' reward for their labor was somewhat based upon faith. The householder said, "Whatever is right, you shall receive." Without a specific contract, they were in a position to be joyful when the goodman settled things with them at the end of the day

All of the laborers needed work, just as all need salvation! We Gentiles, who have come to Jehovah at this late time, so to speak, recognize God's deliverance through Christ as a gift. We didn't have a contract, but our Jewish friends did! They were the first group. You see, they had the Law. They had a covenant with our God to follow the Law. If they did, they would be saved without God's grace being needed. That's why this parable pictures the nation of Israel. They are the first, we Gentiles are the last.

This Bible paradox certainly has come to pass as we look at Jewish history over the last two thousand years. We have seen Israel shrink back, as they for the most part rejected Messiah, while the Gentiles, having embraced him, were the blessed group. Jesus is fully alluding to this prophecy in speaking to the Jews in a way that would be hard to forget. "The first (you Jews) will be last, and the last (Gentiles) will be first!"

But what about an application for us personally? It is important not to despise the grace of God when we see it given another, especially if they seem less worthy. Comparison is a trap our Enemy loves for us to use. Don't do it! Be happy when others are blessed out of proportion to their merit. For the same thing happened to you, when you think about it. Jesus saved you from destruction, so, if He didn't do another thing for you, that would be enough.

Let's look at another parable that we have previously discussed, this time from the point of view of what it says to Israel as well as to the Gentiles.

The Prodigal Son's Brother

The main application to the famous Parable of the Prodigal Son is that of forgiveness and reconciliation as well as demonstrating the Father's love for us. We cried as we considered Him running to embrace the repentant son. Everyone loves this story, especially because of the happy ending. But the parable continues. The rebellious younger son had an older brother who is often left out when this story is preached from the pulpit. That's because Jesus' teaching takes a left turn! The older brother is not happy for his sibling. He too is caught up despising the grace of God (the father) given to his brother.

> Then drew near unto Him all the publicans and sinners for to hear Him. And the Pharisees and scribes murmured, saying, this man receives sinners, and eats with them.
> Luke 15:1-2

The parables of the Good Shepherd, the Lost Coin, and the Prodigal Son were given in response to the Jewish leader's exclusion of "sinners" from the Hope of Israel. When we look at the context and setting of Jesus' words, that is, in response to an attack by the religious elite, we can understand the turn the last portion of this three-in-one parable takes.

> ...But when he was a great way off, his father saw him, and had compassion, and ran, and

> fell on his neck, and kissed him...The father said to his servants, bring forth the best robe, and put it on him; and put a ring on his hand, and shoes on his feet: And bring hither the fatted calf, and kill it: And let us eat, and be merry. Now the elder son was in the field (*the land in Bible typology pictures Israel, while the sea typifies the Gentile nations*): And as he came and drew near to the house, he heard music and dancing. And he called one of the servants, and asked what these things meant. and he said unto him, your brother has come, and your father has killed the fatted calf, because he has received him safe and sound. And he was angry, and would not go in:
> Luke 15:20, 22-28a (italics added)

The older son had faithfully followed in his father's footsteps. He worked the land, he tended to expectations placed upon him. He was working for his father's favor and ultimately for his blessing and inheritance. So, from that point of view, it is easy to see why he became upset. We would be too. But that's the problem. It is me, me, me when it comes to that older son. Like his father, he should have been glad for his brother, but his jealousy won out over any empathy that he could have had. One of the Proverbs speaks loudly against this common paradigm that we can hold: "He that is glad at calamities shall not go unpunished" (Proverbs 17:5). The boy was caught up in a works mentality. We know that is not where the blessing resides in God's economy. No amount of work can be enough secondary to our sinful human nature. The elder son became harsh secondary to his legalism. It is so important to flee judgmentalism! It will kill your love.

> Therefore, his father came out, and intreated him. And he answering said unto his father, lo, these many years did I serve you, neither transgressed I at any time your commandment: And yet you never gave me a kid, that I might make merry with my friends: But as soon as this your son was come, which has devoured your living with harlots, you have killed for him the fatted calf. And he said unto him, son, you are ever with me, and all I have is yours. It was meet that we should make merry, and be glad: For this your brother was dead, and is alive again, he was lost, and is found.
> Luke 15:28-32

The elder son's confusion via legalism is clearly seen in the fact that he felt he never had transgressed against his father. His living by comparison, is emphasized next as he notes his younger brothers' sins as being egregious and thus unacceptable to be forgiven. All of this because he was working for the blessing. Jesus is teaching that God wants to bestow grace and mercy, but He doesn't owe it to anyone. As Isaiah has prophesied, "All of our righteousnesses are as filthy rags" (Isaiah 64:6).

Of course, this parable accurately predicted the behavior of the Jews toward their Father and the Gentiles. Fourteen hundred years of following the Law and then thinking the rules had changed. What they missed, though, is that they were wrong. God had said from the very beginning of His relationship with the children of Abraham that the righteous shall live by faith (Genesis 15:6). Wonderfully, though, we see the Father's love for the Jews as the parable ends, "All that I have is yours, son." At the end of this age, Israel too will have a happy ending. They will recognize Jesus as Lord and, as Paul preaches, "All Israel will be saved" (Romans 11:26).

The application for me is that I need to quit trying to get God to bless me. He will be a debtor to no man. Just enjoying His grace, intimacy, and goodness is what I want to do! I need to remember that I could never do enough to merit His blessing. That would be like swimming across Lake Michigan. Impossible! Also, ultimately, He IS the blessing. I take this by faith now as I cannot see him, but one day it will be my reality!

The Parable of the Unclean Spirit

Jesus received much pushback from the Jews who rejected Him as Messiah. Secondary to His immense popularity and adoration from the common people of the nation, the leaders could not simply dismiss him. They had to challenge him, they had to knock Him down, they had to put out the fire of hope that the Lord had ignited among the people, so they attacked Him at every turn. One such confrontation involved their request for a sign from Jesus validating His claims. To that request, the Prophet told of the sign of Jonah. Just as Jonah was in the belly of the Beast for three days and three nights, so would the Son of man be in the heart of the earth. And just as Jonah came back from the dead, so would he! Then Jesus indicted the scribes and Pharisees for their unbelief by noting that others had heard the gospel and had not rejected it. He spoke of the men of Nineveh who repented at the preaching of Jonah, as well as the Queen of Sheba, who traveled from far away to hear the wisdom of Solomon, observing that the greater than Jonah and Solomon was present before them.

After His tough love, the rejected Savior gave a prophetic parable of their future fate secondary to that refusal to believe His message of life.

> When the unclean spirit is gone out of a man, he walks through dry places (*unclean spirits are found in dry places and are fond of dry places!*), seeking rest, and finds none. Then he says, I will return into my house from whence I came out; and when he is come, he finds it empty, swept, and garnished. Then goes he, and takes with himself seven other spirits more wicked than himself, and they enter in and dwell there: And the last state of that man is worse than the first. Even so shall it be also unto this wicked generation.
> Matthew 12:43-45 (italics added)

A spiritual principle is revealed by this parable. There must be regeneration over reformation. Israel had reformation after their captivity in Babylon. Before that, they worshipped the idols of the heathen but, after coming out of internment, they no longer sought after the false gods of the world. Their house was swept and garnished, if you will. Unfortunately, it was still empty! They had not replaced the bad with the good. They were still an unfilled vessel. In rejecting the Messiah, they were saying "No" to regeneration. In refusing Jesus' gift of life, they chose death. They let seven spirits more wicked than the first come in and reside in their clean but empty house.

This explains so much in the world today. Why do addicts succeed in kicking their habit only to relapse again? Why do prison inmates so often cycle back into crime after their sentence is over? Why does the repentant husband beg forgiveness from his wife after his affair only to stray again after she has released him? It's simple, really. In each case, Israel, the addict, the criminal, and the cheater, no change occurred in the heart! Until the cleaned and empty house is filled with something good, until the Holy Spirit moves in, nothing really has happened. Jesus is teaching that regeneration, the New Birth, is the answer to the wicked heart, to the empty house of man.

So, what does this tell me when I consider helping others? For one, it loudly states that I can't clean the fish until I catch it! Going "all in" against abortion, evolution, alternate lifestyles, or any other non-biblical worldview isn't where I want to direct my efforts. It's all about Christ and Him crucified. It's all about the good news of Jesus Christ, His death, burial, and resurrection (1 Corinthians 15:3-4). Jesus is at the center. Everything else is secondary. His is the name in which men are saved and made new. With this calling, I want to help my fellow man, help the addict, the criminal, and the unfaithful husband, not with counseling and intervention but with love and truth. With grace and the gospel. I want to help them find life and liberty in Jesus Christ, first and foremost!

The Parable of the Great Feast

The gospel of Luke gives interesting details of a dinner party Jesus and His disciples attended that was hosted by one of the chief Pharisees on the Sabbath day. At that meal, many others were also present, including a man who suffered from congestive heart failure, known to the ancients as dropsy. The Pharisees wanted to condemn Jesus for healing the man on the Sabbath but were stopped in their tracks by the brilliance of Jesus' words. He asked, "Is it lawful to heal on the Sabbath? Which of you shall have an ass or an ox fallen into a pit and will not straightway pull him out on the Sabbath day?" As noted, they could not answer this wonderful logic. Jesus then used this platform to give a parable about humility followed by one glorifying service. One of the dinner guests marveled at the Teacher's words by proclaiming "Blessed is he that shall eat bread in the Kingdom of God." To that exclamation, Jesus clarified a problem He perceived His hosts and, by extension, the nation of Israel, were going to have secondary to their dismissal of the King of said Kingdom.

> Then He said unto him, a certain man made a great supper, and invited many: And sent his servant (*An unnamed servant is often a picture of the Holy Spirit in the Bible*) at supper time to say to them that were invited, Come, for all things are now ready.
> Luke 14:16-17 (italics added)

The invited guests speak of the unbelieving portion of Israel. They were the preferred, they were the chosen. They were invited to partake in eternal fellowship with the Father. But read what happens to them. What can often happen to all if we are not paying attention:

> And they all with one voice began to make excuse. The first said unto him, I have bought a piece of ground, and I must go and see it: I pray you have me excused. And another said, I have bought five oxen, and I go to prove them: I pray you have me excused. And another said, I have married a wife, and therefore I cannot come.
> Luke 14:18-20

Excuses cause me to miss out on dining with the Lord. Possessions (the piece of ground), occupation (the five oxen), family (married a wife) are not bad in themselves, obviously, but they can distract me from intimacy with my Lord when He nudges me to come and dine with him. The choice of my priorities will determine my place at the banquet table. Of course, that is the point to unbelieving Israel; they were not paying close attention and missed out on the blessing.

> So, the servant came and showed his lord these things. Then the master of his house being angry said to his servant, go out quickly into the streets and lanes of the city, and bring hither the poor, and the maimed, and the halt, and the blind.
> Luke 14:21

On the day of Pentecost, Peter preached Jesus Christ, Him crucified and resurrected, and three thousand in Jerusalem believed (Acts 2:41). These all were Jews who had come for the feast. The first group of believers, the first group of guests who came to the great feast of this parable were the believing portion of Israel. They were of the city, they were nearby. The Church of Christ is made up of only two groups, Jews and Gentiles. What Christ did is break down the partition, the wall separating them, making the two clusters into one (Ephesians 2:11-15).

You can probably guess who the next group is.

> And the servant said, Lord, it is done as you have commanded, and yet there is room. And the lord said unto the servant, go out into the highways and hedges, and compel them to come in, that my house may be filled. For I

> say to you, that none of those men which were
> invited shall taste my supper.
> Luke 14:22-24

"For God desires all men to be saved and come to the knowledge of the truth" (1 Timothy 2:4). He wants His house to be filled. But He is a perfect gentleman, He will not force himself upon any of us. So sad for the Jews!

Of course, this last group of banqueters is from farther away. They are the Gentiles who were called last and partake of the meal while the first group decline and miss out.

The Parables of the Vineyard

After Christ's triumphant entry into Jerusalem before Passover (fulfilling the prophecy given in Zechariah 9:9), as well as the subsequent cleansing of the Temple by our Lord, the leaders of the nation were desperate to take Him out. The Messianic fire started by Jesus in the hearts of the people, this movement which they perceived would lead to retaliation from the Romans, must be snuffed out. Thus, they grilled Him subtly, yet mercilessly, in an attempt to obtain evidence they could use against him. The brilliance of our Lord rebuffed them at every turn. Jesus ended His rebuttals by asking about John. "The baptism of John, where was it from? Heaven, or of men?" (Matthew 21:25). They could not answer this logic without tripping up themselves, so they refused to say. To that Jesus spoke two parables, which again are one, impeaching the Jewish fathers for their unbelief and prophesying what would therefore occur consequent to their rejection of the Messiah.

> But what think you? A certain man had two sons; and he came to the first, and said, son, go work today in my vineyard. He answered and said, I will not: But afterward he repented, and went. And he came to the second, and said likewise. And he answered and said, I go sir: And went not. Which of the two did the will of his father?
> Matthew 21:28-31a

Jesus was setting them up for a fall indeed. The first son represents the common people; they were the "sinners" who initially did not follow the Law, like their pharisaical leaders, but later repented when they heard the preaching of John. Of course, the second son, the one who said he would go but then did not, speak of the religious leaders. The Savior is unwrapping their hypocrisy unwittingly before their eyes!

> They say unto him, the first. Jesus said unto them, truly I say unto you, that the publicans and the harlots go into the Kingdom of God before you. For John came unto you in the way of righteousness, and you believed him not: But the publicans and the harlots believed him: And you, when you had seen it, repented not afterward, that you might believe him.
> Matthew 21:31b-32

Once again, the paradox of the first shall be last and the last shall be first is clearly seen. John's ministry had been spoken of by Isaiah (Isaiah 40:1-5), yet they refused to listen to him. The time of the appearance of the Messiah had been openly predicted by

Daniel (9:25-26); nonetheless, they turned their backs upon that certain revelation.

The result of their unbelief is next:

> Hear another parable: There was a certain householder, which planted a vineyard (*by now you understand the vineyard is Israel*), and hedged it round about (*the householder nourished it*), and dug a winepress in it (*hoping to see fruit production*), and built a tower (*he gave them His Word*), and let it out to husbandmen, and went into a far country. And when the time of the fruit drew near, he sent his servants (*the prophets*) to the husbandmen, that they might receive the fruits of it. And the husbandmen took his servants, and beat one, and killed another, and stoned another. Again, he sent other servants more than the first: And they unto them likewise. But last of all he sent unto them his son (*showing that Jesus is the last word given by God to Israel*). But when the husbandmen saw the son, they said among themselves, this is the heir; come, let us kill him, and let us seize on his inheritance. And they caught him, and cast him out of the vineyard, and slew him. When the lord therefore of the vineyard comes, what will he do unto the husbandmen? They said unto him, he will miserably destroy those wicked men, and will let out his vineyard unto other husbandmen, which shall render him fruit in their seasons.

Matthew 21:33-41 (italics added)

Incredible! The leaders did not see the obvious! That's what sin does. That's what self-righteousness accomplishes. It blinds me from what others see readily. And look what they did...they pronounced their own prophecy against themselves. "Those husbandmen shall be miserably destroyed and the vineyard given to others." Of course, we know that is exactly what occurred. The unbelieving portion of Israel suffered tragically, being taken out and suppressed shortly thereafter while the Church, made up of believing Jews and Gentiles, was the recipient of God's blessing and has brought forth fruit over the past two thousand years.

In response to their understanding of the flow of the parable while at the same time not comprehending that it spoke of them, the Prophet lowered the boom:

> Jesus said unto them, did you never read in the scriptures, the stone which the builders rejected, the same is become the head of the corner: This is the Lord's doing, and it is marvelous in our eyes? Therefore, say I unto you, the Kingdom of God shall be taken from you, and given to a nation bringing forth fruits thereof.
> Matthew 21:42-43

Ironically, these words are found in Psalm 118:22-23 and are immediately followed by the praises that Christ's followers sang that very day. "This is the day which the Lord hath made; we will rejoice and be glad in it. Save now (Hosanna), I beseech thee, O Lord: O Lord, I beseech thee, send now prosperity. Blessed be He that comes in the name of the Lord" (Psalm 118:24-26).

Looking back, this must have floored the believers which heard this. The Bible was being fulfilled right in front of their eyes at that moment!

The context of Jesus' reprimand is that the chief cornerstone being rejected sang of the days of Solomon when the Temple was being constructed. In that day, the stones for the Temple came up from the rock quarry, pre-fitted. But there was one that didn't seem to match anything, so it was rolled down the Temple Mount into the valley below. Later the builders realized it indeed was the cornerstone, the stone upon which all of the building was centered! Of course, spiritualizing, this song reveals what happened to our Lord. It prophesied of the time of Messiah, the true chief cornerstone, who also would be rejected.

> And whosoever shall fall on this stone shall be broken: But on whosoever it shall fall, it will grind him to powder.
> Matthew 21:44

If I fall upon the chief cornerstone in brokenness, humility, and repentance, in agreement that I am a sinner, then I am saved. But if the chief cornerstone falls upon me, woe is me...for that stone grinds to powder. As noted elsewhere, "Our God is a consuming fire."

This parable reminds me of Daniel's words which also speak of Jesus, the Rock:

> Thou saw until a stone was cut out without hands, which smote the image upon his feet that were of iron and clay, and broke them to pieces. Then was the iron, the clay, the brass, the silver, and the gold (*representing all of*

> *the previous kingdoms of the world*), broken to pieces together, and became like the chaff of the summer threshing floors (*nothing but dust*); that no place was found for them: And the stone that smote the image became a great mountain, and (*his glory*) filled the whole earth.
> Daniel 2:34-35 (italics added)

At this point, the Bible tells us that the priests and Pharisees realized Jesus had been speaking of them all along but it was too late for them. Like Pharaoh in the days of Moses, their hearts were hardened. We learn from Matthew that they wanted to kill Him that very moment but feared the people because they took Jesus correctly as a prophet.

How do you see Jesus, how do I perceive Him? Is He a threat to our comfort and plans or is He a prophet predicting our future? The answer to this question determines our destiny. Like the unbelieving and believing Jews, our future will be misery or majesty based upon the answer to this inquiry!

The Parable of the Fig Tree Given a Second Chance

As we have previously discussed, like the vineyard, the fig tree also speaks of Israel each time it is used in the Bible. Thus, a parable about a fig tree given another chance brings joy to our hearts. We are sad for Israel because we understand that, given the same circumstances, we too could easily trip up as they did. For the chief cornerstone was not what they expected.

Let's see what they did with their second chance. Would they repent?

> There were present at that season some that told Him of the Galileans, whose blood Pilate had mingled with their sacrifices. And Jesus answering said unto them, suppose you that these Galileans, were sinners above all Galileans, because they suffered such things? I tell you, no: But, except you repent, you shall all likewise perish. Or those eighteen, upon whom the tower in Siloam fell, and slew them, think you that they were sinners above all men that dwell in Jerusalem? I tell you, no: But, except you repent, you shall all likewise perish.
> Luke 13:1-4

The news of the day, as in our time today, can be bothersome. It can push against the paradigms we have erected. A common construct we have is that bad things happen to bad people and good things happen to good people. Jesus blows this mindset out of the water, noting that all are sinners and evil and disasters are somewhat random. "Stuff" is going to happen. This is a fallen planet inhabited by sinners. A better way, instead of complaining about the bad, is to marvel at God's grace, that good also abundantly happens. We need to look for the blessings and be grateful when we see them.

Along with leveling the playing field by observing that we all are sinners, the Lord concluded to His listeners, and to us, that repentance is the key. Agree with what God says about our sin, that's repentance, and turn to Him for salvation.

> He spoke also this parable; a certain man (*the Father*) had a fig tree planted in his vineyard (*a fig tree and a vine, clearly speaking of Israel*);

> and he came and sought fruit thereon, and found none. Then said he unto the dresser of his vineyard (*Jesus*), behold, these three years (*the duration of Jesus' public ministry to Israel*) I come seeking fruit on this fig tree, and find none: Cut it down; why bother letting it stand? And he (*Jesus*) answering said unto him, Lord, let it alone this year also, until I shall dig it, and dung it: And if it bear fruit, well: And if not, then after that you shall cut it down.
> Luke 13:6-9 (italics added)

For the entirety of Jesus' time with the Jewish leaders, the Father was not seeing any fruit. Cut them down was the order. Like the souls whose blood Pilate mingled and the men at Jerusalem's Pool of Siloam whom the tower crushed, the nation had been judged and found wanting. But like Moses in the days of the Exodus when he interceded for the people who had been sinning, we see Jesus doing the same. Let me dig it. That is, let me expose the roots of the tree. Let me show my brothers that they are missing the mark. And let me dung it. That is, let them see me dispel myself. Let them learn what I will do for them in dying for their sins. Let's give them this chance. Then after seeing my resurrection, if they bear fruit they will live. If not, then you can cut them down.

Of course, we know this is what happened. Those who chose to believe continued making up the early church of Jesus Christ, while the unbelieving portion of Israel was cut down less than one generation later as Rome leveled the city and the nation.

What does this parable say to me, to you? Clearly, if I expose my sin, if we confess our sin and if dispel myself, if we call Jesus our Lord, we will be in a position like that fig tree to produce fruit.

And bearing fruit glorifies the Father (John 15:8). That's what I want to do.

The Cursed and Then Revived Fig Tree

During the last week of His earthly ministry, Jesus gave an object lesson about the power of faith when He cursed a fig tree that could not please Him with fruit to satisfy His hunger. But a second message, a picture, if you will, of the fate of the nation is also portrayed.

> And on the morrow, when they were come from Bethany, He was hungry: And seeing a fig tree afar off having leaves, He came, if haply He might find anything thereon: And when He came to it, He found nothing but leaves; for the time of figs was not yet. And Jesus answered and said unto it, no man eat fruit of yours, hereafter forever. And His disciples heard it... And in the morning, as they passed by, they saw the fig tree dried up from the roots.
> Mark 11:12-14, 20

The disciples marveled at the quick destruction of the fig tree, which allowed the Teacher to speak of the power of faith to move mountains. But, as mentioned, a second meaning is also present. Remembering that the fig tree always speaks of Israel, this illustrates what would happen to the nation after its rejection of the Messiah. Their inability to please Him with fruit cost the nation its very life.

The same principle is in play for all. The Bible teaches that Jesus is worthy to receive glory, honor, and power, for He has created all things and, for His pleasure, they are and were created (Revelation 4:11). This means that all created things are for His pleasure. Obviously, we were created, thus our purpose is to please Him above anything else we may say or do. When we are not fulfilling that purpose, our purpose, well, then we are missing the meaning of our very lives! Since He is the vine and we are the branches (John 15:5), when we become disconnected from the Source, well, clearly, we will dry up, just as that fig tree did.

Wonderfully, later the very same day, the Prophet once again spoke of the fig tree, this time in the context of the End of this age, predicting that the fig tree would come back to life and, in so doing, would signal the very time of His near return. Let's listen to this wonderful prophecy once again:

> Now learn a parable of the fig tree; when her branch is yet tender, and puts forth leaves, you know that summer is near: So, in like manner, when you shall see all these things come to pass, know that it is nigh, even at the doors. Truly I say to you, that this generation shall not pass, until all these things be done. Heaven and earth shall pass away: But my words shall not pass away.
> Mark 13:28-31

Because Jesus suffered, died, and was raised to life, He miraculously paved the way for the same to happen to the fig tree. Indeed, this is what has transpired. The nation died and for two thousand years was without a homeland. Then, after the Holocaust, the culmination of two millennia of suffering, the nation was reborn on March 14, 1948. Delightfully for us, Jesus then promised that the generation that witnessed that event, that is, those alive when it occurred, would not pass away until they witness His return. That was seventy-three years ago! That generation is getting pretty old. Surely His Coming is nigh. Heaven and earth will pass away before His words will lose their power!

Applying this lesson to my life is easy. The same words of the Master that can raise the dead also can restore things that have died in my life and things gone from yours that you feel can never be returned. Have faith, the mountain of unbelief can be moved by His resurrection power. Lord, help us in our unbelief!

Three Pictures of Resurrection

In one day in the life of Jesus, we see three miracles of healing that typify His deliverance of all people, both Gentiles and Jews.

> And they arrived at the country of the Gadarenes (*Gentile territory*) ...And when He went forth to land, there met Him out of the city a certain man, which had devils a long time, and wore no clothes, neither abode in any house, but in the tombs (*nudity and obsession with death are often signs of Satan's influence*). And when he saw Jesus, he cried out, and fell down before Him (*the devils were in fear before our Lord*), and with a loud voice said, what have I to do with you, Jesus, thou Son of God most high (*they knew who He was*)? I beseech you, torment me not...And Jesus asked him, saying, what is your name? And he said, Legion: Because many devils were entered into him. And they besought

> Him that He would not command them to go out into the deep (*Devils know their ultimate destination of outer darkness, but they did not think this was yet the time*) ...He (*Jesus*) suffered them. Then the devils went out of the man...Then they that saw what was done came to Jesus, and found the man, out of whom the devils were departed, sitting at the feet of Jesus, clothed, and in his right mind.
> Luke 8:26-35 (excerpts; italics added)

The demoniac man from the land of the Gadarenes pictures the Gentiles. They lived outside of the promises of God, outside of the covenants, and were unaware of His directives. Thus, they were easy pickings for the god of this world. You see, without God's Word, we are in the dark. Think of the Bible as God's instruction manual. It gives the directions for life. Without those guidelines, abuse is inevitable. When I am ignorant of important principles of life, Satan can easily influence me negatively. This is what happened to the Gentiles after the Flood. Over time, the memory of Eden and of God was lost, giving Satan free rein to dominate the Gentiles, as seen pictorially by this demoniac man living among the dead. Wonderfully, we see Jesus traveling across the lake to rescue this captive man and, in so doing, He showed what He would do for all Gentiles who would believe. He calls them from death to life.

Immediately on the heels of this picture of the Gentiles' deliverance we see two types of the progressive resurrection of the Jews.

> And it came to pass, that when Jesus returned (*to Capernaum, Jewish territory*), the people

gladly received him: For they were all waiting for Him (*A good thing to do!*). And behold, there came a man named Jairus, and he was a ruler of the synagogue: And he fell down at Jesus' feet, and besought Him that He would come into his house: For he had a daughter, about twelve years of age (*The number twelve, like the vine and the fig always has a picture of Israel imbedded in Bible typology.*), and she lay dying. But as He went the people thronged him. And a woman having an issue of blood twelve years, which had spent all her living upon physicians, neither could be healed of any, came behind him, and touched the border of His garment: And immediately her issue of blood was stopped. And Jesus said, who touched me? ... Somebody has touched me: For I perceive that virtue has gone out of me. And when the woman saw that she was not hid, she came trembling, and falling down before him, she declared unto Him before all the people for what cause she had touched him, and how she was healed immediately. And He said unto her, Daughter, be of good comfort: Your faith has made you whole; go in peace. And while He yet spoke, there came one from the ruler of the synagogue's house, saying to him, your daughter is dead; trouble not the Master. But when Jesus heard it, He answered him, saying, fear not, only believe, and she shall be made whole. And when He came to the house...he took her by the hand,

> and called, saying, maid, arise. And her spirit
> came again, and she arose straightway.
> Luke 8:40-55 (excerpts; italics added)

Twelve tribes of Israel, twelve apostles, etc. Twelve is Israel's number. Thus, when the Bible goes out of its way to include information which would otherwise seem superfluous, that being twelve years of bleeding and a twelve-year-old dying girl, we should pay attention that these stories tell of Israel. Indeed, like the woman with the issue of blood, Israel became an outcast after they rejected our Lord. They were excluded from the life of God after their Temple and their nation was destroyed in 70 AD. They were outcasts wondering in the wilderness of the nations of the world. But in 1948, they touched the hem of God's garment and were healed. Additionally, like Jairus' daughter, they seemingly died. They were without hope, without life. But along came Jesus. He raised that little girl, picturing what He will do at the end of this age for Israel. Today, in our day, Israel is healed, they are the woman no longer bleeding. Soon, they will come back to life spiritually, on that day when they recognize Jesus as Lord and mourn over Him whom they have pierced (Zechariah 12:10). Interestingly to me, we are living today between the prophetic pictures of these three miracles. The Gentiles were first delivered, then the Jews were healed, and now we wait for their spiritual re-birth. Just like the dry bones prophecy of Ezekiel, which we have discussed previously, we are living in the days of prophetic fulfillment. May we have eyes to see!

The True Vine

The Jewish leaders considered themselves, considered Israel, to be God's vine. Clearly, as we have discussed, the scriptures indicated this to be true. But Jesus, seeing a problem for His disciples, secondary to the rejection, for most of their message by the Jews, had a new revelation for His men to consider and to hold tightly to. That being, that he, not Israel, is the True Vine.

> I am the true vine, and my Father is the husbandman...I am the vine, you are the branches: He that abides in me, and I in him, the same brings forth much fruit: For without me you can do nothing.
> John 15:1, 5

This last of the great "I AM" statements of Jesus, found in the gospel of John, must have brought much comfort to His disciples over the years after the Savior's departure back to Heaven. You see, the nation of Israel did not accept Christianity as a legitimate extension of Judaism, even though that is what the early church leaders initially thought would happen. As the progressive revelation of inclusion of the Gentiles was given to the believers by Peter and Paul, it became clear over the decades afterward that Christianity, that the Way, was going to be a separate entity from Judaism. These words of our Lord, that He, not Israel, is the True Vine made it possible for the early believers to disengage from Israel when it became apparent that they were not going to believe the message. As we read the Book of Hebrews, we see this wrestling take place to a great degree. Christ as the better way is the "big idea" of that epistle. He fulfilled the Law and, as such, the Old Testament sacrifices the Jews were clinging to were of no effect. In fact, Hebrews soberly preaches that going back to the sacrifice and the works-based mentality of Judaism was to crucify Christ afresh by not recognizing that His sacrifice was once and for all time (Hebrews 6:4-6).

So, as we end our discussion of Jesus' word to His brothers, the Jews, we are reminded that hard words are sometimes needed to bring us to the place of repentance. Such was certainly the case for the Jewish leaders who had closed themselves down to their Savior because He did not appear as they expected. Corporately, we must learn from this. We, too, in the Christian church of the 21st Century, can get caught up in pharisaical legalism, in religiosity, and miss the simple message of grace given to all by the Lord. We see that, indeed, the first became the last in the history of the Church of the First Century. Let's not let that happen to us. Let's continue to put ourselves last, to humble ourselves and seek only His face. Let's stay attached to the True Vine, for that is the only place of fruit production that will have eternal and lasting value for us.

But, on a personal level, this also holds true. So often, in God's economy of grace, we see the latecomer receiving a blessing out of proportion to his effort or station. Again, this is because grace is not a contract. It's a gift. As I read in God's Word, it is clear that the Giver of Gifts does not like murmuring from His kids, and why should he? We don't like it in our children either! I want to stay away from complaining and just remember how good He has been to me. I want to recognize that every new day is a gift of God's grace to me. I want to unwrap it, I want to embrace it, I want to savor it!

Summary:

1. "Blessed is He who shall not be offended in me" implies that we can misunderstand God's promises, as the Jewish leaders did, when things seemingly don't work out as we feel they should.
2. The hinge point between experiencing the goodness versus the severity of God swings upon faith.

3. The Parable of the Workers in the Vineyard speaks of God's grace. It pictures that grace by definition is not determined by our effort. It is unmerited, undeserved favor.
4. There are three ways one can despise the grace of God. Become jealous when it is extended to others. Murmur against it when it is extolled by others. Disrespect it when it is given to you.
5. The Parable of the Unclean Spirit explains many of the recurring problems we see in our world today. Self-improvement techniques without spiritual transformation are destined to fail!
6. The Parable of the Great Feast demonstrates three areas in my life which, if not prioritized correctly, can interfere with my fellowship with the Lord. Possessions, occupation, and family.
7. The Parables of the Vineyard reveal that the Jewish leaders perceived Jesus as a threat to them, not as a Savior for them. They picture that this is a mistake we do not want to make!
8. The Parable of the Fig Tree given a second chance pictures Jesus' heart for His countrymen. He longs for them to embrace His sacrifice for them.
9. Revelation 4:11 teaches that Christ created everything and that all things are for His pleasure. As created beings, our primary purpose is to bring pleasure to the Lord.
10. The healings of the demonic man, the hemorrhaging woman, and Jairus' daughter illustrate our Lord's deliverance of both people groups, Gentiles and Jews.
11. Jesus as the True Vine fulfilled the Old Testament Law and replaced Israel as God's vineyard.

For Further Study:

1. When reading the Bible, if you come across a passage from God that seems harsh and possibly unloving, what should you do? How can you judge God's tone? Hint: See James 3:15-17. If strife and confusion are released in my heart, then I am missing God's tenor.
2. What should we do when not understanding God's plan and ending a sentence about His ways with a question mark?
3. What are three types from this essay that picture Israel? Hint: Two plants and a number.
4. How has the Bible paradox that the last shall be first and the first shall be last been fulfilled over the past two thousand years?
5. What was the sin of the elder son in the Parable of the Prodigal Son? What were the factors that led to this sin?
6. What eternal principle is revealed by the Parable of the Unclean Spirit?
7. According to Matthew 21:44, why must one respect the chief cornerstone?
8. How many times in the gospels did Jesus curse a fig tree that could not satisfy His hunger with fruit? What does this number picture in Bible typology?
9. Have any curses in your life been canceled out by the power of the Cross and the Resurrection of Christ?

The Comforter

The gospel of John explains Jesus as the Son of God, as God the Son. But a second further revelation to the believers is that of the work of the Holy Spirit. In John, we learn much of the Spirit's ministry to mankind from the lips of the Lord himself.

On the night Jesus was betrayed, He sat at a meal with His disciples. Chapters 13 through 17 tell of the intense drama of that meal. In these five chapters, we realize much new information, revelation from the Prophet, that is not present in the other gospel accounts. We are much the richer after John's reporting. Included in the Teacher's words and actions was an object lesson on the beauty of service as the Lord washed the disciple's feet. He foretold Judas' betrayal as well as Peter's denial, followed by words about Heaven and the promise that believers, those who embrace the Way, the Truth, and the Life, will be there with him. Jesus spoke of the importance of staying attached to him, the True Vine, to produce fruit to the Father's glory. He told His men that, as they continued in His word, He would reveal new truths to them going forward, new revelations. This must have encouraged them because the Savior also prophesied that all who follow Him would run into persecution at one time or another for their faith. He spoke much of the Comforter, the Spirit of truth that would come upon all believers to empower us in our journey and the Son of man prayed to the Father for us all that we would live in unity as we wait for the consummation of all things at the end of the age.

In this chapter, we will focus on our Lord's words about the Comforter which He spoke at that awesome dinner meeting.

> I will pray the Father, and He shall give you another Comforter, that He may abide with you forever; even the Spirit of truth; whom the world cannot receive, because it sees Him not, neither knows him: But you know him; for He dwells with you, and shall be in you.
> John 14:16-17

The context of these words is important. Jesus was making it clear to His men that He was going to leave them. He told them that they would sorrow like a woman in travail, like a woman giving birth, as they witnessed His murder, His sacrifice. But He also promised they would rejoice as that same woman does when she realized the birth of her child. They would have inexpressible joy upon His return to them, upon His resurrection from the dead! After finishing His mission, He told the disciples He would ultimately go back to the Father. This would pave the way for the third person of the Trinity to join them. He was present with them previously but, after this, He would be in them. He would come upon them in new ways and with new power. Jesus noted that the worldlings would not understand this, that it would be like a foreign language to them, so not to be surprised when that occurred. This explains so much. The simplicity and beauty of the gospel seem so clear to us who believe, yet to the unbelieving world it is either a stumbling block or foolishness. This, according to our Lord, is because they are living without the connection to God, without the Comforter who only will come upon those who believe. It's the classic Catch-22... Don't' have the Comforter, don't understand, but need the Comforter to even begin to comprehend. Thank God that He even gives us the faith to believe. As Paul preaches, "For by grace are you saved through faith; and that not of yourselves: It is the gift of God" (Ephesians 2:8). Even the faith it takes to believe comes from God. He does it all!

> These things I have spoken unto you, being yet present with you. But the Comforter, which is the Holy Ghost, whom the Father will send in my name, He shall teach you all things, and bring to your remembrance, whatsoever I have said unto you.
> John 14:25-26

This is huge! Jesus will not leave us alone. With Jesus present, the Kingdom of God was with us. But it was limited by space and time. It was only in one place, wherever the King was. But with our Lord's return to the Father, the Almighty would send the Holy Spirit. And that Spirit would not be limited to just one place, for He would be wherever anyone who called upon the name of Jesus resided. The presence of the kingdom would now go across the globe!

And look at the wonderful work that the Spirit would do. He would teach us all things, everything we need to know. And He would cause us to remember what Jesus had previously taught. This explains the inspiration of the New Testament very well. Written shortly after the events, we can be sure that the words we have are from God because they are empowered by the Spirit himself (2 Timothy 3:16, Proverbs 30:5a).

> Nevertheless, I tell you the truth; it is expedient for you that I go away: For if I go not away, the Comforter will not come unto you; but if I depart, I will send Him unto you.
> John 16:7

"It is for the best that I leave!" I doubt at the time that the disciples would have agreed. The task ahead, the road to travel, seemed so great. That small group of believers was the proverbial mustard seed that Jesus said would grow into a great tree. They were only one hundred twenty believers looking at telling the world about their Lord. But Jesus is teaching that, with His return to the Father, the Spirit would come and the new day would begin. In retrospect, we know that is indeed what has occurred.

> And when He is come...
> John 16:8a

Notice, the Spirit is a "he." The Holy Ghost is a person, just like the Father and the Son. He is not an ethereal entity, He is not a vague force. No, He is a person. Undoubtedly, not the way we think of a person, limited to time and space as we are, but an individual nonetheless. Someone with a personality, a character, a will, and an identity.

> ...he will reprove the world of sin, and of righteousness, and of judgment: Of sin, because they believe not on me; of righteousness, because I go to the Father, and you see me no more; of judgment because the prince of this world is judged.
> John 16:8b-11

Jesus here explains the threefold ministry of the Spirit. The Holy Spirit will act as the conscience for the world. He will be the referee separating truth from error. He will be the umpire calling the motions of the world as either right or wrong, true or false. We see that sin is something He will call out. And specifically, it is the sin of not believing in the Savior. You see, the prince of this world wants all to feel that sin is passé. That it is not really a thing. The Holy Spirit will not allow that. All people have sinned, the Bible teaches. Everyone needs a Redeemer. The Spirit will make it His top priority to keep front and center a person's need to repent, to turn from sin, and to turn to Jesus for grace and forgiveness. It's the only way!

Secondly, He will speak of righteousness because Jesus went to the Father. You see, when Adam and Eve were created, many Bible teachers believe that, after a period of testing, if you will, in the Garden of Eden, had they not sinned they would have been transported up into Heaven. Jesus modeled this on the Mount of Transfiguration. After living a perfect human life for over thirty years, He climbed Mount Hebron and glowed like the sun. He heard His Father's blessing and could have left for heaven at that moment, showing that it was possible to live without sinning. But, thankfully for us, He chose to stay and later to climb Mount Calvary to atone for our sins. The Spirit will speak of righteousness by preaching that Jesus is the Way, the Truth, and the Life. He is the path to the Father. It is not all roads that lead to Chicago, as the Devil would like us to believe. No, some roads lead to Timbuktu. Other roads lead to oblivion. The Spirit will clearly spell that out, whether it is politically correct or not!

Thirdly, the Holy Ghost will testify about Satan's judgment. He will announce to the believers that the hordes of Hell no longer have dominion over us. You see, after Adam sinned, as caretaker of this planet, he gave the title deed over to Satan. Our Adversary became the god of this world. Thus, when Jesus came on the scene four thousand years later, Satan was in the position to offer our Lord all of the kingdoms of the world in exchange for His worship. This would have made no sense if Satan was not the owner. Jesus, of course, did not accept, but instead went to the Cross to buy back the planet. The Devil did not understand the implications of Jesus' sacrifice, as 1st Corinthians 2:6-8 teaches. Indeed, Satan believed he had won by killing our Lord. How insanely furious he must have been when, three days later, the new owner of the planet returned to life. The Spirit will constantly remind us that we are more than conquerors through Christ. That greater is He that is in us, than he that is in the world. That the former prince of the world has been judged and is found wanting!

> I have yet many things to say unto you, but you
> cannot bear them now.
> John 16:12

Jesus came speaking a message of repentance, for the Kingdom of God has come. But He did not speak in much detail of the time after His rejection. He did not reveal much of the Age of Grace in which we are now living. The time between His two advents was hidden in God, as Ephesians 3:9 teaches. There are many mysteries that the Spirit subsequently made known to our early brothers of the New Testament, which we are aware of and living in today.

Examples of previously unknown truths, mysteries in the New Testament which the Spirit revealed, are many. We are now cognizant through Paul of the mystery that blindness would in part happen to the Jews until the fullness of the Gentiles be come in (Romans 11:25). The Holy Ghost revealed in much greater detail the event we now understand as the Rapture. Paul called that a mystery in 1st Corinthians 15:51-54. The truth, the mystery, that the Gentiles would be fellow-heirs and of the same body, and partakers of God's promises in Christ, was revealed in the epistles of Ephesians and Colossians. (Ephesians 3:1-11 and Colossians 1:26-27). The mystery of iniquity is found in 2nd Thessalonians 2:7. This is the revelation that, when the Holy Spirit leaves the planet at the time of the departure of the saints, the Wicked One, also called the Antichrist, will be revealed to the fooled of the world as a great leader, a messiah figure. The mystery of the seven prophetic churches was given to the believers from the Spirit's inspiration to John (Revelation 1:20). Lastly, John also spoke of the mystery of a worldwide false religion based in Rome found in Revelation 17:5, 9, and 18.

In the Bible, a mystery means that God is revealing a truth that up until that point in time was unknown to man, or sometimes even by angels. It doesn't mean that it is a new truth that God has come up with but it is an aspect of God's plan that previously was not known. Mysteries are much like the truths children learn as they grow and mature. Just because I didn't understand physics or romance as a boy didn't mean that those things were not an entity. They were just mysteries to me. What about art history or quantum theory? They exist but they still are a mystery to me! Same for those without the Spirit. Each of the mysteries listed above is far outside of the mind of those who do not call Jesus Lord.

Jesus is clearly teaching that there would be things to come that the Spirit would uncover that they were unable to bear at that moment in time. In retrospect, we can revel in the gravity of these words from our Lord to His disciples.

> Howbeit when he, the Spirit of truth, is come,
> He will guide you into all truth: For He will not

> speak of himself...He shall glorify me: For He
> shall receive of mine, and show it to you.
> John 16:13a, 14

Jesus is the Way, the Truth, and the Life. The Spirit will not speak of himself, He will illuminate, He will magnify Jesus. When a work of the Spirit is active, our Lord is the focal point, not the Spirit himself. In Old Testament typology, pictures of the Holy Ghost were always portrayed in humility. Examples you can check are many. Ezra, Nehemiah, Caleb, the unnamed servant of Abraham who was sent out to find a bride for Isaac, all come to mind. All of these Holy Spirit types glorified another, not themselves. Holy Spirit movements, Holy Ghost revivals, are always subject to suspicion, as the Spirit doesn't speak of Himself. When believers conjure up Holy Spirit meetings, I always wonder if that is the best.

> ...and He will show you things to come.
> John 16:13b

The prophets of old had the Spirit come upon them as they predicted the future. So it is also in our dispensation. Prophecy was given to the believers via the Spirit. We have learned of the Rapture, the Tribulation time frame, the Antichrist, and the Second Coming by the Spirit's inspiration. And the wonderful thing is, since so much prophecy of the Lord's dealings in the world has already come to pass, the promises that are still in the future we can trust also as going to occur. God is faithful and His Word is always fulfilled!

As we mentioned at the outset, John's gospel revealed the work of the Spirit to a much greater degree than was previously known. Let's look at some of the other examples of this which we discover from His wonderful account.

> Then answered the Jews and said unto him, what sign do you show unto us, seeing that you do these things? Jesus answered and said unto them, destroy this temple, and in three days I will raise it up. Then said the Jews, forty and six years was this temple in building, and will you rear it up in three days? But He spoke of the temple of His body. When therefore He was risen from the dead, His disciples remembered that He had said this unto them; and they believed the word which Jesus had said.
> John 2:18-22

How did they remember the words Jesus spoke? Why, the Spirit brought it unto their remembrance. Notice also that Jesus did not correct the Jews concerning their wrong understanding of His words to them. They believed He was talking about the actual Temple while, in reality, the Savior spoke of His body which would be given for the sins of the world. Jesus sort of left it out there, trusting that the Spirit would indeed do His work and bring revelation of the correct meaning to the disciples at the proper time.

Reading through the gospels, we see this phenomenon often; that is, an action of Jesus not making sense to His men at the time but in retrospect, when it was recorded later, the Spirit's editing is clearly seen. Confusion turned to explanation. And often that explanation included a prophetic fulfillment of Jesus which the disciples were unaware of at the time, but later, given the spiritual illumination, were able to point out the connections Jesus made for all of us which have followed.

This is a good word for me. I don't have to always explain everything when I perceive that I am being misunderstood. I should take the cue from my Lord and trust He will by His Spirit illuminate others as He sees fit. Living this way is like a cool breeze. Far less stressful. The tricky part, though, is doing it. It's not natural. But, with practice, it can become a habit. And you know what they say about habits. If you sow a habit, it will become a character.

> Jesus answered and said unto her (*the woman at Jacob's well of Samaria*), if you knew the gift of God, and who it is that says unto you, give me a drink; you would have asked of Him, and He would have given you living water. The woman said unto Him, sir, you have nothing to draw with, and the well is deep: From where then have you this living water? Are you greater than our father Jacob, which gave us this well, and drank of it himself, and his children, and his cattle? Jesus answered and said unto her, whosoever drinks of this water shall thirst again: But whosoever drinks of the water that I shall give him shall never thirst; but the water that I shall give him shall be in him a well of water springing up into everlasting life.
> John 4: 10-14 (italics added)

Living water is a metaphor of the Spirit which Jesus gives to all who ask for it. It is much more than mere water that we need to live our temporary lives. It is spiritual drink that imparts eternal life. Like water to the physical, the living water is the essence of eternal and spiritual life. And it will be like a well of spring water. An endless supply from the fountain of life!

Take note, also, that Jesus clearly implies to the woman that one must ask Him for the living water.

> Ask and it shall be given you; seek, and you shall find; knock, and it shall be opened unto you. For every one that asks, receives: and he that seeks, finds; and to him that knocks, it shall be opened. If a son shall ask bread of any of you that is a father, will he give him a stone? Or if he asks a fish, will he for a fish give him a serpent? Or if he shall ask an egg, will he offer him a scorpion? If you then, being evil, know how to give good gifts unto your children: How much more shall your Heavenly Father give the Holy Spirit to them that ask him?
> Luke 11:9-13

Like Jesus' words to the woman at Jacob's well, this contrast parable that ends with these words clearly teaches that we must ask for the Spirit's filling. The empowerment is not a loose cannon, but it is a powerful weapon for good, given to those who desire to be used by God in the world. It doesn't come upon us by accident, but by conscious and simple request.

Soon thereafter, Jesus not only shared living water, but living bread. Let's listen:

> The Jews then murmured at Him, because He said, I am the bread which came down from heaven...Truly, truly I say unto you, he that believes on me has eternal life. I am the bread

of life. Your fathers did eat manna in the wilderness, and are dead. This is the bread which comes down from heaven, that a man may eat thereof, and not die. I am the living bread which came down from heaven: If any man eats of this bread, he shall live forever: And the bread that I shall give is my flesh, which I will give for the life of the world. The Jews therefore strove among themselves, saying, how can this man give us His flesh to eat? Then Jesus said unto them, truly, truly I say unto you, except you eat the flesh of the Son of man, and drink His blood, you have no life in you. Whoso eats my flesh, and drinks my blood, has eternal life; and I will raise him up at the last day. For my flesh is meat indeed, and my blood is drink indeed. He that eats my flesh, and drinks my blood, dwells in me, and I in him. As the living Father has sent me, and I live by the Father: So he that eats me, even he shall live by me. This is that bread which came down from heaven: Not as your fathers did eat manna, and are dead: He that eats of this bread shall live forever. These things said He in the synagogue, as He taught in Capernaum. Many therefore of His disciples, when they had heard this, said, this is a hard saying; who can hear (*understand*) it? When Jesus knew in Himself that His disciples murmured at it, He said unto them, does this offend you? What and if you shall see the Son of man ascend up where He was before? It is the spirit that

> quickens; the flesh profits nothing: The words that I speak unto you are spirit, and they are life...From that time many of His disciples went back, and walked no more with Him.
> John 6:41, 47-63, and 66 (italics added)

After these spiritual words were spoken, words of spirit and life, many disciples left, they went back to their lives and no longer followed him. What did Jesus do? Clearly, He did not chase after them. We didn't see Him running after His followers saying "Wait, you misunderstood me! Eating my flesh and drinking my blood is a metaphor, it's not literal. It's about taking into yourselves my very life. Please come back!" No, this is not what the Lord did. He was relaxed, again trusting that the Spirit would reveal the appropriate meaning of His vivid word picture at the right time. As He said... "it is the Spirit that quickens."

This is another application for us who want to be used by our Lord, too. I want to share truth and trust the Father, through the Spirit, to draw people to himself. We are witnesses, not defense attorneys! All we need to do is speak the Word, and the Spirit will make the application in people's hearts. We plant and water, but He gives the increase!

> In the last day, that great day of the feast (*the eighth day of the Feast of Tabernacles*) ...
> John 7:37a (italics added)

Understand that the Feast of Tabernacles was the greatest of the three major feasts on the Jewish calendar. It occurred in September or early October and celebrated the wilderness wanderings of the Jews in the days of Moses, commemorating God's deliverance and provision. But it also looked forward to that future liberation at the hands of the Messiah. During their time in the wilderness, perhaps the greatest miracle, among a multitude of signs, was when Moses was instructed to smite the rock and out gushed forth water that satisfied the thirst of the people. In Jesus' day, the priests had a ritual that illustrated this beautifully. For the first seven days of the feast, they would proceed down from the Temple Mount with much pomp and ceremony to the Pool of Siloam (Siloam means Sent One). There, the high priest would gather up water in a golden pitcher from the pool and bring it up to the mount where, in front of all of the worshippers who were sitting in the open square, he would pour it out as an offering, thanking God for His past provisions. But on the eighth day, the great day, the high priest would bring an empty pitcher, he would pour it, with nothing present, and pronounce their hope and belief in the future provision that would be ushered in by Messiah. The people would then recite a promise found in Isaiah's words to them: "Thus saith the Lord that made thee, and formed thee from the womb, which will help thee: Fear not, O Jacob, my servant, and thou Jeshurun (*another name for Israel*), whom I have chosen. For I will pour water upon him that is thirsty, and floods upon the dry ground: I will pour my spirit upon thy seed, and my blessing upon thine offspring" (Isaiah 44:2-3, italics added).

With this background, what happened next is awesome!

> ... Jesus stood and cried, saying, if any man thirst, let him come unto me, and drink. He that believes on me, as the scripture has said,* out of his belly shall flow rivers of living water. (But this spoke He of the Spirit, which they that believe on Him should receive: For the

> Holy Ghost was not yet given; because that Jesus was not yet glorified.)
> John 7:37b-42 (* Proverbs 14:27, Isaiah 58:10-11)

The audacity of this scene. It's completely quiet, very somber. The people had just recited Isaiah's words, everyone is waiting for the high priest to pronounce that future blessing of Messiah. You could hear a pin drop. Then suddenly, from the middle of the sitting crowd, stands up the True High Priest, rises up one who screams at the top of His lungs what you have just read. Imagine the power and the presence that Jesus possessed at that moment. All were stunned! All were flabbergasted. The very picture this ceremony was illustrating was taken to a new level. It indeed was fulfilled at that very moment. The Rock that was smitten in the Exodus account, releasing water for the people was picturing the true Rock of Ages, being smitten and thereby releasing the torrents of living water, forever quenching the believer's thirst. Indeed, on the eighth day (eight being the number of new beginnings in the Bible) Messiah pronounced their provision, an endowment based upon belief in him!

Shortly after the Lord was glorified, these words were fulfilled actively:

> And when the day of Pentecost was fully come, they were all with one accord in one place. And suddenly there came a sound from heaven as of a rushing mighty wind, and it filled the house where they were sitting...And they were all filled with the Holy Ghost...And there was dwelling in Jerusalem, Jews, devout men, out of every nation under heaven.

> Now when this was noised abroad, the multitude came together, and were confounded, because that every man heard them speak in his own language. And they were all amazed and marveled, saying one to another, behold, are not all these which speak Galileans? And how hear we every man in our own tongue, wherein we were born? ... we do hear them speak in our own tongues the wonderful works of God. And they were all amazed, and were in doubt, saying one to another, what does this mean? Others mocking said, these men are full of new wine. But Peter, standing up with the eleven, lifted up his voice, and said unto them, you men of Judea, and all that dwell in Jerusalem, be this known unto you, and hearken to my words: For these are not drunken as you suppose, see it is but the third hour of the day (*9 am*). But this is that which was spoken by the prophet Joel: And it shall come to pass in the last days, saith God, I will pour my spirit upon all flesh: And your sons and your daughters shall prophesy, and your young men shall see visions, and your old men shall dream dreams...And it shall come to pass, that whosoever shall call on the name of the Lord shall be saved.
> Acts 2:1-17, 21 (excerpts, italics added)

Peter then boldly preached the gospel in the power of the Spirit and three thousand Jews were saved! Joel's words concerning the outpouring of the Spirit (Joel 2:28-32) were set in motion upon that day, just as Jesus said it would occur.

Lastly, in considering our Comforter, greetings of Paul to the believers in Corinth give a wonderful amplification of the Spirit's working in our lives to encourage others.

> Blessed be God, even the Father of our Lord Jesus Christ, the Father of mercies, and the God of all comfort: Who comforts us in all of our tribulation, that we may be able to comfort them which are in any trouble, by the comfort wherewith we ourselves are comforted of God.
> 2nd Corinthians 1:3-4

We can comfort one another even when we have not experienced the same trials as others because we have seen the Comforter's work in our lives in the tribulations we have endured, and thus can leverage those experiences of God's faithfulness to help others. This is important to remember regarding ministry. Don't believe the lie that you cannot help another who is going through a trial that you have never experienced. Our Adversary wants us to sit on the sidelines feeling inadequate when this promise says otherwise. Just because I have never had a miscarriage, for instance, does not disqualify me from ministering to a sister undergoing this pain as God has worked mercy into my life via other challenges I have experienced. This work of the Spirit dares us all to live in the present and to operate in the here and now, knowing we are indeed up to any opportunity for ministry we may face.

So let us thank the Father and the Son for sending the Comforter. With His work in our world, we are more than conquerors, separating truth from error, showing the way of salvation, pronouncing the judgment of evil, and telling of things to come while we wait patiently, yet expectantly, for the return of our wonderful Savior, Jesus Christ.

Summary:

1. Jesus told His disciples that, after He left, He would send the Comforter to those who believe in Him. The Holy Spirit would bring to remembrance things He had said.
2. The Holy Ghost has a threefold ministry: To reprove the world for the sin of not believing in Jesus, to demonstrate the righteousness of the Lord in living a beautiful life, and to tell of the judgment of Satan.
3. The Comforter speaks of Jesus and of things to come in the future.
4. The "living water" passages of John 4 and 7 are metaphors of the Holy Spirit.
5. The Comforter empowers believers to be witnesses for Christ (Acts 1:8) and a comfort during trials to others.

For Further Study:

1. What happened to Satan's control over you and the world when the Comforter judged him?
2. What are some of the truths the Spirit has revealed to us that Jesus was unable to tell His disciples when He was with them?
3. Do you think the words of Paul and John concerning the Rapture and the End Times are inspired?
4. Why did Jesus not feel the need to correct listeners who misunderstood Him?
5. How does a believer become empowered by the Spirit?

Success

How would you define success, describe living a rich and fulfilling life? How would you define a life well lived? Would it be a lifetime with little pain and much pleasure? Or a lifespan filled with accolades and financial rewards? Would being remembered favorably after death be a marker of success? Or making a difference in the lives of others, would that qualify as an achievement? Well, of course, all of these examples are opinions that some might hold forth as proper definitions of a successful life. But, toward the end of His life, the One who came to set us free also shared His opinion on the definition of a life lived well. It is a pathway, a recipe for success that we all can emulate, for the route to success is found in Jesus' high-priestly prayer to His Father, found in John, Chapter 17.

> These words spoke Jesus, and lifted up His eyes to heaven, and said, Father, the hour is come; glorify Your Son, that Your Son also may glorify you.
> John 17:1

Am I living or just existing? Am I intentional in my actions or am I sleepwalking through life? Jesus looked up toward God. He was dependent upon His Father, for He knew that a life dependent upon God experiences the supernatural power of God. As has been said by Robert Morris, "Only a life dependent is a life that is capable." Independence is a lie, first propagated in the Garden of Eden and still fed to us in overflowing amounts every day and in every way from the god of this world, from people, from the world's system, and even from our loved ones and parents! "You should take charge," we hear. We are taught to have that "can-do attitude." No, no, no! Jesus understood that it is far better to live with a sense of divine destiny, trusting the Father, depending on the Father, for everything in His life, even the end! Jesus knew that this was His hour for greatness! It was His hour to glorify God.

What about me, about you? Am I desirous to elevate God? Is my purpose to bring praise to the Father? That was our Lord's drive, to bring exaltation to God. That was His definition of a successful life.

To follow in this prayer are the markers Jesus used to define success. To outline how He saw a life well lived. This is a blueprint we may want to remember and walk in as we seek to emulate our wonderful Savior.

> I have glorified thee on the earth:
> John 17:4a

Have I glorified the Father during my days given to me upon this orb? How do I even do that?

The answer to that is given just a few verses earlier by Jesus when He spoke His final words to His men on the night He was betrayed.

> Herein is my Father glorified, that you bear much fruit.
> John 15:8

That's the key! I want to be a fruit bearer and, in doing so, I will glorify God, I will be a success.

And just what is fruit-bearing?

First of all, fruit is not for the branches, it is others-oriented. Fruit is a blessing to others, it brings refreshment and nourishment to hungry souls. It is seen in Paul's words to the Galatians:

> But the fruit of the Spirit is love, joy, peace, longsuffering, gentleness, goodness, faith, meekness, temperance...
> Galatians 5:22

The fruit of the spirit is love, which is then characterized by its components of joy, peace, patience, gentleness, kindness, faith, meekness, and self-control. Living a lovely life is one example of fruit-bearing, of bringing exaltation to the Father, of living a successful life.

Fruit production can also be tasted on our lips as we praise the Godhead with thankful words: "By Him therefore let us offer the sacrifice of praise to God continually, that is, the fruit of our lips giving thanks to His name" (Hebrews 13:15). Thus, we learn that a life filled with thanksgiving and praise to God is also one that would be characterized as successful by our Savior.

Am I generous? That also is an example of fruit production. "For even in Thessalonica you sent once again unto my necessity. Not because I desire a gift: But I desire fruit that may abound to your account" (Philippians 4:16-17). Being big-hearted with my time and money, with the gifts God has given me is fruit that glorifies God and contributes to my success.

How about the way I walk, the way I carry myself, the way I live? Am I striving to move in the spirit and live by His precepts or am I base and crass, living in the flesh and embarrassing the people of God by my earthy lifestyle? "But now being made free from sin, and become servants to God, you have your fruit unto holiness, and the end everlasting life" (Romans 6:22). Living holy is a marker of success because it, too, glorifies our God.

And not only is living a life avoiding evil important, but one filled with good deeds is also beautiful and glorious to God. "That you might walk worthy of the Lord unto all pleasing, being fruitful in every good work" (Colossians 1:10). A life filled with virtuous acts is also a successful one.

Lastly, did I share the gospel of Jesus Christ with others? Did I speak of Christ crucified for our sins and conquering death? Did I tell people that to trust in Him, to call Him Lord, and to confess one's sinful state is the way to redemption, the way to life? This is fruit production of a high degree. "I oftentimes purposed to come to you...that I might have some fruit among you also, even as among other Gentiles" (Romans 1:13). Soul winning is fruitful and brings glory to God, being another marker for success.

So we see that walking in the spirit, praising the Lord, being generous and holy, living a life of many good deeds, and sharing the gospel with others is fruit unto our accounts and glorifies our Father. These things are treasure in heaven for the believer, your retirement plan, if you will, and in God's economy, it is what success is all about.

> I have finished the work which you gave me
> to do.
> John 17:4b

What a question! Will I be able to say this when my life is complete? Did I finish the work the Father has given me to do? Did I finish strong? Did I run through the tape? This is so important! The world is constantly attempting to get me off of this goal.

Retirement, pleasure, family dynamics, trivia, as well as non-eternal worries like world stage issues and financial concerns, all compete to slow me down.

Then, of course, there is the other team. Demons can't get away with outright lying to me very often, as I know truth from error. No, what they do are the two "D's," delay and distraction! "Don't worry about that nudge from the Lord, you can get to that later." Guess what, later sometimes doesn't come! Or, "I was going to spend time with the Lord this morning but the rain last night left some dirt residue on my car and I needed to wash it." Worldly distractions can sideline me for weeks sometimes. Don't let that happen!

Now you may remember that often distractions are ministry opportunities, so, how do you tell the difference? Here's a phrase from Jon Courson that really says it all: "When it comes to ministry prospects, if you don't know, get up and go! When it comes to worldly endeavors, if in doubt, opt out!" Have "Yes" be your default setting when it comes to the things of the Lord and be a little choosy when it comes to the many, many things the world has to offer to fill our time.

Jesus finished the work God gave Him to do. You can do the same by paying attention and being intentional. Again, I say, don't sleepwalk through life. Keep the goal in view!

> I have manifested your name unto the men
> you gave me.
> John 17:6a

Jesus manifested God's name. He illustrated it with His words and actions. You see, the name of God reveals the nature of God. God is love, light, and life. He is the Prince of Peace and our Provider. He is the Friend of Sinners and the Wonderful

Counselor. He is the Good Shepherd and the Rose of Sharon. He is the Bright and Morning Star and the Bread of Life. He is the Great High Priest and the Lamb of God. This is what I want to do. What you can do, too! We can manifest God's name by walking and living in His nature. We can love people and live at peace with them. I can extend mercy to fellow sinners like me and share His words of truth with other seekers on our journey through life. You can lead little ones along and live whimsically, causing others to want what you have discovered. And we can feed people the words of life, sharing that the ultimate nature of God is one of mercy and grace, one of patience and kindness, one of goodness and truth (Exodus 34:6). Yes, as Jesus said to Phillip, "He who has seen me, has seen the Father" (John 14:9). I want folks to see God in my life, too. The same can be said for you!

> For I have given them the words which you have given me.
> John 17:8a

Did I give out God's Word to people in my circles of life? And, more properly, did I give out the "rhema" or spirit-filled word I receive moment by moment from the Lord? Did I speak words of wisdom to the weary in season and out? Did I have the tongue of the learned and speak the words of God as He inspired me (Isaiah 50:4-6)? Of course, this heavenly ability is predicated upon a soul that is attentive to the Father. One that wakes most mornings asking Him to bless others and committing to staying close to Him throughout the day to hear His voice over the noise of the world. What we are talking about here is revelation from God. Special words, special wisdom, given at the proper time in response to the needs of others. This is what Jesus specialized in and what we can emulate to some degree.

So how does one receive revelation from God? Going to the written Word will give the answers on hearing from the Lord. First, listen at night, when you are in twilight sleep. God in His word often spoke to His children in dreams and visions during their sleep time. Second, extend mercy to others. The Bible says that He will meet His people at the "mercy seat." Next, worship. In Psalm 22:3, we learn that God inhabits the praises of His children. This is another way to open the floodgates of revelation. Fourthly, live a life of obedience to Him. Truly, we are saved by grace, but sin has repercussions that are stifling to our ears (Isaiah 59:1-2). The following promise from Jesus tells it all in regards to obedience and revelation. "You are my friends, if you do whatsoever I command you. Henceforth I call you not servants; for the servant knows not what his lord does: But I have called you friends; for all things that I have heard of my Father I have made known unto you" (John 15:14-15). Galatians 4:1 notes that an heir is treated like a servant until he comes of age. This is what the Lord is saying. If you act like a mature child, you will get the benefits that come with adulthood. Believers living in their fleshly nature are still saved, but they miss out on hearing from the Teacher!

After obedience, living in the fear of the Lord will open my ears to hearing from God. Psalm 25:14 promises, "the secret of the Lord is with them that fear Him; and He will show them His covenant." Sharing the Word with others is another road to revelation. Preachers tell me often that right in the middle of a sermon or a prep time, new insights will scream out to them. I know this to be true. As an author, almost every time I sit down to write, something I had never thought of will pop into my conscious that I had not considered previously. When I go back over my writings, I am constantly aware of the many things I've written down that were new to me at the time they were penned! Jesus said this would be the case. Let me show you:

> Take heed what you hear: With what measure you give out, it shall be given to you; and you that hear, shall more be given.
> Mark 4:24

How perfect is this! As I give out what I am learning, what I am reading, what I am hearing, He will give me more. Talk about compound interest! This is God's economics for sure!

Lastly, my list of avenues to revelation from God includes times of trouble, times of pain and suffering, times of tribulation. When did Shadrach, Meshach, and Abednego walk with the Lord, when did they commune with Jesus? Why, when they were in the fiery furnace. And walking in that heat caused others to see the Lord in all of His glory. As hard as it may be to hear, we are told to embrace difficulties, for it is in these times that we shine the brightest for the Lord. Those are the times that we can look back on, knowing that God was doing a work in our souls that bettered not only ourselves but others.

> While I was with them in the world, I kept them in your name: Those that you gave me, I have kept, and none of them is lost...
> John 17:12

Like Jesus, the Father has given me, has given you, people to keep in our hearts. Praying for our tribe, blessing and enlarging others, building up and shoring up those souls God has given us to influence and lead. I want to embrace this calling by living a life that directs my people to God and not away from him. Keeping people means frequently bringing them before the throne of grace in prayer and living a life that propels individuals forward, not stumbling them backward by a poor example of a loveless and distracted lifestyle. Keeping the things of God front and center is part of keeping the persons God has given me. Eyes are upon you, dear believer; it matters what you do. Monkey see, monkey do, is not just a nursery rhyme. It is a fact of life. My people will end up doing the things they see me do, either good or bad. Thus, it's extremely important to keep my soul by leading with a good example.

> I have given them your word.
> John 17:14

In Verse 8, Jesus gave His men the words God gave Him moment by moment; here in Verse 14, He is talking about the written word. The Law, the Poetry, and the Prophets. Jesus taught and divided the Word of God in a way that was enlarging and spirit-filled. He told His followers that looking at a woman with lust was the same as adultery. He proclaimed that unrighteous anger was the same as murder. He defined divorce as nearly impossible except for unfaithfulness. He explained the Sabbath and He taught that an eye for an eye was not the best way, but turning the other cheek was the intent of God.

What about me, what about you? Do I explain, do I divide the Word to my followers, to my family, to my kids? This is crucial! This is one of the things my Lord thought to be important. Sharing the Word of God to others. Speaking, interpreting the Bible to my group.

The good news is that this is not a bummer, not a hardship, it's easy. Just as I go about my day, opportunities pop up left and right. Being sensitive to the many times when conversation will lead to an opportunity to talk about the things of God is all that is needed. Oh, one more thing. Trust over fear. If I worry about what others will think or say, I am tempted to keep quiet. But if I prefer what the Lord thinks, then speaking is not an issue, but a joy. And, after the word is released, you will feel great as God's glory will descend upon your heart, no matter how your words are received.

So, give out the Word. This is another aspect of success in our Lord's thinking.

> I have declared unto them your name, and I will declare it: That the love wherewith you have loved me may be in them, and I in them.
> John 17:26

In Verse 6, Jesus manifested God's name, His nature, to His followers and disciples. Here in Verse 26, He declares the Name. It is a new name that didn't show itself in the scriptures they had available to them two thousand years ago. The name Jesus declared was "Abba."

Papa is the closest we have in English to Abba. It was a name of endearment that lovers of God had not been introduced to until that time. Intimacy and trust are taken to a new level as we consider this name of the Father which Jesus had declared to His brothers.

This is for us also. We can live in the "Abba" lifestyle as we walk in intimacy with our Lord, realizing that God is the Husband of Israel, those governed by God, and He is the Groom of the Church. We are His bride!

This closeness is the apex of this life and thus, important to tell and show others. I want to declare Abba to others as this too is on the highway to heaven, on the road to success.

Along with characterizations of success from Jesus' final recorded words to His Father, we see Jesus praying earnestly for His men, for His children. A look into what He prayed gives us another template of things we too will want to lift up to God concerning those He has entrusted us with to lead and to love. But, more important, the seven things Jesus will pray for are a pathway to beholding the glory of God. For each request, when answered in a believer's life, builds upon the prior request like a stairway to heaven!

> ...keep through your own name those whom you have given me, that they may be one as we are.
> John 17:11b

God is a compound unity. He is "Elohim." He is plural. Elohim is a plural word implying a group of more than two. God is Father, Son, and Holy Spirit. He is three, yet He is one! Think of a cluster of grapes or the classic example of the shamrock. More than one, yet one.

So too, that is what Jesus is asking of the Father. "Make them a group of one just as we are. Give them the same mind, i.e., the mind of Christ, and give them the same purpose, i.e., to glorify you, Father." The Bible sings, "Behold, how good and how pleasant it is for brethren to dwell in unity" (Psalm 133:1). How does that happen? The next verse carols the answer. "It is like the precious ointment upon the head, that ran down upon the beard, even Aaron's beard: That went down to the skirts of the garments." Ointment is always a type of the Holy Spirit in the Bible. Here we see it upon the head of the high priest Aaron, who, of course, typifies Jesus. We, as the body of Christ, receive the spirit as it flows down from the head, as it is received from

Jesus. Thus, unity of the brethren comes as we walk in the spirit, following our Lord's leading. When we do our own thing, Jesus' prayer goes unanswered.

> I pray not that you should take them out of the world, but that you should keep them from evil.
> John 17:15

You know that our fallen world is full of evil, don't you? There are many opportunities to be taken down and wiped out, many pitfalls that can disqualify us from moving out in the spirit effectively. Oh, God doesn't condemn us if we are saved (Romans 8:1) but sin has repercussions. Sin moves me away from the spot where God's blessings flow. Jesus knew that well, hence He prayed for our protection from evil. Implied, of course, in this prayer, is protection from the Evil One! From Satan and his crew!

> Sanctify them through your truth: Your word is truth.
> John 17:17

"Thy word I have hid in my heart, that I might not sin against thee" (Psalm 119:11). The Word of God is truth, it separates truth from error. It gives us the compass we need in the forest of the world. As has been said by Michael Todd, "Without the manual for life, abuse is inevitable!" The Bible warns, "My people are destroyed for lack of knowledge." Indeed, Satan can easily take advantage of us in areas where we are ignorant. Jesus' prayer is for the believer to overcome evil, to be protected from the Evil One, by being rooted and grounded in His Father's Word. Hiding the Word in your heart is so crucial. When I look at our Leader's example, every time He was tempted, He went to the Word, as it was in His heart and ready to be released. That's where the power dwells. The Bible is like a lion in a cage; let it out and watch what happens!

Not only does the Word divide truth from error, but wonderfully it moves a believer away from His former lifestyle of sin and self to one that is sanctified and holy. To be sanctified is to be set apart for God, to be in a position to be used by God for His glory and to build His Kingdom. Jesus is asking the Father to use the Word to protect the believers and also to move them forward in service spreading the gospel.

As this prayer of Jesus was answered, it brings us to the exciting prayer of verse twenty. For this next prayer is the one our Lord prayed specifically for you and me!

> Neither pray I for these alone, but for them also which shall believe on me through their word.
> John 17:20

As disciples are sanctified, as they are set apart for the Master's use, reproduction naturally occurs. A single-minded believer cannot keep quiet! Jeremiah said the Word was a fire in his belly when he kept still. The disciples told the Jews that they cannot but preach the things they had seen and heard. We believers throughout the ages are the answer to this prayer of Jesus. And delightfully, we get to be part of this ongoing request as we move forward in time, telling future generations of our awesome King. How cool is that!

> That they may be one; as you, Father, are in me, and I in you, that they also may be one in

> us: That the world may believe that you have
> sent me.
> John 17:21

The priestly prayer circles back to unity again. Unity among the brethren in the beginning and unity in the church presently. How does that happen? Is this prayer going unanswered? It certainly can be said that there are fractures among the different groups that make up the body of Christ. Well, I submit that Jesus' prayer was and is being answered nonetheless. That is because the differences are on the non-essentials. Do we baptize as a baby or an adult, do we speak in tongues or not, do we sing hymns or worship to drums and guitars? But the essences are the same in all groups. The Lord's Table, the Death and Resurrection of the Christ, the Hope of Heaven, these are all unified beliefs among all who call upon Jesus as Lord.

It is this unity, His death for our sins and His resurrection for our life, that proclaims Jesus to the world. Certainly, it would seem that Jesus' prayer has been received. Jesus Christ is the most famous person who has ever lived. At the time this prayer was uttered, only a few thousand people had ever heard of Him, yet now, two thousand years later, His name has significance to nearly every soul on earth!

> I in them, and you in me, that they may be
> made perfect (*mature*) in one; and that the
> world may know that you have sent me, and
> have loved them, as you have loved me.
> John 17:23 (italics added)

Belief in simplicity of the gospel, belief in the death and resurrection of our Lord is what perfects the follower of Christ. It's not difficult. It's not hard. It's not deep and esoteric. Maturity comes from the simple acknowledgment that I need a Savior. Calling out to Him as Lord and holding fast to the understanding that He alone has the power over death.

With that simple truth comes the "out-of-this-world" next part of Jesus' prayer. That is, that the world would know that God loves them as much as He loves Jesus! What if I really believed that! Would I act and pray differently? Certainly, there would be no pressure to perform. I simply could rest in His love for me. Well, God does love His adopted children just as much, to the same degree, as His begotten Son. This is wonderful! This is freeing! This is good news!

> Father, I will that they also, whom you have given me, be with me where I am; that they may behold my glory, which you have given me: For you loved me before the foundation of the world.
> John 17:24

This is the hope of Heaven. To be with Jesus, to be with our loved ones. To be in that place where there are no more tears, no more sorrow, no more pain. What a day that will be. Thank you, Jesus, for praying this last prayer. And look how He ends it. That we may behold His glory! Do you know, His glory is what you are really craving? The glory, the "Chabod" in Hebrew, the weight and substance of God, is what we all long for. Jesus ends this wonderful prayer by requesting His Father immerse us all in the very presence of His life, love, and light. What we lost in Eden will be restored in Paradise!

So we see this prayer building beautifully. Unity and protection lead to sanctification and then evangelism. This, in turn, brings forth corporate unity producing maturity and the sense of God's great love for us. All of this culminates in the great goal, the great desire. That we would and will behold His glory!

So, we understand that Jesus' definition of a successful life is far different than the world's. But how do we get to the holy place where He walked seemingly all of the time? Well, one step at a time, one day at a time. Our lives are made of days and weeks, of hours and moments. This is the key to success. It is moment by moment. Opportunity by opportunity. And the wonderful thing is that, even when we fail, God still loves us, so just get up, dust off, and start back on the path of success, for the reality of life is that a successful day or a successful life is not accomplishing the things on my schedule or my five-year plan, but it is to remain in fellowship and communication with my Lord as much as possible!

Summary:

1. Success in Jesus' eyes looks different than success as viewed by the world.
2. Seven statements summarize Jesus' success. He glorified the Father, He finished the work given Him, He manifested God's name, He gave out the words given to Him by the Father, He kept those He was given, He gave out the Word, and He declared the love of Abba.
3. Fruit-bearing is others-oriented.
4. Delay and distractions are two things the Devil, the world, and the flesh will use to get you off of your goal.
5. The names of God reveal His nature. To manifest God's name means to live life in a way that reflects God's nature.
6. Revelations Jesus received from the Father, He gave to others.

7. Keeping those given to me includes praying for them, blessing and enlarging them, as well as leading them by example.
8. Jesus made seven requests to the Father which build upon each other and culminate in beholding the glory of God. Keep them as one, keep them from evil, set them apart by the Word, keep those they preach to and keep them as one also, give them all maturity and a sense of your love for them. Finally, He prayed to let them all see His glory!
9. The glory of God is what we all innately crave.

For Further Study:

1. What are some examples of producing fruit that will bring glory to God?
2. Again I ask: How does finishing strong in life look to you?
3. How do you tell the difference between worldly distractions from those that are actually opportunities for good?
4. What are some ways men and women receive revelation from God? What do you do with it when you hear it?
5. How does 2nd Timothy 2:15 help you give out the Word of God to those entrusted to you?
6. Is it easy or hard for you to think of God as Papa? Does believing that He loves you as much as He loves Jesus help you in that regard?
7. How does knowing principles and precepts of God's Word simplify one's life?
8. Here are two questions for you to think about after reading Jesus' markers for success. First, who are you? Second, what are you doing here?

Epilogue

"It is finished." These were the words our Savior spoke as He died for the sins of the world, as He accomplished the mission He came to our planet to complete. He took our place and died the death we all deserve due to our sin and stupidity. Then, wonderfully, three days later, our Lord conquered death as He rose from the grave, showing for all time that sin and death had been put aside, that our ancient enemies had lost their sting.

Indeed, Jesus Christ lived beautifully and died courageously. As the Lamb of God (John 1:29), He paid the debt of our rebellion and, as the Wisdom of God (Colossians 2:3), He taught us the proper response to His awesome gift of life. But, as we have frequently emphasized, we do not always rise to the principles of His kingdom but our efforts must always be directed toward living in His words of instruction as best we can. Truly, to emulate the Lord to the greatest of our ability is our fitting goal.

In addition, we have often spoken of how Jesus' words, parables, and teachings are counter to the ways of our world. We are living in a "matrix," in a paradigm, that is opposed to the things of God in most respects. Jesus came to set us free from our delusions and false worldviews. Oh, how important it is to take in, study, and then give out His words. As you, as I, do this, we will set ourselves and others free. As He has said, "if we continue in

His word...we shall know the truth, and the truth shall make us free" (John 8:31-32).

Shortly thereafter (forty days), He ascended to Heaven, where He sits at the right hand of the Father, interceding for us. During those days, Jesus spoke of the Kingdom of Heaven to His followers (Acts 1:3) as well as showing himself alive to hundreds of chosen ones (1 Corinthians 15:6), proving the veracity of His resurrection. We don't have the words He preached during that awesome interval but we do have love letters the Spirit of Jesus has given to us via the early believers. Specifically, Peter, John, Paul, James, and Jude have given us further insights from the ways and words of our Teacher.

In closing this book, I would like to include some last instructions Jesus gave to John to offer to the seven churches of the Revelation. Many see these seven letters to seven literal Christian churches of Asia Minor as directives to the entire Christian church of the last two thousand years. Jesus has many words of affirmation and warning to which we would do well to pay attention. In addition, promises to the believers of rewards in His future Kingdom are given as motivation to keep and treasure these splendid words.

First, the Lord told the believers in Ephesus that they had left their first love. That saddened him. He implored them to remember what they had lost, to repent of their moving away, and to return to that spot they were previously living and walking. Obviously, this is a pertinent word to many of us today. We too can get distracted and drift away from the Lover of our Souls. As we perceive this as happening, our response is to get ourselves back to that place we were when we were hot for His Kingdom and in love with being His follower. Jesus promised those in Ephesus that the intimacy they had once experienced would again be restored on that great day to come, as they returned to their King.

To the persecuted church of Smyrna, the Author of Life said not to fear men. He predicted that tribulations would occur in this life but that those who overcame would not be hurt by the second death. Later, that death is graphically revealed to John as part of his revelation (Revelation 20:11-15).

Solomon told us the same thing, did he not? The fear of man brings a snare (Proverbs 29:25), while the fear of the Lord is the beginning of wisdom (Proverbs 9:10). That is, to fear the Lord is the origin, the starting point of all other wisdom. We have talked of the fear of the Lord extensively in the book. It is my prayer that many of you will live as Jesus did in that regard. That is, live a life that is terrified at the prospect of being separated from our God.

Next, to the confused church of Pergamos, the Word of God (Revelation 19:13) told His followers to stay separate from the pernicious ways of the world. As they, as we do that, Jesus promises fellowship with Him as close friends in the kingdom to come.

Clearly, we live in a world, in a time, where the things of God and the things of men do not mix. As oil and water will not blend, so too, we are to stay separate from this world. As the Bible paraphrases, "we are in the world, but not of the world."

Jesus' fourth message was to the wealthy and dominant church of Thyatira. That city was wholly given to idol worship as they followed false spiritual leaders. "Don't do that" was His command. We can know a tree by its fruit and we can also know a true leader from one who is false by the fruit we see produced in his or her life. The King of Kings, the True Head of the Body, promised great responsibilities in His kingdom to those who overcome this tendency we have to follow wolves dressed in sheep's clothing.

The fifth church was in the midst of a city built upon a cliff. Sardis was seldom conquered during her long history due to this fortification. In fact, only twice was it defeated. Both were night-time surprise raids that caught them unaware. The One whose ways are not our ways and thoughts are not our thoughts told those believers not to rest on their laurels. Keep moving forward, keep pressing in, keep the fires hot. I'm a golfer. Another way of saying this that my playing partners will understand is, "You are not as good as your last shot, you are as good as your next shot!" We want to finish strong, to run through the tape, as I have said more than once in this book. Jesus promises to confess our names to the Father on that day if we continue to fight the good fight.

The City of Brotherly Love, that is, the church of Philadelphia, was told to hold fast to the Word. Great honor in the Kingdom was the promise to those overcomers. We, too, must give worth to God's Word, not compromising it, as the world so often will push us to do. Issues that the world proclaims as correct, e.g., killing fetuses in the name of autonomy, living in sexual sin under the guise of freedom of expression, as well as many other questions, are plainly contrary to God's ways and must be avoided and called out by His followers. As Mark Batterson has written, "Moral courage is the rarest type of courage today, for we live in a world where it is wrong to say what is wrong." That ought not to be!

In addition, the Philadelphians were told to walk through the doors that the Good Shepherd would open for them. Jesus opens doors for us daily, nudges us often, to move out in ministry, to live on mission. The church in Philadelphia did that, and we want to answer that call also!

Lastly, Jesus had some hard words for the lukewarm church of Laodicea. Illustratively, that city had a cold river that mixed with a hot aqueduct a few miles above it, rendering the water that arrived to them as tepid. Like Pergamos before, don't live with one foot on earth and one in Heaven. Don't be hot on Sunday and cold on Monday. Stay steady, keep engaged, make a decision, who are you going to follow? Jesus poignantly stated to those wishy-washy believers that their lukewarm state wanted only to make Him vomit! Go upstream, where the water is hot was His reprimand and the result would be to rule with Him in His future Kingdom. Again, this can be the battle we face day in and day out. Who am I going to make the Lord of my life today? Will it be me, my agenda, my fleshly desires, or will it be the Way, the Truth, and the Life? As He has said, He is the Vine and, apart from Him, we can do nothing of eternal value (John 15:5).

Now, as we conclude this book of Jesus' parables and teachings, the Great Physician's prescription for life, I can't help but be reminded that He promised that He would come back. I want to be ready, to be watching. I want to live expectantly realizing, as my late friend Pastor Peter John Courson was fond of saying, "The Lord could come back today, and if not today, then tomorrow!" Look up, dear believer, our redemption draws near!

Acknowledgments

Pilate asked Jesus "What is truth," not realizing it was personified in His presence. For that which is consistent with the mind, will, character, and glory of God is truth! Truth is truth and thus it cannot be plagiarized.

With that in mind, I need to clear something up.

In January of 2019, I retired from a busy medical practice and began working part-time as a traveling physician. If you will, I was "on mission" to little hospitals in the Northwest and to patients to which the Lord would lead me. And I found myself with much more free time than in my previous life. About that time, I was reading John Eldridge's book *Beautiful Outlaw* and was inspired by his presentation of Jesus' many and varied personality traits. I was also reading in the Old Testament about Solomon and his intent to build something great for the Lord since he was given a time of peace and tranquility. And third, at that time Levi Lusko preached a sermon on the Good Samaritan that reminded me that we so often misunderstand Jesus' words and parables, interpreting them as things we need to do, instead of realizing that many times they speak of things of which He has already done! We are not the Good Samaritan, Jesus is!

So, I purposed to write a book about Jesus' parables and teachings. I've been influenced by many great preachers and authors over the years and I am certain that many little phrases and thoughts, which I have long forgotten of where I heard and learned them, have made it into the body of this book and hence are not noted. I would like to thank many for their indulgence in this. Along with Eldridge and Lusko, I want to acknowledge, Jon, Ben, and Peter John Courson, Tom Sabens and Jim Wright, C.S. Lewis, Mark Batterson, Sarah Young, and Joyce Meyers, Robert Morris, Michael Todd, John Bevere, and William Young. These come to mind; I'm sure there are others. Ultimately, though, this is a Holy Spirit-inspired book and I hope you will receive this work in that light. It is my desire that many of you will read, study, and share these truths as your own, all for His glory!

For more see, www.danieltomlinson.org".

CPSIA information can be obtained
at www.ICGtesting.com
Printed in the USA
BVHW070724240322
632312BV00001B/3